Dealing with Censorship

Edited by

James E. Davis
Ohio University

National Council of Teachers of English
1111 Kenyon Road, Urbana, Illinois 61801

NCTE Editorial Board: Thomas K. Creswell, Kermeen C. Fristom, Rudine Sims, Donald C. Stewart, Ann C. Terry, Robert F. Hogan, *ex officio,* Paul O'Dea, *ex officio*

Staff Editor: Philip Heim

Book Design: Tom Kovacs

NCTE Stock Number 10622

Copyright © 1979 by the National Council of Teachers of English. All rights reserved. Printed in the United States of America.

It is the policy of NCTE in its journals and other publications to provide a forum for the open discussion of ideas concerning the content and the teaching of English and the language arts. Publicity accorded to any particular point of view does not imply endorsement by the Executive Committee, the Board of Directors, or the membership at large, except in announcements of policy, where such endorsement is clearly specified.

Library of Congress Cataloging in Publication Data

Main entry under title:

Dealing with censorship.

  Bibliography: p.
  1. Text-books—United States. 2. Censorship—United States. 3. Sexism in text-books—United States. 4. Racism in textbooks—United States. I. Davis, James E., 1934–   II. National Council of Teachers of English.
LB3047.D4   379'.156   79-4053
ISBN 0-8141-1062-2

Dealing with Censorship

NCTE Committee Against Censorship

Edward B. Jenkinson, Chair, Indiana University
Gertrude Berger, Brooklyn College
Lee Burress, University of Wisconsin—Stevens Point
Gary Cox, Haworth High School, Kokomo, Indiana
James E. Davis, Ohio University
Kenneth L. Donelson, Arizona State University
Diane P. Shugert, Central Connecticut State College
Frances M. Russell, *ex officio*, Winchester High School, Winchester, Massachusetts
Charles Suhor, *ex officio*, NCTE Deputy Executive Director
Richard P. Kleeman, Association of American Publishers, Inc., consultant
Judith Krug, Director, Office for Intellectual Freedom, American Library Association, consultant

Contents

Acknowledgments   vii

Preface   ix

I. The Current Climate   1

1. Dirty Dictionaries, Obscene Nursery Rhymes, and Burned Books   2
   Edward B. Jenkinson

2. A Brief Report of the 1977 NCTE Censorship Survey   14
   Lee Burress

3. Censorship and the Classroom Teacher   48
   Allan Glatthorn

4. Censorship and English: Some Things We Don't Seem to Think About Very Often (But Should)   54
   Robert C. Small, Jr.

5. Obscenity and the Chill Factor: Court Decisions about Obscenity and Their Relationships to School Censorship   63
   Kenneth L. Donelson

6. Legal Decisions and Censorship: A Game of Chance   76
   Robert T. Rhode

II. Issues and Pressures   85

7. Some Thoughts on Censorship in the Schools   86
   Robert F. Hogan

8. Clouds on the Right: A Review of Pending Pressures against Education   96
   J. Charles Park

9. How the Mel Gablers Have Put Textbooks on Trial   108
    Edward B. Jenkinson

10. Is Secular Humanism the Religion
    of the Public Schools?   117
    Robert T. Rhode

11. Hester Prynne and Linda Lovelace, Pure or Prurient   125
    Gertrude Berger

12. Issues of Censorship and Research on Effects of
    and Response to Reading   131
    Richard Beach

III. What to Do   161

13. Censorship in the 1970s: Some Ways to Handle It
    When It Comes (And It Will)   162
    Kenneth L. Donelson

14. Basic Training and Combat Duty—Preventive
    and Reactive Action   168
    Charles Suhor

15. Teach the Parents Well: An Anti-Censorship
    Experiment in Adult Education   180
    June Berkley

16. How to Write a Rationale in Defense of a Book   187
    Diane P. Shugert

17. The Iowa Model Policy and Rules for Selection
    of Instructional Materials   202
    Larry Bartlett

18. A Body of Well-instructed Men and Women:
    Organizations Active for Intellectual Freedom   215
    Diane P. Shugert

    Selected Bibliography   222

    Contributors   226

Acknowledgments

"Issues of Censorship and Research on Effects of and Response to Reading" by Richard Beach and "Obscenity and the Chill Factor: Court Decisions about Obscenity and Their Relationships to School Censorship" by Kenneth L. Donelson. From the *Journal of Research and Development in Education* 9 (Spring 1976). Copyright 1976 by the College of Education, University of Georgia. Reprinted by permission of the authors and the publisher. Material from *How Porcupines Make Love: Notes on a Response-Centered Curriculum* by Alan C. Purves. Reprinted by permission of John Wiley & Sons, Inc. "A Position Statement on Teaching English" by Mari Ann Doherty et al. From *Louisiana English Journal* 10 (Summer 1975). Copyright 1975 by the Louisiana Council of Teachers of English. Reprinted by permission of the publisher. "Basic Training and Combat Duty—Preventive and Reactive Action," originally titled "Censorship and the Saber-Toothed Gadfly," by Charles Suhor. From *Media and Methods* 15 (November 1978). Copyright 1978 by North American Publishing Company. Reprinted by permission of the author and the publisher. "Some Thoughts on Censorship in the School" by Robert F. Hogan and "Censorship and English: Some Things We Don't Seem to Think About Very Often (But Should)" by Robert C. Small, Jr. From *Focus: Teaching Language Arts* 3 (Fall 1976). Copyright 1976 by the Southeastern Ohio Council of Teachers of English. Reprinted by permission of the Southeastern Ohio Council of Teachers of English.

"Legal Decisions and Censorship: A Game of Chance" and "Is Secular Humanism the Religion of the Public Schools?" by Robert T. Rhode first appeared in *Indiana English* 1 (Fall 1977). "Censorship in the Seventies: Some Ways to Handle It When It Comes (And It Will)" by Kenneth L. Donelson first appeared in *English Journal* 63 (February 1974). "Censorship and the Classroom Teacher" by Allan Glatthorn first appeared in *English Journal* 66 (February 1977).

Preface

Censorship is certainly not new in this country. The earliest censors proscribed sacrilege at least as strictly as obscenity. In Massachusetts in 1664 Thomas á Kempis's *Imitation of Christ* was declared papist and therefore proscribed. Obscenity cases in the colonial period generally were based on legal precedents in the English courts, although the Massachusetts Bay Colony Act recognized obscenity as an offense even before it was recognized in English common law. The criteria of intent of the accused and corruption of youth were present from the very beginning. The first federal legislation was the Customs Law of 1842—aimed against the importation of indecent and obscene prints, paintings, lithographs, engravings, and transparencies. Printed matter was not included. In 1865 Congress enacted a law declaring that the mailing of obscene publications was a criminal offense.

The man who is credited with leading the fight for the censorship of literature in the United States in the nineteenth century is Anthony Comstock. With the help of a powerful, wealthy supporter, Morris K. Jessup, president of the Young Men's Christian Association and founder of the American Museum of Natural History, Comstock formed the YMCA Committee for the Suppression of Vice. Law enforcement officials were very cooperative. In 1873, when Comstock became secretary of the New York Society for the Suppression of Vice, he was even empowered to make arrests. He was made a special agent of the Post Office and in that office engineered the passage of a more stringent Federal Obscenity Bill. Comstock was later directly involved in the formation of the New England Society for the Suppression of Vice. He was very harsh in his methods, once boasting that he had caused fifteen suicides and had destroyed 160 tons of obscene literature.

It is no accident that an increase in censorship in the late nineteenth century coincided with an increase in literacy. Although magazines were still by and large under the influence of the "genteel" tradition, other materials were becoming available for the common people. A broader field of concern was thus opened up for the censor. The common people long had been assumed to be particularly susceptible to the "evils" of obscenity, so a work was far more likely to be attacked once it was reprinted in an inexpensive edition. Many judicial decisions since that time have reflected this distrust of the common people.

In the twentieth century practically every decade has had its several writers decrying "increasing incidents of censorship." But censorship incidents in the schools in the seventies seem to represent something new in both degree and kind. The great benchmark incident occurred in the mid-seventies in West Virginia. School board member Alice Moore raised objections to parts of the three hundred different language arts textbooks which the Textbook Selection Committee had submitted to the five-member Kanawha County (Charleston) School Board in April 1974. She began a censorship campaign which would be heard about throughout the country. Moore failed in her effort to get the board to veto the books, but this did not deter her. With the help of various fundamentalist religious groups and an organization called Christian American Parents (CAP), she began a crusade against the books, which she said ridiculed a child's faith, called Biblical stories fables, and implied that the Bible was not to be taken literally. She also objected to the use of four-letter words, to moral relativism, and especially to questions and activities that tended to invade the privacy of the home and to "subvert family relationships." The protest spread, with hundreds joining in marches and demonstrations. Three ministers were arrested for demonstrating on school property.

The various anti-textbook groups decided to boycott the opening of the schools in September. Their picketing and strikes led to the closing of the public bus system, a trucking terminal, mines, and several stores and factories. A compromise was offered by then Superintendent Kenneth Underwood the stop the violence. Under his plan the texts would be removed from the classrooms and reviewed for a thirty-day period. The anti-textbook leaders would accept nothing less than permanent removal. The extent to which these leaders believed in the righteousness of their course is revealed in a September 20 news item in the *Charleston Daily Mail* in which the Reverend Charles Quigley is reported to have said, "I am asking Christian people to pray that God will kill the giants that have mocked and made fun of dumb fundamentalists. I know of several Biblical incidents where men tried to stop the work of God and died."

Objections seemed to fall into the following categories: (1) anything which might be construed as ridiculing faith, (2) calling Biblical stories fables or myths, (3) use of four-letter words, (4) any selection or question implying moral relativism, (5) any techniques or procedures in teaching that might involve invasion of privacy, (6) treating God as human, (7) anything that would tend to subvert family relationships, (8) any treatment of sex, (9) any anti- or un-American stance, (10) nonstandard English, (11) anything that might show disrespect (or questioning) of authority, (12) cruelty and violence in stories, (13) unhappy endings and pervasive sadness in stories, and (14) over-concern with minority racial and ethnic groups.

In the face of growing agitation of the anti-textbook group a pro-textbook group called Citizens Concerned for Quality Education was formed. Two ministers were its leaders, James Lewis (Episcopal) and Ronald English (Baptist). Lewis accused the anti-textbook groups of breaking the very laws they pretended to uphold. The West Virginia Council of Churches, also aligned with the pro-textbook faction, warned against any attempt to impose religious ideas on public institutions as against the fundamental concept of religious freedom.

Following the explosive opening of school, further demonstrations, strikes, boycotts, and violence continued through the fall. An elementary school was bombed, cars were bombed, board members were attacked, and fear reigned. In November the School Board voted by a vote of four to one (Alice Moore alone dissented) in a televised meeting to return most of the controversial texts to the classroom. Parents who objected to their children using the books were given the right to request that others be substituted. Some of the most controversial books were placed in the library to be checked out only with written parental permission.

The Kanawha County crisis was the most violent, far-reaching, long lasting, and surely the best publicized of the censorship cases of recent years. But it was by no means the only one, nor was it at all isolated. Some of the same national groups—the Ku Klux Klan, the John Birch Society, the National Committee on the Crisis in Education, Carl McIntire's Christian Crusade, Citizens for Decent Literature, Citizens for Decency Through Law, the Heritage Foundation, and the National Parents League—involved in Kanawha County were active as well in cases in Oklahoma, Texas, Georgia, Indiana, and other states.

Censorship protests are on the increase, as are the number of people involved in a single protest and the amount of violence in the protests. This might reflect the frustrations of people who feel they are a part of a society over which they have little influence. Many seem to sense that society has moved in the wrong direction. Their tendency is to lash out at institutions over which they feel they still have some control—institutions like the school which are emblematic of the whole system. Thus protests nowadays are likely to involve issues that go far beyond textbooks.

The National Council of Teachers of English and its state and regional affiliates have long been concerned with matters related to censorship and the teaching of English. Their record of publication verifies this. *English Journal* regularly publishes articles on censorship, and NCTE has published such works as *Obscenity, the Law, and the English Teacher* (1966) and *Meeting Censorship in the Schools: a Series of Case Studies* (1967). *The Students' Right to Read* has been around for many years, with its most recent revision, by Ken Donelson, in 1972. Another extensive revision is in process. State and regional affiliates such as Wisconsin (1963), New England (1969), Arizona (1969 and 1975), Iowa (1975), Southeastern Ohio (1976), and Indiana (1978) have devoted entire issues of their publications to censorship.

But at least since the well-publicized outbreak in West Virginia and the reporting of that conflict at the National Council of Teachers of English convention in New Orleans (1974), there have been increasing requests for new materials on how English teachers may cope with censorship. With incidents of censorship spreading all over the country, the requests for help have accelerated even more. When the NCTE Committee on Censorship was reconstituted and recharged in the fall of 1976, with Edward B. Jenkinson as chairperson, one of its first decisions was to publish helpful materials for English teachers to use in solving censorship problems. *Dealing with Censorship* is the result.

> James E. Davis
> Ohio University

I The Current Climate

Many English teachers have not had to deal with censorship, and they need to know what is currently happening in case they do face censorship in the future. Those who have faced or are facing censorship need to know they are not alone. They may also get some helpful ideas from knowing what others have done.

Jenkinson's introductory article hypothesizes that censorship is on the rise. He offers four reasons for this rise, identifies prominent censors and what is being censored, and expresses his major fear—that students might lose the right to learn through exploring ideas. Burress points out that surveys of censorship and the English teacher have been done on a fairly regular basis at least since 1963. His 1977 NCTE survey affirms that censorship in the schools is accelerating. Glatthorn's 1977 article points out that the wave of censorship has not yet crested and offers suggestions on how the profession should respond. Small concentrates on some dimensions of censorship that he thinks do not usually get enough attention—the historical, social, educational, and human. Small says that we must attempt to understand censors and work not to alienate them—after all, we do not want to lose their interest in schools. Donelson's article alerts teachers and others to some of the basic issues and problems involving definitions of obscenity and how these relate to school censorship. There is no unambiguous definition of obscenity, as his survey of legal decisions reveals, so the teacher must learn to gauge community standards to some extent, while, at the same time, trying to keep those standards from limiting too severely what is offered in schools. Books cannot fight for themselves. The section concludes with Rhodes' characterization of court cases as a game of chance, which the English teacher may or may not win. The game is risky, but it can be won if teachers play well and do not make the mistake of thinking that the opposition is less than able.

1 Dirty Dictionaries, Obscene Nursery Rhymes, and Burned Books

Edward B. Jenkinson
Indiana University

When parents complained that "seventy or eighty" words in *The American Heritage Dictionary* were obscene or otherwise inappropriate for high school students, the school board ordered the dictionary removed from the high school in Cedar Lake, Indiana.[1] In Eldon, Missouri, when twenty-four parents filed a complaint noting that thirty-nine words in *The American Heritage Dictionary* were objectionable, the school board voted to remove the dictionary from a junior high school.[2]

The dictionary protesters obviously ignored nearly all of the 155,000 words in the 1550 pages of the *AHD* and focused only on the so-called dirty words. One parent in Eldon was reported as saying: "If people learn words like that it ought to be where you and I learned it—in the street and in the gutter."[3] A board member in Cedar Lake noted: "We're not a bunch of weirdo book burners out here, but we think this one [the *AHD*] goes too far."[4] One of the more frequently criticized words in the Cedar Lake controversy was the word *bed*. "Among the nine definitions listed are 'a place for lovemaking' and 'a marital relationship with its rights and intimacies.' "[5]

After registering an initial response of outrage upon hearing about the fate of the *AHD*, a lover of language might dismiss the bannings as the acts of school boards in small towns. Many people believe that most censorship activity takes place only in small towns. Such is not the case. A recent study indicates that "censorship disputes are twice as likely to grow up in large cities (with over 100,000 residents) than in small communities having fewer than 2,500 residents. Large cities are also 50 percent more likely to spawn such cases than are either middle-sized or small urban communities."[6]

In 1976, the *AHD* joined four other dictionaries on the no-purchase list for the entire state of Texas. According to the *Newsletter on Intellectual Freedom:*

> Education Commissioner Marlin Brockette halted an expected protest against five dictionaries *(American Heritage Dictionary, The Doubleday Dictionary, Webster's Seventh New Collegiate Dictionary, The Random House College Dictionary,* and *Webster's New World Dictionary of the American Language)* by stating that no works would be purchased that "present material which would cause embarrassing situations or interfere in the learning atmosphere of the classroom." Complaints were expected against definitions for "bed," "knock up," "faggot," and other expressions with sexual meanings.[7]

Commissioner Brockette's announcement was reported in various Texas newspapers on November 12, 13, and 14, 1976. Four months before his announcement, Brockette received bills of particulars from various groups of citizens about the dictionaries that had been submitted for adoption by the State of Texas. One of the letters called attention to these objectionable entries in *Webster's New World Dictionary of the American Language:*

> 1. bed - p. 81 vt, bedded, bedding - 3. to have sexual intercourse with, bed and board 2. the married state
> 2. fag - p. 341 2. slang, a male homosexual; term showing contempt, also faggot.
> 3. horny - p. 459 4. slang, sexually excited - horniness, n.
> 4. hot - p. 460 3. d) having strong sexual desire - lustful
> 5. knock - p. 529 (knock up) 2. slang, to make pregnant.
> 6. queer - p. 785 slang, homosexual; term showing contempt
> 7. rubber - p. 838 3. c) slang, a condom
> 8. shack - p. 881 shack up with (slang) to share living quarters with (one's lover)
> 9. slut - p. 908 1. a dirty, untidy woman; slattern 2. a sexually immoral woman • sluttish adj. sluttishly adv. sluttishness n.[8]

Calling attention to two items in a Texas proclamation about textbooks, the dictionary protesters stated:

> After reviewing the above referenced dictionary, we are of the opinion this is in violation of both sections 1.7 and 1.8. [According to the protesters, this is the wording of those two sections of the Texas proclamation: 1.7 "Textbooks offered for adoption shall not include blatantly offensive language or illustrations." 1.8 "Textbooks offered for adoption shall not present material which could cause embarrassing situations or interference in the learning atmosphere of the classroom."] Many of the

words listed on the attached list could not be printed in a newspaper or said on television or on the radio. We find the words very offensive and embarrassing and feel many people would agree. Every word on the attached list violates the Proclamation as stated above and we respectfully request these words be deleted or else this book be turned down for adoption.[9]

The removal of the dictionaries from the purchase list in Texas was hailed by Norma and Mel Gabler, the self-styled textbook analysts who operate Educational Research Analysts. The Gablers wrote:

God gave parents a number of victories. In Texas alone, the State Textbook Committee did a good job of selecting the best of the available books. Then, the State Commissioner of Education removed 10 books, including the dictionaries with vulgar language and unreasonable definitions.[10]

When many parents and teachers with whom I have spoken hear about the banning of the dictionaries, they begin asking questions about censorship activity in the United States. Their questions provide a useful framework for the rest of this article.

Question: Is Censorship Activity on the Rise?

In my estimation, there are more attempts at censorship now than ever before. There are more than fifty state and national organizations that are concerned about all the educational materials used in the schools. And I believe that the work of such organizations is prompting many citizens to protest textbooks, library books, films, and homework assignments. I have read several recent surveys of teachers of English in which the researcher attempted to determine the scope of censorship activity. When the researchers compared the results of recent surveys with previous surveys, they noted that teachers are now reporting more incidents of censorship.

Question: Why Is Censorship Activity on the Rise?

I think there are at least four major reasons for the increasing attempts at censorship. First, many parents do not recognize the subject matter we now call English. They think that English is diagramming sentences, writing innocuous themes, and reading *Silas Marner*. When some parents do take the time to look at their children's textbooks or to talk with them about homework assignments, the parents do not always understand what their children are doing, nor do they understand why students are being asked to read certain contemporary works of literature. Consequently, the parents may become upset after they read sentences out of context or after they try to compare what they did twenty or thirty years ago with what their children are doing today.

Second, some parents neither read nor like contemporary literature. They object to seeing four-letter words in print, and they also object to any stories that show conflict between teenagers and adults. One familiar cry of the censors is that today's books are anti-Christian, anti-parent, anti-government, immoral, and obscene.

A third reason that censorship is on the rise is that more and more organized groups are involved in attempts at censorship. On the one hand, we have groups—frequently calling themselves "Concerned Citizens" and frequently obtaining materials and advice on censorship from specific organizations—who object to books that they call anti-God, anti-authority, and so forth. On the other hand, we have groups that object to books that they label sexist or racist. I have heard this latter kind of censorship referred to as "good censorship." But to me, censorship is censorship whether it be labeled good or bad.

A fourth reason for the rise in censorship is that the schools are a convenient target for unhappy citizens. Many people feel that they cannot fight Washington, the state capitol, or even city hall. When they become unhappy because of inflation, federal or state laws, the so-called moral decline, or anything else, they want to lash out. But they don't always know how to attack the problems that really trouble them. So they vent their spleen upon the schools.

Whether elected or appointed, school boards must conduct public meetings. Citizens who feel that they cannot fight Washington can complain to school boards because they are accessible. And the schools themselves are open every weekday, at least nine months out of the year. Parents can go to a school and demand an audience with the principal, and he or she can't refuse to see them. Nor can a classroom teacher refuse to see parents.

Because the media have given the schools so much publicity since the student protest movement of the sixties, taxpayers have a tendency to feel that almost everything that's wrong with society stems from the schools. So the schools have become a target for irate taxpayers, and censorship is one of their weapons.

Question: Who Attempts to Censor Materials in the Schools?

Note how that question is phrased. The word *attempts* is significant since only a person in authority can actually censor materials. But anyone can bring sufficient pressure to bear on a person in authority so that books will be censored.

People and organizations who attempt to censor school materials can be classified as follows. First, we have the students. Some take books home and show their parents a few four-letter words or controversial ideas, knowing that the parents will explode. In some cases, I think the students are simply trying to get out of work or stir up trouble. Other students honestly object to books because the language or ideas offend them. But I think that teachers would find substitute books for those students if only the students would ask for them.

Second, we have those parents who are concerned with the language their children are reading or with the ideas they are being exposed to. I think parents have a legitimate concern about what their children see and hear. But the question that always arises in my mind is this: As a parent, do my rights of censorship or selection of materials for my children extend to the children of others? I believe the answer to that question is no.

Third, there are some teachers who censor books. Sometimes teachers censor books for the same reasons that parents and students do; other times, I think teachers censor books out of fear. For example, in one very large school I know well, one parent objected quietly to *Of Mice and Men*. The teachers quit teaching that novel and removed it from the classroom shelves. When I mentioned this incident at a conference, a teacher from another school talked with me afterward and reported that the same thing occurred in the school in which she teaches.

The fourth group of censors is school librarians. Many librarians, like many classroom teachers, fight any attempt at censorship. But others, perhaps out of fear of losing their jobs, quietly remove books from the library shelves.

Fifth, we have those school administrators who censor books sometimes without reading them. In one case that was reported to me, a superintendent demanded that classroom teachers stop teaching *Flowers for Algernon* because a "leading citizen" objected to the book. The superintendent admitted that he had not read the entire book, but he ordered his teachers to stop teaching "that filthy book." In a second case, the superintendent in Oakland, California, ordered *Daddy Was a Number Runner* removed from the junior high school library shelves on the basis of one parental complaint and over the objections of her personally selected panel of experts. The grand irony in that incident is that the superintendent had been the director of the National Right to Read Program.

The sixth group of censors is school board members. In Island Trees, New York, the newly elected school board censored at least a dozen books. That case is in the courts. The school board in Strongsville, Ohio, lost a case after removing books from the schools. Other school boards throughout the country have ordered books removed from classrooms or library shelves. Some have been successful; others, fortunately, have failed.

The seventh group of censors is the clergy. Several incidents have been precipitated by clergy. Probably the most famous is the Kanawha County, West Virginia, battle that was ignited by a school board member who was the wife of a minister and that was fanned by several ministers. On the other hand, ten clergymen in Kanawha County fought attempts at censorship.

The eighth group of censors is the organizations that precipitate censorship incidents. Appendix 8 of James C. Hefley's *Textbooks on Trial* gives this information about Mel and Norma Gablers' Educational Research Analysts, Inc., in Longview, Texas: "As the major textbook clearinghouse, the Gablers have thousands of textbook reviews—their own, plus reviews from many other states. Most are by page, paragraph, and line, prepared by parents for parents, and consider the age level and knowledge of the students. They concentrate on pointing out questionable content. . . ."[11]

Other organizations that supply reviews for concerned parents are America's Future in New Rochelle, New York, the John Birch Society, PONYU (Parents of New York—Unite), and the many concerned citizens groups that are springing up across the country. Organizations actively involved in attempting to remove books that are racist or sexist are the National Organization of Women (NOW) and the Council on Interracial Books for Children.

Question: What Is Being Censored?

It is tempting to answer that question with one word: everything. And that single-word answer would not be an exaggeration nor would it be misleading. But to be more specific, I usually cite these fourteen targets of the censors.

1. Novels for adolescents. The organized censors do not approve of the subjects that novelists today select for treatment in stories for teenagers. Parents prone to censor books do not think their children should be reading S. E.

Hinton's *The Outsiders,* John Donovan's *I'll Get There, It Better Be Worth the Trip,* Nat Hentoff's *I'm Really Dragged But Nothing Gets Me Down,* Paul Zindel's *My Darling, My Hamburger,* or his *The Pigman,* Judy Blume's *Are You There God? It's Me Margaret,* and dozens of other popular books. Many protective parents do not want their sons and daughters reading books about student conflicts with parents, drug use and abuse, sex, homosexuality, teenage violence, the horrors of the ghetto, teenage pregnancy, and so forth. Such parents seem to remember the books they read when they were young, and they want the school to focus attention on those books. The irate parents would have the schools remove the works of such authors as Judy Blume, Nat Hentoff, and Paul Zindel and replace them with the novels of Betty Cavanna, Anne Emery, Rosamund DaJardin, and John R. Tunis.

2. Realistic dialogue. Proponents of the back-to-basics movement do not want their children reading sentences that are not grammatically correct. They object to stories in which authors have characters speak substandard English. In other words, some censors believe that all characters in all books must speak standard English at all times. Otherwise, the censors contend, their children will be taught to use substandard English, since they will imitate the language of the characters in books.

3. The works of "questionable" writers. The organized censors have a tendency to label authors as "questionable" if the censors do not agree with the ideas of the writers. The organized censors decry anthologies that contain stories, poems, and essays by such writers as Langston Hughes, Dick Gregory, Ogden Nash, Richard Wright, Joan Baez, and Malcolm X. Such writers are also often labeled subversive.

4. The literature of homosexuals. Here is a portion of a message distributed by members of a Save Our Children group:

> Save Our Children wishes to thank those members of your community who, with their contributions, helped sweep us to victory in Florida. The battle has only begun, however, and soon we will carry our campaign all over the nation. . . . For years homosexuals have been hogging the news with their demands for equal rights, and it is time we pushed back. It is time that, along with thieves and murderers, they be branded for the sinners they are and removed from

Dirty Dictionaries 9

society. . . . You can fight to eliminate homosexual literature from our schools and libraries. This includes works by such homosexuals as Emily Dickinson, Gertrude Stein, John Milton, Willa Cather, Virginia Woolf, Hans Christian Andersen, Tennessee Williams, Walt Whitman, Marcel Proust, Oscar Wilde, Andre Gide, Horatio Alger, Jr., T. E. Lawrence, Jean Cocteau, Truman Capote, Jean Genet, Gore Vidal, Rod McKuen.

5. "Trash." Books that are frequently labeled "trash" include *The Catcher in the Rye, Flowers for Algernon, Soul on Ice, Forever, Black Boy, Laughing Boy, Go Ask Alice,* and most contemporary novels for adolescents.

6. Ideas, teaching methods, and books that are examples of "secular humanism." In the foreword to James C. Hefley's *Textbooks on Trial,* Congressman John Conlan writes: "Bad textbooks full of immoral content and violence, biased toward increasing the centralized power of a secular humanistic state, will ultimately destroy the family, decent social standards, and basic principles of decentralized government that safeguard every American's individual freedom." Throughout *Textbooks on Trial,* the author indicates that secular humanism is a religion running rampant through America's schools.

7. Ethnic studies, drug education, and so forth. Concerned parents can obtain petitions that they can present to an administrator or teacher that call for the removal of their children from classes in which a variety of topics are discussed or a variety of methods are used. This petition, or a variation of it, was presented to teachers and/or administrators in Tulsa, Oklahoma, in 1975, in Culver, Indiana, in 1976, in Deer River, Minnesota, in 1977, and in Austin, Texas, in 1977:

This letter is to inform you that certain rights and privileges with regard to the instruction of our child _____ are permanently and specifically reserved by us, the parent(s). The familial relationship involving personal relationships, attitudes, responsibilities, and religious and social training are the sole prerogative of the parents.

Therefore, you are hereby notified that our child _____ will not be enrolled, instructed, or made to participate in any course or class, workshop, study group, etc., which includes: instruction in any training or education in sex and/or sexual attitudes, personal and family emotional development, introspective examination of social and cultural aspects of family life, group therapy or group criticism of family life, "sensitivity training," "magic circles," Human Development programs, social awareness, self-awareness or self-understanding, situation ethics, value judgment, values clarification, moral value alteration, Behavior Modification, Reality Therapy, ethnic studies, "Humanities," the philosophies of the Humanist religion, the Occult, or any combination or degree thereof, without the consent of the undersigned by express written and signed permission.

That petition virtually rules out the teaching of English as we know it. Any theme assignment could be construed to be attempts at "self-understanding" or "personal . . . emotional development," and many theme assignments could be construed to be "introspective examination of social and cultural aspects of family life." Literature can also be so construed. So that leaves the diagramming of sentences which, I was told, teachers of English in a heavily censored school system found to be the one safe activity they could assign to students.

8. Role playing. In Park Rapids, Minnesota, parents attending a meeting of concerned citizens received a set of guidelines for the selection of public school material that included this statement: "Classroom materials, textbooks, etc., must not use psycho-drama (role playing) as a teaching tool." A bill was introduced into the Indiana State Senate that called for the abolition of role playing as a teaching method for "the purpose of classifying, controlling, or predicting behavior." The sponsor of that defeated bill introduced another bill that would have prohibited teaching materials that presented "sadistic or degrading behavior," that invaded "the privacy of the pupil, the pupil's home and parents," and that contained "either profane statements or disrespectful statements or pictures regarding the religious or ethical beliefs of others." Many people could subscribe to the major tenets of the proposed bill. However, the critical questions are these: Who decides what is "degrading behavior," for instance? Would a novel be rejected because of the "degrading behavior" of one of the characters? Who would enforce the bill? Would the enforcement of this and similar bills lead to a police state atmosphere?

9. The absence of grammar rules. Item 7 of "A Policy Statement of the Kanawah County Board of Education" states that textbooks "used in the study of the English Language

shall teach that traditional rules of grammar are a worthwhile subject for academic pursuit and are essential for effective communication among English speaking people." The same rule is a part of the Texas adoption requirements which James C. Hefley notes were proposed by Norma and Mel Gabler when they were called into Kanawha County in 1974.

10. Materials that contain negative statements about parents. The guidelines distributed at a meeting in Park Rapids, Minnesota, noted that classroom "materials, textbooks, audio and/or visual aids must not portray parents as unloving, stupid, hypocritical, old fashioned, possessive nor in any other negative way." Similar statements have been made by censors elsewhere in the United States.

11. Phase-elective English programs. Proponents of the back-to-basics movement are calling for the abolition of phase-elective programs. People who cannot describe phase-elective programs are blaming them for the declining SAT scores, for the failure of Johnny to write well, and for the failure of Susie to read well.

12. Sex education. Long a target for the censors, courses in sex education are still prime targets for unhappy parents.

13. Sexist stereotypes. Members of the feminist movement are objecting to school materials that stereotype women.

14. Racist statements. The Council on Interracial Books for Children has objected to books that contain racist slurs. The Council has actively campaigned for fairer treatment of all races in textbooks, but it has also listed books, including novels, that should be removed from school shelves.

Question: What Are the Results of Attempts to Censor Books or Other Teaching Materials?

It is impossible to say exactly what might come from a censorship incident. But, based on an analysis of several censorship incidents, here are some possible results:

1. A community tends to be polarized. People side with the censors or with the censured. Few adopt a neutral position.
2. Teachers and administrators are frequently demoralized when they become the targets of an attack because they

teach certain materials or because certain materials are taught in their schools. Some leave their positions; some suffer breakdowns; others refuse to discuss the censorship incidents; and a few decide never to teach anything that might be construed to be controversial.

3. Teachers frequently find that they have lost stature in the community.
4. The books under attack become the bestsellers within the community. Students who would not ordinarily read the books under attack make every attempt to do so. Thus, the censors frequently succeed—unwittingly, of course—in encouraging students to read books that the censors don't want them to read.
5. When the censors call for teachers to use felt-tip pens to black out objectionable words in books, the results are frequently not what the censors wanted. For example, a passage with a *damn* or *hell* in it might take on an entirely new meaning if the offensive word is deleted. The imaginative mind can substitute many words for the deleted one. Consider the effects of the felt-tip pen on the following:

    Mary had a little _____.
    Its _____ was _____ as _____,
    And everywhere that Mary _____,
    The _____ was sure to _____.

6. A successful censorship attack leads to more attacks within the same community, and it also leads to "censorship fallout." In other words, a book that is banned in one community will certainly become a target for censors in another community.

Question: After Studying Censorship for Several Years, What Do You Fear Most?

I fear that students might lose the right to learn, the right to read, the right to explore ideas. Whenever I see petitions and guidelines like those mentioned in this article, I shudder. I certainly hope that my children will not have to grow up in a society in which they are denied the right to study any subject, to read any book they deem worth their attention, and to speak out on any topic they think worthy of discussion.

I fear the mentality that would urge the burning of books. When school boards order the destruction of books (by burning or shredding), I wonder if the school board members have read history. I wonder if they have considered the consequences of their acts. And I worry about the consequences of the board of directors in the Line Mountain School District in Pennsylvania ordering the destruction of *Go Ask Alice, Bonnie Jo, Go Home,* and *The Cheese Stands Alone.*

I hope that American children will not have to witness nor read about the burning of more books; rather, I hope that they will grow up free to read.

Notes

1. *Newsletter on Intellectual Freedom* 25 (November 1976):145.
2. *The St. Louis Post-Dispatch,* 18 April 1977, p. 4A.
3. Ibid.
4. Ibid.
5. Ibid.
6. Bruce A. Shuman, "A Geography of Censorship: A Regional Analysis of Recent Cases," *Newsletter on Intellectual Freedom* 26 (January 1977):3.
7. *Newsletter on Intellectual Freedom* 26 (March 1977):47.
8. Letter dated July 6, 1976, from Mr. and Mrs. Earnest Baruch and Mrs. Carl S. Droste to Dr. Marlin Brockette, Commissioner of Education, Austin, Texas.
9. Ibid.
10. See green printed sheet distributed by the Gablers entitled "The Mel Gablers—Consumer Advocates for Education."
11. James C. Hefley, *Textbooks on Trial* (Wheaton, Ill.: Victor Books, 1976), p. 205.

2 A Brief Report of the 1977 NCTE Censorship Survey

Lee Burress
University of Wisconsin—Stevens Point

Beginning at least as early as 1963, the National Council of Teachers of English or its affiliates or individual members of NCTE have attempted to assess censorship problems encountered by English teachers in their use of learning resource materials. The term "censorship" is a shorthand term that implies more exactness than perhaps is the case for the variety of problems that teachers may have encountered. To quantify complaints or their results is difficult. The statistics that follow in this report should be regarded as indicative rather than as absolutely conclusive. However, since approximately the same population has been questioned several times with approximately the same set of questions, the patterns that have emerged suggest the survey has some degree of dependability, if for no other reason than its consistency.

In February 1977 the NCTE office mailed out 2,000 questionnaires to a sample of secondary school teachers who were members of the council. After a reminder letter was mailed out, a total of 630 questionnaires was returned, or slightly over 30 percent. This was a somewhat lesser return than the 1966 survey sponsored by NCTE, which produced a return of 38 percent of 1600 questionnaires. The questionnaires circulated for the same length of time in both surveys. But the 1977 questionnaire was nine pages in length and asked several more questions than did the six page 1966 survey.

The majority of returns was from east of the Rocky Mountains —therefore regional comparisons for the entire country are somewhat incomplete. Nevertheless, those regional differences that did show up are similar to the patterns shown by other studies. Also, the survey succeeded in reaching a fair cross-section of the types of schools found throughout the country. Enrollment totals in respondents' schools varied as follows:

Enrollment	No. of Respondents
0–299	127
300–599	130
600–999	128
1,000–1,499	96
1,500–up	109

Types of schools by grades varied as follows:

Grades	No. of Respondents
1–12	67
7–12	86
9–12	297
10–12	111
Other	53

Kinds of area served by schools varied as follows:

Area Served	No. of Respondents
Metropolitan (250,000)	51
Suburban (peripheral to metropolitan)	135
Urban (above 10,000)	98
Rural (below 10,000)	304

In the 1977 survey, there were four basic questions: Have you or teachers in your department, since September 1, 1975, had objections to (1) a book or book title? (2) a magazine? (3) a film or AV material? or (4) the school newspaper or creative writing publication? The form of the question was the same in 1966, except that items (3) and (4) were not included. Following each of these basic questions was a detailed set of questions asking about the objector, objections, and results of the complaint. The questionnaire also included a list of one hundred books composed of fifty innocuous titles and fifty controversial titles. The list served as an instrument for comparing the holdings of the respondents' school libraries.

Because the 1977 survey expanded the number and kinds of questions, the willingness of respondents to answer the total questionnaire was tested heavily. For this reason the total responses to several of the questions is less than 630, the number of questionnaires returned. Tabular summaries of data relating to book censorship, periodical censorship, AV censorship, and censorship of student publications are included in respective sections below.

Statistical analysis of information obtained from the questionnaires was performed by the Academic Computer Services of the University of Wisconsin, Stevens Point. The survey questionnaire is appended to this article.

I. Books

Approximately 49 percent of the returns indicated some kind of attempted or completed censorship, when all four basic categories are considered (see Table 1). If book censorship alone is considered, the 1977 survey shows that slightly over 30 percent of the returns reported book censorship pressures. In raw numbers, 188 respondents reported objections to books used in their schools; 427 respondents reported no objections. In contrast, the NCTE survey of 1966 showed just over 20 percent of the returns reporting censorship pressures on books. The 10 percent increase seems a significant difference.

The northeastern part of the United States reported the highest incidence of censorship pressure on books—34 percent of reporting schools; the south reported the lowest incidence of attempted

Table 1

Source of Objections
(All Media)

Source	No. of Objections	Percent of Objections
Parent	245	73%
School		
Librarian	10	2.9%
Teacher	25	7.4%
English dept. chair	4	1.2%
Administrator	35	10.4%
Board of education	3	.8%
	77	23%
Clergy	12	3.5%
Student	2	.6%
	14	4%
Total	336	100%

censorship—28 percent; the midwest and great plains states were in between—32 percent. The regional variances seem partly explicable when related to factors of school size and number of books in the school library. These are the factors uncovered by the survey as most clearly influencing the incidence of book censorship.

There were 145 titles that appeared as the object of complaints in the 1977 report, 142 in the 1966 report. A number of the 1977 titles appeared in previous surveys, and the objections are quite similar in nature and distribution to those of earlier surveys.

While quantifying the objections presents some difficulty, it appears that the most common objection was to the language of the books (see Table 2). This objection is ambiguous; it sometimes refers to the grammar or dialect, or it may refer to profanity, or to so-called obscenity. (It is the belief of the author of this report that none of the titles objected to would be found obscene by a court. The complete list of titles is below; readers may decide for themselves.) It appears that to many objectors grammar has a moral connotation; bad grammar is equivalent to bad morals.

Next in frequency to objections to language were objections to sex, or erotic qualities in the books. The two sets of objections, to language and to sex, tend to overlap; taken together, they make up about 75 percent of the total number of objections. That is quite similar to previous surveys on this subject. If the books objected to for sexual matter are examined, it seems a reasonable conclusion that any reference to sex or any presentation of erotic qualities in a book, or for that matter in periodicals, is objectionable, to some persons. It is not obscenity that is objectionable; any presentation in literature of sex or sexuality may be objected to, no matter how decorous the reference.

It is noteworthy that relatively few objections of an ideological sort appear. Two possible explanations may be offered. One is that many persons in our society accept the notion that the school or the library should present a complete spectrum of ideas. Complementary to this is the notion that obscenity is not protected by the Constitution, and should not be presented in the schools. Therefore it is proper to object to a book or magazine for its obscenity, not for its ideas. It is also quite possible that many persons direct their objections against language or obscenity, when actually they may be objecting to the ideas in a book.

There were some objections to books because of racial matters, or because of religious references, but relatively few persons explicitly objected on these grounds. However, when the list of titles that have been objected to is examined, it is noteworthy that books with racial implications appear relatively often: *Manchild in the Promised Land, Down These Mean Streets, Nigger, Native Son, I Know Why the Caged Bird Sings,* and *Ann Frank, the Diary of a Young Girl.*

On the other hand there are few objections to books on the grounds of violence. Only about 4 percent of the objections cite violence as the grounds of complaint. This is similar to previous surveys. However, to anticipate the discussion of objections to films and AV materials, violence appeared relatively often as grounds for objection to those media. Apparently violence in books is not as provocative as violence in films.

An examination of the answers to the question "Who objected?" (see Table 2) shows that in 1977, 78 percent of the objections to books was by parents; 19 percent was by members of the school staff—teacher, principal, superintendent, librarian. This is in marked contrast to the 1966 report in which 48 percent of the objections were reported by parents and approximately 42 percent were reported by members of the school staff. If the 1977 report is correct, then the increase in school censorship pressures would seem to have come from parents, not from the school staff. Perhaps the efforts that various professional groups have made in the last ten years have resulted in greater awareness of the need to act in professional ways on the part of members of the school staff.

It must be noted however that, as previous surveys showed, when parents complain, more often than not the attempted censorship does not occur. Thus according to the 1977 survey only about 34 percent of the parental requests to censor a book were carried out. However, when members of the school staff complained, in about 71 percent of the cases the book was censored. The school staff is apparently much more effective than parents in getting materials removed.

So far as this survey shows, most censorship pressure on the schools is from parents or school staff members. Rarely does a clergyman, or some other professional person, or member of the community complain about book use in the schools. The survey failed to ascertain what may have motivated the parent or school staff member to complain. In this respect, this survey is similar to previous ones. Only infrequently have the surveys reported that some organized group that monitors the use of school materials has been the source of objections reported on the questionnaire. The 1977 survey specifically asked a question concerning such

1977 NCTE Censorship Survey 19

groups, but the respondents apparently did not perceive that their difficulties emanated from such groups.

To the present writer no characteristic of censorship seems more evident than its capriciousness. There is however a tendency in schools and libraries to believe that by "careful book selection" censorship may be prevented. This term is very close to euphemism for self-censorship, or pre-censorship. Several respondents did not hesitate to say that they did intend to censor the materials used in the schools. One respondent from North Dakota wrote that "Teachers, principals and superintendents have a perfect right to censor books used in the schools."

In order to test the proposition that book selection practices in school libraries—such as excluding controversial books—were in fact influencing the incidence of censorship, a list of one hundred titles was included in the questionnaire. Half of the titles were books that had been reported on previous surveys as the objects of complaint; they were therefore considered controversial. The other half were considered innocuous. Both lists were taken from sources that would suggest a strong possibility of their being in a school library. The lists were combined in alphabetical order. Respondents were asked simply to indicate which of the titles were in their school library. A ratio of controversial titles to non-controversial titles was then determined for each of the respondents' schools. A statistical analysis of these ratios showed that the differences were not significant in comparing schools reporting censorship with schools not reporting censorship. The ratio of controversial titles to non-controversial titles for schools reporting censorship was 36:40; and for schools not reporting censorship the ratio was 35:39.

One Hundred Book Titles with the Percent of Schools
Reporting Each Book
(*indicates non-controversial books)

67.9	1.*ACROSS FIVE APRILS, I. Hunt	94.3	5. ANIMAL FARM, G. Orwell
95.6	2. ADVENTURES OF HUCKLEBERRY FINN, THE, M. Twain	75.6	6.*ANNA AND THE KING OF SIAM, M. Landon
26.0	3.*AMERICAN NEGRO FOLKTALES, R. M. Dorson	93.2	7.*ANNE FRANK: DIARY OF A YOUNG GIRL, A. Frank
68.1	4. ANDERSONVILLE, M. Kantor	61.4	8. AUTOBIOGRAPHY OF MALCOLM X, Malcolm X

83.2 9. BELL FOR ADANO, A, J. Hersey
93.2 10. BIBLE
63.7 11. BIG SKY, THE, A. B. Guthrie, Jr.
59.5 12. BLACK BOY, R. Wright
83.3 13. BLACK LIKE ME, J. H. Griffin
71.7 14.*BLESS BEAST & CHILDREN, G. Swarthout
85.9 15.*BORN FREE, J. Adamson
86.3 16. BRAVE NEW WORLD, A. Huxley
88.6 17.*BRIDGE OF SAN LUIS REY, T. Wilder
94.1 18.*CALL OF THE WILD, THE, J. London
90.5 19. CANTERBURY TALES, THE, G. Chaucer
76.5 20. CATCHER IN THE RYE, THE, J. D. Salinger
80.0 21.*CHRISTY, C. Marshall
88.7 22.*CONNECTICUT YANKEE IN KING ARTHUR'S COURT, M. Twain
75.9 23.*CYRANO DE BERGERAC, E. Rostand
93.7 24.*DAVID COPPERFIELD, C. Dickens
89.2 25.*DEATH BE NOT PROUD, J. Gunther
31.6 26. DELIVERANCE, J. Dickey
86.3 27.*DON QUIXOTE, M. De Cervantes

20.0 28. DOWN THESE MEAN STREETS, P. Thomas
63.7 29.*DROPOUT, J. Eyerly
31.3 30.*ESCAPE FROM FREEDOM, E. Fromm
93.7 31. EXODUS, L. Uris
71.6 32.*FAHRENHEIT FOUR FIFTY-ONE, R. Bradbury
87.6 33. FAREWELL TO ARMS, E. Hemingway
10.0 34. FEMALE EUNUCH, THE, G. Greer
48.1 35. FIXER, THE, B. Malamud
47.8 36. FOUNTAINHEAD, A. Rand
80.0 37.*GIANTS IN THE EARTH, O. E. Rolvaag
73.5 38. GO ASK ALICE, Anonymous
56.2 39.*GO, TEAM, GO, J. Tunis
71.7 40.*GO TELL IT ON THE MOUNTAIN, J. Baldwin
92.4 41. GONE WITH THE WIND, M. Mitchell
91.9 42. GOOD EARTH, THE, P. S. Buck
92.2 43. GRAPES OF WRATH, THE, J. Steinbeck
45.6 44.*GREAT ESCAPE, THE, P. Brickhill
61.0 45.*GREEK WAY, THE, E. Hamilton
75.4 46. HAWAII, J. Michener
80.2 47.*HOBBIT, THE, J. R. Tolkien

80.0 48. *HOT ROD, H. G. Felsen
88.9 49. *ILIAD, THE, Homer
81.6 50. *INCREDIBLE JOURNEY, THE, S. Burnford
70.8 51. INVISIBLE MAN, R. Ellison
93.3 52. *JANE EYRE, C. Bronte
87.5 53. *JOHNNY TREMAIN, E. Forbes
73.5 54. JOY IN THE MORNING, B. Smith
79.7 55. *KAREN, M. Killilea
80.2 56. *LANTERN IN HER HAND, A, B. S. Aldrich
51.7 57. LEARNING TREE, THE, G. Parks
57.6 58. *LITTLE BRITCHES, R. Moody
87.8 59. LORD OF THE FLIES, W. Golding
73.8 60. *LORD OF THE RINGS, THE, J. R. Tolkien
36.8 61. LOVE & THE FACTS OF LIFE, E. M. Duvall
69.4 62. LOVE STORY, E. Segal
65.4 63. *MAGNIFICENT OBSESSION, L. C. Douglas
52.7 64. MANCHILD IN THE PROMISED LAND, C. Brown
45.6 65. MISTER ROBERTS, T. Heggen
76.8 66. *MRS. MIKE, B. & N. Freedman
41.9 67. NIGGER, D. Gregory
88.9 68. NINETEEN EIGHTY-FOUR, G. Orwell
8.7 69. O, BEULAH LAND, M. L. Settle
88.3 70. OF MICE & MEN, J. Steinbeck
93.7 71. OLD MAN & THE SEA, E. Hemingway
86.5 72. *OLD YELLER, F. Gipson
91.0 73. *OLIVER TWIST, C. Dickens
64.3 74. ONE DAY IN THE LIFE OF IVAN DENISOVICH, A. Solzhenitsyn
77.1 75. ON THE BEACH, N. Shute
75.7 76. *OUTSIDERS, THE, S. E. Hinton
83.0 77. OX-BOW INCIDENT, W. Clark
93.7 78. *PEARL, THE, J. Steinbeck
87.3 79. *PRINCE AND THE PAUPER, M. Twain
78.4 80. *PYGMALION, G. B. Shaw
63.5 81. *RASCAL, S. North
95.1 82. RED BADGE OF COURAGE, THE, S. Crane
94.1 83. SCARLET LETTER, THE, N. Hawthorne
67.3 84. *SCARLET PIMPERNEL, THE, E. Orczy
85.7 85. SEPARATE PEACE, A, J. Knowles
82.7 86. *SEVENTEENTH SUMMER, M. Daly
84.1 87. *SHANE, J. Schaefer
63.0 88. SIDDHARTHA, H. Hesse

54.1	89.	SLAUGHTERHOUSE-FIVE, K. Vonnegut
62.4	90.	STRANGER, A. Camus
17.9	91.	STUDS LONIGAN, J. Farrell
59.0	92.*	SWIFTWATER, P. Annixter
85.6	93.*	SWISS FAMILY ROBINSON, THE, J. Wyss
92.4	94.	TO KILL A MOCKINGBIRD, H. Lee
77.3	95.*	TO SIR, WITH LOVE, E. R. Braithwaite
82.1	96.*	TRAVELS WITH CHARLEY, J. Steinbeck
63.8	97.*	TUNED OUT, M. Wojciechowska
77.6	98.	THE UGLY AMERICAN, E. Burdick & W. Lederer
70.5	99.	WEST SIDE STORY, I. Shulman
92.5	100 *	WUTHERING HEIGHTS, E. Bronte

The questionnaire also asked for the total number of books circulated in the school library. This question, like the previous library related question, required special effort from the respondent, and understandably elicited fewer responses than other items in the questionnaire. Nevertheless, given the data received, a statistical analysis by use of a T test showed that it was significant at the level of .035 in comparing schools reporting censorship with schools not reporting censorship. The average number of books in the library of schools reporting censorship (from 116 reports) was 10,812, while the average number of books in the library for schools not reporting censorship (from 251 reports) was 9,252.

The volume of books in the school library may be related to school size. The survey established that there is a highly significant relationship between school size and the incidence of censorship. The larger the school the more likelihood of censorship. This relationship, on the basis of a Chi square test, was significant at the level of .00. The survey therefore supports the hypothesis that the larger the school and the greater the number of books in the school library the more censorship pressure.

Apparently censorship is a phenomenon that may occur anywhere, and is not particularly characteristic of the so-called backwoods communities of the country. In fact, data from the survey question identifying the area served by the respondent's school—whether metropolitan, suburban, urban, or rural—turned out to be inconclusive. Furthermore, the survey fails to support any presumption about the kinds of material likely to provoke censorship. In concurrence with previous surveys, it gives evidence that the censorship phenomenon is capricious. Any book, it seems, may become a focus for objection.

In addition, it should be noted that while a few titles receive much attention from the would-be censors—*The Catcher in the Rye,* books by Steinbeck, *Brave New World, 1984,* and a few others—the great majority of titles receive only one complaint. Of the several hundred titles reported as the object of censorship since 1963 on various surveys, probably 70 percent were the object of a single complaint. Thus if a librarian is to be free from complaints, a typical library would have to remove hundreds of titles, since we know that many books have characteristics that arouse the sensitivities of censorious persons. On the current survey 75 percent of the titles were the object of a single complaint.

Readers may wish to examine the list of 145 titles included below and ponder the qualities of the books for themselves. As Nyla Ahrens pointed out in a 1965 doctoral dissertation that examined the same population as the present survey, the main objects of attack are contemporary books by American authors that examine the problems of our society realistically. It seems safe to conclude that the most careful pre-censorship will not protect the schools or libraries from complaints or attempted censorship, unless the pre-censorship goes so far as to preclude all recent American literature as well as a substantial body of English literature, including Shakespeare and the Bible.

What effect do these censorship pressures have? No easy answer can be made to this question, but it does seem the effect must be very depressing, at least from the standpoint of attempting to achieve the most effective education. In this survey no teacher was reported to have lost a position as a result of book selections, though there was one report of a person who came close to being dismissed over a complaint. The national media have reported dismissals in North Dakota, Wisconsin, Pennsylvania, and Indiana recently, as many teachers are aware.

It is clear from the survey that on a number of occasions teachers have been prevented from using their best judgment in the selection of books and films. As the chart beneath shows, in more than a third of the cases, when there was a complaint, the objectionable book was censored in some way—removed from classroom use, the title taken from a list of recommended books, the book removed from the library, or put on closed shelf. There are sixty-six titles of books that were censored as a result of complaints. Some of these books are clearly ephemeral, *Semi-Tough,* for example. But if teachers cannot select ephemeral books that they believe may interest a particular student or class, or may fit into a particular curricular unit, then the educational process is severely handicapped. Among the books that were censored are many of the greatest books of our literature, including *The Scarlet Letter, A Farewell to Arms, The Sound and the Fury,* and *The Grapes of*

Wrath. It is hard to understand a school system that prevents high school students from reading these books.

There are, however, some grounds for optimism. Though the number of reported complaints is higher than on previous surveys, the ability of the school system to deal with the complaints seems improved. 296 respondents reported their school systems had a planned procedure available, while 276 reported they had none. On a related question, 395 respondents' school systems apparently have a planned procedure for selecting resource materials; only 181 do not. This survey shows more rejections of censorship attempts, and more offers of alternative assignments (see Table 3), than were reported in 1966. Perhaps the school systems are learning more effective ways of dealing with parental complaints. It is somewhat hopeful to note that of the 145 titles objected to, only 66 were in fact denied to students in various schools throughout the land. It would be much better, of course, if none of those titles had been censored, but that the schools were able to withstand the degree of censorship pressure that currently exists, as well as they apparently did, gives hope of continued improvement in dealing with this problem.

List of All 145 Books Objected To
(*indicates that number of objections to book is given in parentheses)

ALIVE, P. Read, 1975
ALL THE LITTLE LIVE THINGS, W. Stegner, 1968
AMERICAN ENGLISH TODAY—12, H. Guth & E. Schuster, 1970
ANDERSONVILLE, M. Kantor, 1955
THE ANDROMEDA STRAIN, M. Crichton, 1969
AND THEN THERE WERE NONE, A. Christie, 1940
ANNE FRANK: THE DIARY OF A YOUNG GIRL, A. Frank, 1948
BEING THERE, J. Kosinski, 1971
A BELL FOR ADANO, J. Hersey, 1944
BIBLE
BIG SKY, A. Guthrie, Jr., 1947
BLACK BOY, R. Wright, 1942
BLACK LIKE ME, J. H. Griffin, 1961
*BLESS THE BEASTS AND CHILDREN, (3), A. Swarthout, 1970
BLUES FOR MR. CHARLIE, J. Baldwin, 1964
*BRAVE NEW WORLD, (4), A. Huxley, 1932
BREAKFAST OF CHAMPIONS, K. Vonnegut, 1973
BURIED ALIVE: THE BIOGRAPHY OF JANIS JOPLIN, M. Friedman, 1974
BUTTERFLY REVOLUTION, W. Butler, 1975
CALL OF THE WILD, J. London, 1903
CANTERBURY TALES, G. Chaucer, ca. 1400

*CATCH 22, (4),
J. Heller, 1961
*THE CATCHER IN
THE RYE, (25),
J. D. Salinger, 1945
CAT ON A HOT TIN ROOF,
T. Williams, 1953
CAT'S CRADLE,
K. Vonnegut, 1963
THE CHEERLEADER,
R. MacDougall, 1973
THE CHOCOLATE WAR,
R. Cormier, 1975
CHOIRBOYS,
J. Wambaugh, 1975
THE CRUCIBLE,
A. Miller, 1953
CRYING OF LOT 49,
T. Pynchon, 1966
A DAY NO PIGS WOULD
DIE, R. Peck, 1972
DEATH OF A SALESMAN,
A. Miller, 1949
DEEP VALLEY, B. W. &
E. C. Aginsky, 1971
*DELIVERANCE, (3),
J. Dickey, 1971
THE DEVIL AND DANIEL
WEBSTER, S. Benet, 1937
DOWN THESE MEAN
STREETS, P. Thomas, 1967
THE EXORCIST,
W. Blatty, 1971
THE FAMILY, E. Sanders,
1975
A FAREWELL TO ARMS,
E. Hemingway, 1929
THE FICTION OF
EXPERIENCE, M. Lesser &
J. Morris, eds., 1962
FIVE SMOOTH STONES,
A. Fairbairn, 1966
THE FIXER, B. Malamud,
1966
*FLOWERS FOR
ALGERNON, (5),
D. Keyes, 1970

FOREVER, J. Blume, 1976
FRANNY AND ZOOEY,
J. D. Salinger, 1961
THE GANG WHO COULDN'T
SHOOT STRAIGHT,
J. Breslin, 1971
A GATHERING OF GHETTO
WRITERS, IRISH, ITALIAN,
JEWISH, BLACK AND
PUERTO RICAN, W. Miller,
1972
THE GENETIC CODE,
I. Asimov, 1962
GHOSTS, H. Ibsen, 1881
THE GIRLS OF
HUNTINGTON HOUSE,
B. Elfman, 1972
*GO ASK ALICE, (10),
Anonymous, 1971
GOD BLESS YOU,
MR. ROSEWATER,
K. Vonnegut, 1968
THE GODFATHER,
M. Puzo, 1969
GOODBYE COLUMBUS,
P. Roth, 1970
THE GOOD EARTH,
P. S. Buck, 1931
GO TELL IT ON THE
MOUNTAIN, J. Baldwin, 1953
THE GRADUATE,
C. Webb, 1971
*THE GRAPES OF
WRATH, (12),
J. Steinbeck, 1939
THE GREAT GATSBY,
F. S. Fitzgerald, 1925
THE HEART IS A LONELY
HUNTER, C. McCullers, 1940
HERO/ANTI-HERO,
R. Rollin, 1973
THE HORSE DEALER'S
DAUGHTER, D. Lawrence,
1922
HUCKLEBERRY FINN,
M. Twain, 1884

HUMANITIES IN THREE CITIES, E. Fenton, 1969

HURRY SUNDOWN, K. Gilden, 1966

I KNOW WHY THE CAGED BIRD SINGS, M. Angelou, 1970

I'LL GET THERE, IT BETTER BE WORTH THE TRIP, J. Donovan, 1969

IMAGES OF WOMEN IN LITERATURE, M. Ferguson, ed., 1976

IN COLD BLOOD, T. Capote, 1966

IN THE NIGHT KITCHEN, M. Sendak, 1970

IS THERE A LIFE AFTER GRADUATION, HENRY BIRNBAUM?, C. Balducci, 1971

I NEVER LOVED YOUR MIND, P. Zindel, 1970

JAWS, P. Benchley, 1974

*JOHNNY GOT HIS GUN, (4), D. Trumbo, 1959

JOY IN THE MORNING, B. Smith, 1963

*LAST SUMMER, (3), E. Hunter, 1974

THE LEARNING TREE, G. Parks, 1963

LISA BRIGHT AND DARK, J. Neufeld, 1970

LITERATURE OF THE SUPERNATURAL, R. Beck, ed., 1975

THE LONELINESS OF THE LONG DISTANCE RUNNER, A. Sillitoe, 1972

*LORD OF THE FLIES, (7), W. Golding, 1959

*LOVE STORY, (5), E. Segal, 1970

LYSISTRATA, Aristophanes, 411 B.C.

*MANCHILD IN THE PROMISED LAND, (3), C. Brown, 1965

MAN, MYTH, and MAGIC, R. Cavendish, 1969

THE MARTIAN CHRONICLES, R. Bradbury, 1958

MASH, R. Hooker, 1975

MEAT ON THE HOOF, G. Shaw, 1973

MONK, M. Lewis, 1975

MR. AND MRS. BO JO JONES, A. Head, 1967

*MY DARLING, MY HAMBURGER, (6), P. Zindel, 1969

MY SWEET CHARLIE, D. Westheimer, in print 1977

NATIVE SON, R. Wright, 1940

NEW AMERICAN AND CANADIAN POETRY, J. Gill, ed., 1971

THE NEW AMERICAN POETRY, D. Allen, ed., 1960

NIGGER, D. Gregory, 1970

NINE STORIES, J. D. Salinger, 1948

*1984, (4), G. Orwell, 1949

95 POEMS, e. e. cummings, 1971

NOT WITHOUT LAUGHTER, L. Hughes, 1969

*OF MICE AND MEN, (12), J. Steinbeck, 1938

ON THE BEACH, N. Shute, 1957

*ONE DAY IN THE LIFE OF IVAN DENISOVICH, (6), A. Solzhenitsyn, 1963

*ONE FLEW OVER THE
CUCKOO'S NEST, (8),
K. Kesey, 1962
THE OTHER, T. Tryon, 1971
THE PAINTED BIRD,
J. Kosinski, 1965
THE PATCH OF BLUE,
G. Hill, 1934
PATTON, I. Peck, 1973
THE PIGMAN, P. Zindel, 1968
POEMS OVER LINE AND
LONGER [sic]
RED SKY AT MORNING,
R. Bradford, 1968
THE REDS, J. Thomas, 1970
THE REINCARNATION OF
PETER PROUD, M. Ehrlich,
1975
ROSEMARY'S BABY,
I. Levin, 1967
RUN SOFTLY, GO FAST,
B. Wersba, 1972
SARAH T., PORTRAIT OF
A TEENAGE ALCOHOLIC,
R. Wagnen, 1976
THE SCARLET LETTER,
N. Hawthorne, 1850
SEMI-TOUGH,
D. Jenkins, 1972
*A SEPARATE PEACE, (3),
J. Knowles, 1961
SEVEN CONTEMPORARY
SHORT NOVELS, C. Clerc
& L. Leiter, eds., 1969
*SLAUGHTERHOUSE-
FIVE, (4), K. Vonnegut, Jr.,
1969
SNOWBOUND, B. Pronzini,
1973
THE SOCIAL REBEL IN
AMERICAN LITERATURE,
R. Woodward & J. Clark, eds.,
1968
THE SOUND AND THE
FURY, W. Faulkner, 1929

SOUL ON ICE, E. Cleaver,
1967
THE STERILE CUCKOO,
J. Nichols, 1972
STRANGER IN A STRANGE
LAND, R. Heinlein, 1968
SUMMER OF '42,
H. Raucher, 1971
THE SUN ALSO RISES,
E. Hemingway, 1926
SYBIL, F. Schreiber, 1974
TELL ME HOW LONG THE
TRAIN'S BEEN GONE,
J. Baldwin, 1968
TELL ME THAT YOU
LOVE ME, JUNIE MOON,
M. Kellogg, 1968
THAT WAS THEN, THIS IS
NOW, S. Hinton, 1971
THIS PERFECT DAY,
I. Levin, 1975
TO SIR, WITH LOVE,
E. Braithwaite, 1959
ULYSSES, J. Joyce, 1922
UP THE DOWN STAIRCASE,
B. Kaufman, 1964
VOICES IN LITERATURE,
LANGUAGE, AND
COMPOSITION, J. Cline,
et al., eds., 1974
WELCOME TO THE
MONKEY HOUSE,
K. Vonnegut, 1968
WHERE ARE THE
CHILDREN?, M. Clark, 1976
WHITE DOG, R. Gary, 1970
WHY WAIT UNTIL
MARRIAGE, E. Duvall, 1965
THE WORD, I. Wallace, 1972
WORKING, S. Terkel, 1975
THE WORLD OF
DELACROIX, (1789-1863),
T. Prideaux, 1966

Table 2
Objectors and Objections to 145 Books
(Numbers total across; percentages total down)

Objections	Parent n=245	Lib. n=10	Teacher n=25	Eng. Dept. Chair. n=4	Administration n=35	Bd. of Ed. n=3	Clergy n=12	Student n=22	Total No. of Objections
Sexual references	51 20.8%	2 20.0%	5 20.0%		6 17.1%		4 33.3%	4 18.1%	72
Obscene, bad language	118 48.9%	4 40.0%	6 24.0%	1 25.0%	19 54.2%		5 41.6%	12 54.5%	165
Violence	4 1.6%		2 8.0%					2 9.1%	8
Religious ideas	16 6.5%				3 8.5%	2 66.6%		2 9.1%	23
Political ideas	3 1.2%				2 5.6%				5
Racial ideas	3 1.2%		1 4.0%		1 2.8%				5
Trash	2 .8%				1 2.8%				3
Not appropriate, not suitable	4 1.6%	1 10.0%	1 4.0%	1 25.0%	1 2.8%				8
Too vague to classify	6 2.4%	1 10.0%	6 24.0%		2 5.6%		1 8.3%		16
Not accurate	1 .4%								1
Added nothing to curriculum	1 .4%		1 4.0%	1 25.0%					3
Critical of parents	1 .4%								1

Table 2–Continued

Objections	Parent	Lib.	Teacher	Eng. Dept. Chair.	Administration	Bd. of Ed.	Clergy	Student	Total No. of Objections
Moral values	5 2.0%					1 33.3%	1 8.3%		7
Vulgar	9 3.2%			1 25.0%				2 9.1%	12
No reason	7 2.8%		2 8.0%						9
Drugs	1 .4%								1
Subject matter, graphic detail	5 2.0%		1 4.0%						6
Emotionally close	1 .4%	1 10.0%							2
Picture of tarot card	1 .4%								1
Condoned bad behavior	4 1.6%								4
Treatment of marriage and family		1 10.0%							1
Distorted view of life	2 .8%								2
Obscene pictures							1 8.3%		1
Total	99.8%	100.0%	100.0%	100.0%	99.4%	99.9%	99.8%	99.9%	

Table 3

Results of 287 Censorship Events
Dealing with 145 Books

Results	No. of Cases	Total No. of Reported Occurrences
No Censorship		141
Request denied	73	
Alternate assignment	68	
Censorship		109
Book removed from class use, from library, or from recommended list	97	
Book put on closed shelf	12	
Inadequate information or case still being considered		37
Total		287

II. Periodicals

An examination of the censorship pressures occasioned by periodicals supports some of the conclusions arrived at concerning book censorship. Complaints were reported by forty-eight respondents; 540 reported none. Thirty-one popular magazines were the object of attempted censorship. It is noteworthy that the objectionable titles are not titles that could be conceivably the subject of obscenity trials; they are the popular magazines of our time. *Time* was reported most often as objectionable; in fact, of the eighty-nine objections reported, thirty were to the popular news magazines— *Time, U.S. News and World Report, Newsweek,* and *Sports Illustrated.*

It is a striking evidence of the power of these censorship pressures that twenty-six out of thirty complaints resulted in some form of censorship of these news magazines. Sometimes the subscription was ended; occasionally a page was torn out; often magic marker was used to delete so-called offensive material. Apparently magic marker is an indispensable tool in some libraries for censoring objectionable periodicals (see Table 4).

The data on censorship of periodicals seem to indicate a strong desire to protect young people from knowledge of the grimy, gritty, unpleasant realities of the world outside the schoolhouse. It seems another form of the old tendency to kill the messenger because he brings bad news. The data also support the finding with books that censorship is capricious and irrational. Why prevent students in school from reading magazines which must be in the homes of many of the students?

List of All Periodicals Objected To

American Child	Newsweek
Bay Guardian Newspaper	Paris Match
Books	People
Bride's Magazine	Photography
Christian Science Monitor	Plain Truth
Crawdaddy	Planned Parenthood
Essence	Popular Photography
Esquire	Psychology Today
Glamour	Rolling Stone
Mad	Sports Illustrated
Mademoiselle	Teen
Modern Photography	Time
Ms.	Truth
National Lampoon	U.S. News and World Report

III. Films and AV Materials

Reports of censorship pressure on films and AV materials were fewer than reports on the other media surveyed (see Table 7). Perhaps the schools use relatively less such material; or more likely, access to films and AV material is largely limited to students, so that the constituency most likely to complain—parents—do not see the material, and so do not complain. For whatever reason, there were only forty-five reports of censorship pressure against films. It should be noted also that the questionnaire went to English teachers; a fuller report might have been obtained if the questionnaire had been addressed to speech or communications teachers. As it was, there were forty reports of objections to AV material; 545 respondents reported no objection. The largest number of objectors was parents, followed by members of the school staff (see Table 5).

Table 4

Disposition of Objections to Periodicals

		Periodicals Censored				
Objectors	Number of Reports of Complaints	Subscription Ended or Issue Removed	Issue Edited, Page Torn Out Black Marker Used	Put on Closed Shelf	Magazines Not Censored	Other or No Information
Administrators (principal, superintendent)	34	19	6	1	7	1
Librarians	34	13	7	10	3	1
Teachers	21	6	3	2	3	9
Parents	22	7	6	1	5	3
School employee (secretary or not specified)	6	2	2	2		
Clergy	2	1		1		
Local citizens	1					1
Student	1					1
Total	121	48	24	17	16	16

Note: total censored 89 (74%); total not censored 16 (13%); not known 16 (13%).

Objections are similar to those encountered with regard to books and periodicals (see Table 6). References to sexuality lead the list of complaints. As previously suggested, violence is found much more objectionable in films than in books. Objections to films because of their ideas seem to appear more often than is true for books. Are people more willing to accept the notion that the function of a library is to present a wide range of ideas in books than they are to accept a similar philosophy for films? It should be remembered too that national policy does support legal constraints on films and television. Many cities or states have film censorship laws or agencies; very few such laws or agencies exist for the print media. Moreover, the Federal Communications Commission has extensive regulations concerning television. These precedents may account in part for the different attitude toward the use of films in the schools, as compared with the attitude toward the use of books. This subject calls for further thought and investigation.

List of AV Materials Objected To

Amblin
Bless The Beasts and Children
The Boarded Window
Bonnie and Clyde
Conrack
Cooley High
Deliverance
Emperor of the North
Future Shock
Growing Up (girl's hygiene)
Having A Baby
Hello Mustache
Illustrated Man
The Longest Yard
The Lottery
(Polanski's) Macbeth
Making of Butch Cassidy and the Sundance Kid
Man Called Horse
On Death and Dying
Outer Space Connection
Romeo and Juliet
(Portions of) Roots
Sanctuary
Serpico
Summer of '42
Tommy
Understanding Your Love Feelings
Venereal Disease

All materials with the word *man* in the title
About Hitler's atrocities—exterminating Jews
About teenagers hitchhiking across country
Had to do with family life education
Showed birth of baby
Unsure - about abortion

Table 5

Reports of 45 Attempted Film and AV Censorship Events

Objector	Number of reports
Parents	25
Administrators (principals and superintendents)	10
Teachers	9
Member of board of education	4
Clergyman	1
Member of John Birch Society	1
Female speaker from women's group	1

Note: total exceeds 45 since there were several objectors on some occasions.

Table 6

Objections to AV Materials

Reasons for Objection to Material	Number of Objections
Sexual references	13
Homosexuality	2
Drugs	2
Language	9
Ideas	9
Secular humanism	1
Values presented contradicted those of the school	1
German people made to look bad	1
Male chauvinism	1
Derogated hunting	1
Evolution	1
Death	1
Unpopular religious beliefs	1
Race (*Roots*)	1
Violence	8
Showed mother being stoned by children	2
Rated R	2
Not suitable	2
Outdated (*Romeo and Juliet*)	1
Not clear	1

Note: total exceeds 45 since several objections were given in some cases to one film.

Table 7

Results of Objections to Films and AV

Final Action	Number of Cases
Censored (removed from class or recommended list, sent back, was not reordered)	25
Not censored	16
Unclear, undecided	4

IV. School Publications

The questionnaire asked about both creative writing publications and newspapers published by the school. Reports of both items are included in this discussion, since there was little difference in the nature of objections. There were very few reports concerning school creative writing publications. In total, there were 171 reports of pressure against school publications; 367 respondents reported no incidents.

This material is more difficult to deal with, since an analysis of the responses cannot be verified by examining the material objected to, as is the case with the other three media discussed in this report. The conclusions therefore must be more tentative, since there is no way of knowing, for example, whether or not a given publication dealt in a biased way with the material it supposedly reported on. Nevertheless a number of interesting implications do emerge.

It is noteworthy that censorship pressures on the school newspaper seem a prominent part of school life, second only in frequency of report to censorship pressures on books (see Table 10). There were 170 questionnaires that reported censorship pressures.

There were significant differences in the sources of complaints and in the nature of complaints. The newspaper is the only school media that does not arouse much parental complaint. Of the 227 complaints reported only 33 were from parents, or slightly over 14 percent, markedly in contrast to the source of complaints about books or films. The school staff provided the great bulk of complaints—58 percent of the complainants were teachers, principals, superintendents. Many others complained, including members of the Board of Education, businessmen, janitors, and others. The list beneath is worth examining in detail (see Table 8).

The reasons for objecting differ also in significant ways (see Table 9). There were very few objections to sexual references in school publications—only seven in all. But there were many objections to the tendency of school newspapers to be critical of the school, its administration, of teachers, of local businessmen, and of school activities—athletic or musical. There were many comments like the following: "The principal objected because it made the school look bad." In another case both a teacher and a principal objected because a reporter "expressed a personal opinion about the lack of service from guidance personnel." Another objection was to printing "information about how to change your schedule without getting caught." Local businessmen objected to criticism of the bus service, of supplies furnished the school, and other services. Janitors complained because the school paper did not support the janitors' strike. Do school newspapers have the same right to be critical of institutions that other newspapers have? Many school staff members and interested citizens apparently do not think so.

There were relatively few objections to the content of the paper of an ideological sort. More serious was a large group of complaints based on allegations of bad journalistic practices. No judgment could be formed from the questionnaires about the validity of these charges. Sometimes the respondents themselves believed the charges correct; sometimes they did not.

There were relatively few charges based on the use of language; here one finds the same ambiguity that appears in the objections to books. Is bad English immoral? Less than 10 percent of the charges were based on this objection; apparently the processes by which school papers are prepared result in generally conservative language.

Conclusion

A major conclusion of this report is that censorship pressure is a prominent and growing part of school life. Why this is so is a subject that needs further thought by interested persons. Academic freedom is rather well established in the institutions of higher learning, though even there occasional violations may be observed. But there is not as yet general acceptance of academic freedom for students or teachers at the elementary or secondary level of education. A few recent court cases suggest a growing body of law that may ultimately support the belief that academic freedom and the Bill of Rights apply as well to the lower level schools as they do to the institutions of higher education. The Supreme Court case of *Tinker vs. Des Moines Independent School District,* 393 U.S. 503 (1969) and the case of *Minarcini vs. Strongsville City School District,* 541 F. 2d 577 (6th Cir. 1976) offer some encouragement for the belief that the courts may yet protect teachers and students from the capricious threats revealed in this report.

A question that has concerned professional associations is whether the kind of material reported here should in fact be published. Some persons fear that these lists will be used to identify books and other learning resource materials for pre-censorship. In the opinion of this writer, that danger is negligible. Those inclined to be censors will find ready assistance from a host of organizations that do not believe in academic freedom. Publishing the actual lists of attempted or completed censorship cases will, we may hope, alert the general public to what is happening and arouse support for the selection by teachers and librarians in the schools of those books and periodicals they deem most useful.

Mark Twain observed that laughter is the human race's best weapon. The lists published above seem laughable indeed to this writer. Let us publicize these lists in the hope that the laughter they cause may blow away the humbuggery of censorship.

Table 8

Sources of Objections to School Publications
(Newspaper, Creative Writing Publications)

Objector	Number of Cases
Teachers	61
Administrators	73
Principals	61
Superintendents	6
Department chairs	6
Parents	33
Students	22
Librarians	4
Board of education	17
Coach of another school	1
Businessmen	3
Supplier	1
Bus operator	1
Local businessman	1
Local Bible class	1
PTA	1
Local citizens	4
Clergy	3
School news reporter	3
Janitors	2
Total	238

Note: sometimes two or more persons complained about the same publication.

Table 9
Objections to School Publications

Objection	Number of Cases
Paper was critical	58
Of the school	18
Of the administration	11
Of teachers	11
Of students	5
Of local businessmen	3
Of local clergy	1
Of basketball team	2
Of football team	1
Of band or director	2
Of unspecified persons	4
Other kinds of content	16
Sexual references	7
Objectionable ideas	9
Too controversial	2
Unpatriotic	2
Too conservative	1
Anti-establishment	1
Did not support janitor strike	1
Sexist	1
Ethnic discrimination	1
Language	22
Poor taste	14
Bad English	3
Offensive language	5
Bad journalistic practices	48
Biased writing	12
Information not accurate	15
Use of material without permission	2
Claimed to be able to publish whatever staff wished	1
Judged to be libellous	5
Judged to be libellous; suit threatened or underway	2
Editorializing	1
Not appropriate	5
Unspecified	5

Table 10
Results of Objections to School Publications

Final Action	Number of Cases
Possible censorship	64
Material prevented from being published	39
Printed material not distributed	6
Material rewritten or re-edited	4
Publication discontinued	3
Administrative control changed	10
System of censoring future issues	2
Possible prevention of censorship	65
Request denied	35
No action taken	30
Other action taken	55
Apology or retraction printed	18
Personal apology made	3
Report of dissatisfaction to writer, editor, sponsor	18
Offended party wrote a rebuttal	7
Action not reported or unclear	9

Note: sometimes two or three actions were taken concerning a single complaint.

QUESTIONNAIRE ON PROBLEMS INVOLVED IN SELECTING AND USING LEARNING RESOURCE MATERIALS — BOOKS, NEWSPAPERS, MAGAZINES, FILMS, AND OTHER A.V. MATERIALS

Please return to Lee Burress, English Department, University of Wisconsin, Stevens Point, Wisconsin 54481.

School Name _____ Street Address _____

City _____ State _____

(Although you are asked to identify your school, no material from this questionnaire will be attributed to particular schools.)

1. What is the enrollment in your school? (Check one)
   ( ) 0–299
   ( ) 300–599
   ( ) 600–999
   ( ) 1,000–1,499
   ( ) 1,500–up

2. What grades are included in your school?
   ( ) 1–12
   ( ) 7–12
   ( ) 9–12
   ( ) 10–12
   ( ) Other (Specify) _____

3. Is the area served by your school?
   ( ) Metropolitan (250,000)
   ( ) Suburban (peripheral to a metropolitan area)
   ( ) Urban (above 10,000 in population)
   ( ) Rural (10,000 or below in population)

4. Have you or teachers in your department, since September 1, 1975, and the present, had objections to a book or book title you are using?
   ( ) Yes   ( ) No

5. If your answer to question 4 was yes, please list below each of those books about which objections have been raised:
   Book 1: Author _____ Title _____
   Book 2: Author _____ Title _____
   Book 3: Author _____ Title _____

6. What action did the objector ask for:
   Book 1: ___ Book 2: ___ Book 3: ___ Remove from classroom use
              ___   ___   ___ Remove title from recommended list
              ___   ___   ___ Remove from library
              ___   ___   ___ Placed on closed shelf

1977 NCTE Censorship Survey 41

7. Who raised the original objection to the book or books?
   Book 1: ___ Book 2: ___ Book 3: ___ Parent
        ___   ___   ___ Clergyman
        ___   ___   ___ Student
        ___   ___   ___ Newspaper reporter or editor
        ___   ___   ___ School librarian
        ___   ___   ___ Another teacher
        ___   ___   ___ English department chairman
        ___   ___   ___ Principal
   Book 1: ___ Book 2: ___ Book 3: ___ Superintendent
        ___   ___   ___ Member of the Board
                              of Education
        ___   ___   ___ Local organization (Which?)
                                _____
        ___   ___   ___ National organization (Which?)
                                _____
        ___   ___   ___ Other (Specify) _____

8. What reason was given for the objection? Please quote if possible.
   Book 1: _____
   _____

   Book 2: _____
   _____

   Book 3: _____
   _____

9. Indicate below whether the objector claimed to have read the book or books.
   Book 1   Book 2   Book 3
   ( ) Yes   ( ) Yes   ( ) Yes
   ( ) No   ( ) No   ( ) No

10. What disposition was made of the case?
    Book 1   Book 2   Book 3
    ( )   ( )   ( )   Request denied
    ( )   ( )   ( )   Book removed from classroom use
    ( )   ( )   ( )   Book removed from recommended list
    ( )   ( )   ( )   Book placed on closed shelf
    ( )   ( )   ( )   Book removed from library
    ( )   ( )   ( )   Other—Please describe below

_____
_____
_____

11. On what administrative level was the decision made in regard to the cases cited above?

    Book 1 Book 2 Book 3
    ( )   ( )   ( )   Teacher
    ( )   ( )   ( )   Department Chairman
    ( )   ( )   ( )   Librarian
    ( )   ( )   ( )   Principal
    ( )   ( )   ( )   Superintendent
    ( )   ( )   ( )   School Board
    ( )   ( )   ( )   Other—Please describe below

    _____
    _____
    _____

12. Have you had complaints about periodicals in the library between September 1, 1975, and the present?
    ( ) Yes   ( ) No

13. Who raised the original objection to the periodicals?

    Period-   Period-   Period-
    ical 1: ___ ical 2: ___ ical 3: ___   Parent
       ___   ___   ___   Clergyman
       ___   ___   ___   Student
       ___   ___   ___   Newspaper reporter or editor
       ___   ___   ___   School librarian
       ___   ___   ___   Another teacher
       ___   ___   ___   English department chairman
       ___   ___   ___   Principal
       ___   ___   ___   Superintendent
       ___   ___   ___   Member of the Board of Education
       ___   ___   ___   Local organization (Which?)
                                            _____
       ___   ___   ___   National organization (Which?)
                                            _____
       ___   ___   ___   Other (Specify)
                                            _____

14. If you answered question 12 with yes, please list the title below:

    Periodical 1: _____
    Periodical 2: _____
    Periodical 3: _____

15. What action did the objector ask for:

    Periodical 1   Periodical 2   Periodical 3
    ( )   ( )   ( )   Cease subscribing to the periodical
    ( )   ( )   ( )   Place periodical on a restricted shelf

16. What disposition was made of the case?

Periodical 1	Periodical 2	Periodical 3	
( )	( )	( )	Request denied
( )	( )	( )	Subscription ended
( )	( )	( )	Periodical placed on closed shelf
( )	( )	( )	Other—Please describe below

_____
_____

17. On what administrative level was the decision made in regard to the cases cited above?

Periodical 1	Periodical 2	Periodical 3	
( )	( )	( )	Teacher
( )	( )	( )	Department Chairman
( )	( )	( )	Librarian
( )	( )	( )	Principal
( )	( )	( )	Assistant Superintendent
( )	( )	( )	Superintendent
( )	( )	( )	School Board

18. Have you or teachers in your department, since September 1, 1975, and the present, had objections to films or other A.V. materials that you are using?
    ( ) Yes ( ) No

19. If your answer to question 18 was yes, please list below each of those films about which objections have been raised:

    Film 1. Title _____
    Film 2. Title _____
    Film 3. Title _____
    (Please use the back for additional titles if needed.)

20. What action did the objector ask for:

    Film 1 ___ Film 2 ___ Film 3 ___ Remove from classroom use
    ___ ___ ___ Remove title from recommended list
    ___ ___ ___ Remove from library
    ___ ___ ___ Place on closed shelf

21. Who raised the original objection to the film or films?

    Film 1 ___ Film 2 ___ Film 3 ___ Parent
    ___ ___ ___ Clergyman
    ___ ___ ___ Student
    ___ ___ ___ Newspaper reporter or editor
    ___ ___ ___ School librarian
    ___ ___ ___ Another teacher
    ___ ___ ___ Department chairman
    ___ ___ ___ Principal

___   ___   ___   Superintendent
___   ___   ___   Member of the Board
                  of Education
___   ___   ___   Local organization (Which?) _____
___   ___   ___   National organization (Which?) _____
___   ___   ___   Other (Specify) _____

22. What reason was given for the objection? Please quote if possible.
    Film 1. _____
    _____

    Film 2. _____
    _____

    Film 3. _____
    _____

23. What disposition was made of the case?
    Film 1   Film 2   Film 3
    ( )   ( )   ( )   Request denied
    ( )   ( )   ( )   Film removed from classroom use
    ( )   ( )   ( )   Film removed from recommended list
    ( )   ( )   ( )   Film placed on closed shelf
    ( )   ( )   ( )   Film removed from A.V. library
    ( )   ( )   ( )   Other—Please describe below
    _____
    _____

24. On what administrative level was the decision made in regard to the cases cited above?
    Film 1   Film 2   Film 3
    ( )   ( )   ( )   Teacher
    ( )   ( )   ( )   Department Chairman
    ( )   ( )   ( )   Librarian
    ( )   ( )   ( )   Principal
    ( )   ( )   ( )   Superintendent
    ( )   ( )   ( )   School Board
    ( )   ( )   ( )   Other—Please describe below
    _____
    _____

25. Do you have a school sponsored (i.e., financed) newspaper?
    ( ) Yes   ( ) No

1977 NCTE Censorship Survey   45

26. Do you have a school sponsored (i.e., financed) creative writing publication?
    ( ) Yes   ( ) No

27. Do you have an independent (not school financed) writing publication of any kind?
    ( ) Yes   ( ) No

28. If the answer to question 27 is yes, please describe briefly.
    _____
    _____
    _____

29. Have you experienced complaints about material published in the school newspaper?
    ( ) Yes   ( ) No

30. Have you experienced complaints about material published in the creative writing publication?
    ( ) Yes   ( ) No

31. Have you experienced complaints about material published in the independent writing publication?
    ( ) Yes   ( ) No

32. What action did the objector ask for:
    Publication 1   Publication 2   Publication 3
    ( )   ( )   ( )   Prevent inclusion of the material before publication
    ( )   ( )   ( )   Prevent distribution of the printed material
    ( )   ( )   ( )   Publish a retraction or apology
    ( )   ( )   ( )   Dismiss the editor or writer of the objectionable material
    ( )   ( )   ( )   Cease publication of the entire periodical
    ( )   ( )   ( )   Change the administrative control of the publication
    ( )   ( )   ( )   Other (Specify) _____

33. Who raised the original objection to the material?
    Publication 1   Publication 2   Publication 3
    ( )   ( )   ( )   Parent
    ( )   ( )   ( )   Clergyman
    ( )   ( )   ( )   Student
    ( )   ( )   ( )   Newspaper reporter or editor
    ( )   ( )   ( )   School librarian
    ( )   ( )   ( )   Another teacher

( ) ( ) ( ) Department chairman
( ) ( ) ( ) Principal
( ) ( ) ( ) Member of the Board
of Education
( ) ( ) ( ) Local organization (Which?)

( ) ( ) ( ) National organization (Which?)

( ) ( ) ( ) Other (Specify) _____

34. What reason was given for the objection?
    Publication 1 _____
    _____
    Publication 2 _____
    _____
    Publication 3 _____
    _____

35. What disposition was made of the case?
    Publication 1   Publication 2   Publication 3
    ( )   ( )   ( )   Request denied
    ( )   ( )   ( )   Prevent inclusion of the
                                          material before publication
    ( )   ( )   ( )   Prevent distribution of the
                                          printed material
    ( )   ( )   ( )   Publish a retraction or apology
    ( )   ( )   ( )   Dismiss the editor or writer
                                          of the objectionable material
    ( )   ( )   ( )   Cease publication of the entire
                                          publication
    ( )   ( )   ( )   Change the administrative
                                          control of the publication
    ( )   ( )   ( )   Other (Specify) _____

36. On what administrative level was the decision made with regard to the case above?
    Publication 1   Publication 2   Publication 3
    ( )   ( )   ( )   Teacher
    ( )   ( )   ( )   Department chairman
    ( )   ( )   ( )   Principal
    ( )   ( )   ( )   Superintendent
    ( )   ( )   ( )   School Board
    ( )   ( )   ( )   Other—Please describe below

1977 NCTE Censorship Survey

_____
_____
_____

37. Does your school system have a planned procedure for dealing with objections to the use of learning resource materials?
    ( ) Yes   ( ) No

38. Does your school system have a planned procedure for selecting learning resource materials?
    ( ) Yes   ( ) No

39. Please provide a brief description of any incident which may have occurred in your school when you, or members of your department, had complaints about learning resource materials. Please indicate the effect the occurrence had on the school(s). Were any personal issues involved in addition to the question of objectionable materials? Was the school board involved? If so, what was its attitude? _____
_____
_____
_____

You will need to ask the librarian to answer the two questions beneath.

40. Please report the number of printed volumes allowed to circulate, that is, go out of the library. Do not report reference books, films, records, and other non-print media.

41. Please indicate which of the following books are in the school library. The list is suggestive, intended to discover something of the range of books in the school library. Please check against the actual holdings listed in the card catalogue.

(The list is included on pages 19-22.)

3 Censorship and the Classroom Teacher

Allan Glatthorn
University of Pennsylvania

We are in the midst of a wave of censorship and educational controversy that has not yet crested. The vicious battle in West Virginia, the Congressional attacks on *Man: A Course of Study,* and the large number of local conflicts over textbooks and curricula are sure indications that the phenomenon is widespread, not localized, and long-lasting, not temporary.

And the effects of such controversy, of course, pose serious problems for all of us. Individual teachers and administrators have been attacked. School systems and communities have been torn asunder. School boards have adopted much more restrictive policies. And publishers have reacted, predictably, by imposing their own brands of prior censorship. We therefore cannot dismiss the problem airily or wish it away with tolerant smiles. We need to understand its roots and consider our response.

Where does the new censorship come from? Some of the would-be censors are political opportunists who will ride any wave that promises to carry them to victory. Many of the critics attacking school textbooks and modern curricula are also attacking the federal bureaucracy, school busing, and any other target that might capture the attention of a bored constituency.

And part of the censorship movement, obviously, is a specific and pointed attack on questionable material. Parents who are not captive of any given ideology are simply unhappy with the books being studied. And I, for one, think such concerns are in part justified, for we have made some bad choices. The new freedom granted by elective courses has led to a kind of curriculum anarchy. And our genuine concern for finding books with a high appeal for TV addicts led us to choose some books better left on the drugstore rack. (A young man carrying a copy of *Fear of*

Flying recently assured me it was required reading for an elective called "The Literature of Flight.")

So there are some questionable books and a few political mountebanks. But we would be ill-advised to consider the problem local or the issue specific. There are larger forces at work that need to be examined.

Some of the censorship, of course, is a thinly disguised racism, a counter-attack by whites unhappy with the current concern for black culture.

Some of the censorship is simply a manifestation of a vague malaise that affects us all. These are difficult times. The bills pile higher, children become more sullen, the traffic gets worse, and we all go about muttering "things fall apart, the center cannot hold." In times like these, people need a scapegoat. But there aren't many scapegoats left these days. We don't have Mr. Nixon to kick around any more, the law won't let us lynch black folk, and the Arabs are too remote and too powerful to attack. But schools and teachers are handy and defenseless targets. So many of the attacks of the censors are an attempt to hold the schools and the teachers responsible for the problems of our society. Kids use drugs; it's the school's fault. Young people are bored; the classes have turned them off. Teenagers act immorally; so it must be the textbooks. Censorship becomes one more form of scapegoating.

But perhaps the most important source of all is an ideological warfare of which censorship is only one battle. The working class people of middle America are convinced that they are a beleaguered minority who have been systematically attacked for the past fifteen years. First the blacks demanded power; then the young revolted. Next, women marched in the streets; and then homosexuals demanded equal treatment. The results were predictable. For, in years gone by, to be white, middle-aged, and manly meant that you demanded instant respect; now, in the seventies, it means only that you are immediately suspect. So we are experiencing a white backlash as middle America decides it can survive only by fighting back. And the battle over textbooks is, I believe, the first in a series of confrontations yet to come. To the coal miner in West Virginia, I am the enemy.

So what response do we make? I think three answers are called for—*dialog, change,* and *resistance.* Let me speak briefly about each.

Obviously, there is a need for a new dialog between schools and the communities. But such dialog needs to go far beyond the patronizing condescension and manipulation that too often pass for school public relations. There is a need first of all for a new humility among us educators. We don't know all the answers. We don't know what is best for all teenagers. We aren't sure about the effects of pornography. We don't know which books might be too disturbing for that troubled adolescent. We are trained teachers—but most of us are not experts in adolescent psychology or juvenile literature. And such a humility should lead us to respect our saner critics. Except for a few deranged individuals, most of the parents attacking textbooks are sincere people who are aching to be heard. But we aren't listening very well. Some of the textbook defenders in West Virginia certainly inflamed the controversy by describing the critics as Hitlers . . . and by seeing in this grassroots protest a sinister conspiracy.

But there is also a need for firm honesty in such dialog. To a troubled community, we need to say, "We are all accountable—our young people are in trouble and we are to blame." The school has no problems that are not those of the larger society. Young people are in trouble—and the school is only the place where their sickness becomes epidemic. The schools have no drug problem; young people are still using too much alcohol and drugs. The school has no race problem; our society is racist and young people have caught that disease. The school does not breed permissiveness; young people have become spoiled by indulgent parents.

Such honest dialog should not result simply in more blaming, but should lead instead to a sense of shared responsibility and an open admission of our own failings. Such an admission will then move us to the second step of changing. For I truly believe that the rash of attacks suggests to us that some changes are needed.

For one thing, we as English teachers need to show more acceptance and respect for values other than our own. Most of us are intellectuals who see ourselves as liberated; but too often such intellectual independence becomes distorted into a smug conviction that the traditional values of church, country, and family are childish aberrations that must be corrected. So we set about to indoctrinate with our own brand of humanistic relativism. Sometimes the indoctrination is subtle, as we choose books that reflect only that perspective. And sometimes the indoctrination is explicitly direct in the case of the radical teacher who meets his ego needs by ridiculing the faith of a troubled adolescent. And you don't need to be very smart to make a sixteen year old look foolish. We do need an open English classroom, an open forum for the expression of all ideas—even the most traditional and the most religiously fundamental.

I think a second change we need is a new respect for the privacy of the young. Here again a legitimate concern to help the young know their values and discuss their feelings has too often become an insistent prying into the recesses of their own hearts. The critics have justifiably attacked those English classes that more closely resemble sensitivity groups. It seems to me that self-realization always involves a dynamic tension between the private and the public, the open and the closed, the engaged and the withdrawn. And we need to make the English class a place where silence is valued, where loneness is given its time, where privacy has room.

And we ourselves should heed this advice of Amiel, the French diarist who tells us:

> 2nd December 1851. Let mystery have its place in you; do not be always turning up your whole soil with the ploughshare of self-examination, but leave a little fallow corner in your heart for any seed the winds may bring, and reserve a nook of shadow for the passing bird; keep a place in your heart for the unexpected guest, an altar for the unknown God. Then if a bird sing among your branches do not be too eager to tame it. If you are conscious of something new—thought or feeling—wakening in the depths of your being, do not be in a hurry to let in light upon it, to look at it; let the springing germ have the protection of being forgotten, hedge it round with quiet, and do not break in upon its darkness; let it take shape and grow, and not a word of your happiness to anyone. Sacred work of nature as it is, all conception should be enwrapped by the triple veil of modesty, silence, and night.
>
> Amiel's Journal.

I think we need finally to do a better job of self-censorship. And here we need to keep firmly in mind that the classroom is not the newsstand, the English textbook is not a girlie magazine, the teenager is not the adult. My own bias is that the society can tolerate almost absolute freedom as to what is published for private consumption by mature adults. But I become more and more convinced that a required book studied by all students in the English classroom must meet very different criteria. We make a grave mistake if today's best-seller list becomes tomorrow's exclusive required reading.

For one thing, we see Gresham's law of literature developing—with the bad driving out the good. We have only so much time and so many dollars, and every period, every dollar spent on *The Godfather* is one less for Shakespeare.

A second concern is that our lusting after the most recent fad book means that we often spoil the fun of reading with the drudgery of studying. Vonnegut is to be read, not analyzed. *Watership Down* is a personal book that makes its own private connections and should not be twisted with the heavy hand of the symbol-hunter. Or as one teenager complained, "Every time a good book comes along, English teachers spoil it."

A final concern, of course, is that some of our choices seem just not appropriate for all the young adolescents in our classes. I do not subscribe to the belief that there is a direct connection between what we read and how we act, but I do know that we are subtly influenced by all powerful books, and that the teenage mind is easily impressed. Consequently, I believe that books that reek of violence, that flaunt sexual perversion, that perpetuate ethnic stereotypes, or that preach occult nonsense may be entitled to two weeks on the supermarket rack, but do not belong on anyone's required reading list.

Just in case I might be misunderstood, I would like to make it clear that I do see the need to use books that are contemporary and that help young people understand the reality of an evil world—but I do think that some of us have made some foolish mistakes in the hope of finding relevant literature. We need to develop some reasonable guidelines that will protect us from the attacks of our critics and save us from our own foolishness. If we don't develop our own guidelines, then others will develop them for us, and we will be working under restrictions like those imposed by the Kanawha County School Board.

But finally, I believe, we must take a stand. After all the dialog has been held and after the needed changes have been made, we must at some place draw the line. For the battle has been joined. We are locked in a struggle over the fundamental principles of freedom and liberty. It is not simply the struggle to defend our professional freedom to choose books. It is the larger struggle to ensure that the public school classroom remains a forum for free inquiry. If angry parents can turn the public school into a closed system for inculcating their narrow vision, then surely we are all in trouble.

In such a struggle, surely the National Council of Teachers of English and its local affiliates must play an active role. Help is needed by the classroom teacher besieged by angry critics. We need help in developing good selection policies, in finding better materials, in beginning the dialog so sorely needed. And there are two areas where the power and influence of NCTE can especially be brought to bear. One is to lobby against any legislation which would result in unduly restrictive policies. And the other is to create a legal defense fund for those teachers who find themselves in the courts over issues of censorship.

Perhaps an even more important role can be played by teacher associations that are more astute about the politics of power. Such associations seem all too ready to strike for selfish ends but have been conspicuously absent in the censorship fray. Perhaps new leaders will have the vision to realize that academic freedom is truly a non-negotiable demand.

But at the last, the battle is a lonely and private one; one which individuals, not organizations, can only fight, and I would not presume to tell you where you take a stand. I can only remind you and myself that people are measured by the battles they fight and certainly no case is greater than what Jeffers calls "the cold passion for truth."

So we call ourselves *teacher* and the classroom is our world. It is there that the battle is joined. In our own way we must struggle to guarantee that the English classroom most of all remains a place where all issues can be examined, all voices heard.

Surely the risks are great. We will be pilloried and slandered. We may suffer physical violence. And we may lose our jobs.

But the costs of remaining silent are even greater. If we capitulate to the forces of censorship, the foundation of liberty will have been eroded. And in the process we shall have lost our souls.

Ortega reminds us that "to live is to feel ourselves fatally obliged to exercise our liberty, to decide what we are going to be in this world."

So the choice is clear. We can exercise our liberty by speaking out, not remaining silent—by protesting, not acquiescing—by defending, not capitulating. Some of us will fight to eliminate sexism from books. Some will struggle to extirpate all vestiges of racism. Some will be in the forefront of the public battle over censorship. Others will work quietly in the less glamorous arena of the classroom. But each of us in our own way will join in the defense of freedom, so at the end it can be said of us, "While others talked about liberty, they struggled that it might survive."

4 Censorship and English: Some Things We Don't Seem to Think About Very Often (But Should)

Robert C. Small, Jr.
Virginia Polytechnic Institute and State University

With all of the publicity censorship receives, it would seem that every dimension of the controversy should already have been explored thoroughly. Yet, there are several major aspects to which few writers have given very much attention. A careful review of hundreds of the articles on censorship which have appeared in the journals included in the *Education Index* during the past twenty years has revealed that writers about censorship and the schools have usually dealt with one of the following:

1. the details of specific censorship cases and their causes, including discussions of the types of materials or subjects under attack (the specific dimension);
2. arguments against censorship and a defense of the "freedom to read" (the freedom dimension); and
3. advice to teachers and schools about how to prepare for censorship attacks and what to do when under attack (the professional dimension).

In a similar fashion, many teachers of English seem limited in their awareness of the many dimensions to the topic of textbook censorship. They can discuss specific cases and are often familiar with the details of such cases, especially ones that seem absurd. They can present arguments against censorship, often with references to Milton and Jefferson. Finally, they can make a case for themselves as the appropriate selectors of English school materials and laud themselves as defenders of the school against censorship attacks. Like the articles just mentioned, they can deal effectively with three dimensions of censorship: the specific dimension, the freedom dimension, and the professional dimension. Each of these is an important aspect of any school censorship crisis.

Each of these dimensions is familiar to us all. We have heard each one expounded by colleagues and by experts. We have read about each. We have discussed each. But missing from the articles reviewed and the teachers' discussions is an awareness that schools, and therefore, censorship in schools, have an historical background. Such discussions of censorship fail to recognize that schools have a relation to the society that causes them to come into existence and that schools have an educational purpose, the direction of which is not absolute but rather a matter of opinion. Also lacking in discussions among those of us who are English teachers is an understanding that questions of the purpose and worth of the study of works of literature are not answered merely because English teachers have developed their own answers. Finally, and most sadly for a discipline that prides itself on its humanism, there has usually been missing from discussions of censorship and the schools an awareness that those who would censor are human beings of as much value as any other human beings. Thus to the three dimensions of censorship usually dealt with one must add three others of equal worth but, unfortunately, rarely considered: the historical and social, the educational, and the human.

The Historical and Social Dimension

First, it seems important for educators to realize that schools have traditionally been places where students were, at least officially, protected from many aspects of the world, not exposed to them or prepared for them. Certain clear, generally agreed upon notions about what was right and good and clean and, thus, what was appropriate for children governed the curriculum of American schools for most of their history. Although much has changed in American society and in the make-up of the school since those early days, these general notions about the appropriate have probably changed little, at least among parents. Traditionally, then, moralistic concepts about the suitable have dominated education and still dominate popular thinking about it. It is only in recent years that schools have not been more or less the willing servant of such ideas. At the same time, the historical role of the school has been to uplift and improve. Revisionist historians may argue whether schools did, in fact, ever fulfill that role. Achieved or not, however, that is what generally was seen as the role of the school. What the students read and studied and discussed in school, it was believed, should be better than what they might encounter elsewhere, not a reflection of it, certainly not an examination of the worst life had to offer. School studies should present an idealized view of life, not deal with the less than ideal lives the students lead.

In such an historical context, any material in textbooks which was not idealized, aimed at perfecting, uplifting, and free from the sordid, ugly, or unpleasant aspects of life was obviously poorly chosen. It was, in fact, clearly inconsistent with the historical aims of the school. When citizens of a community march upon the school to demand removal of stories with curse words, novels that are partly about the sex lives of characters, and poems that show America to be less than perfect, they do so, therefore, in, not against, the historical tradition. Nearly every general curriculum text deals with the relation of society to the school. Saylor and Alexander, for example, have stated in *Curriculum Planning for Modern Schools:*

> The school is an agency established by a social group to serve a group purpose. The society has certain ends in view for the development of the individual. These ends in view become the basic factor in the determination of the aims of education (p. 84).

Admitting that the school thus owes a duty to society, they point out that ". . . the fundamental obligation of the school as a social instrumentality is to achieve the goals that the citizens have in mind as they establish and operate the schools" (p. 89).

What then can we make of teachers who act as if such an intimate connection between society and the aims of education does not exist? Seen from one point of view, professional control of the curriculum may obviously be right and proper. Seen from another, however, it is an arrogant seizure by teachers of that instrumentality of society that Saylor and Alexander mention. "We pay for the schools," citizens say; "we send our children to them. We should be able to say what can and can't go on there." Crudely put, perhaps, but such comments say what Saylor and Alexander also have said. In the view of many parents, teachers have come more and more to see the schools as places where their children are not improved, but changed to fit a model the teachers see as better; and more and more that model only partly resembles the parents' ideal, if at all. At a time when many citizens dislike the changes which they see in the country, when attitudes and behavior which they have always thought were to be condemned are now at least accepted and perhaps praised, such citizens wonder why the schools do not redouble their efforts to counteract such trends. Instead, they detect those same elements present in their own schools, and they rebel.

Inarticulately and, unfortunately, with violence, such citizens are voicing real and profound, but difficult, questions about education that philosophers have struggled with for ages. Unfortunately, they are questions that many of us, concerned with what we will do tomorrow, with the latest curriculum gimmick, with each new, shiny teaching toy, have refused to be bothered with. Try to philosophize about schools and society and the duties of each to the other, try to examine the historical role of the school, and you will be labeled a fuddy-duddy out of touch with the reality of the school and of no practical help—too "theoretical," as the saying goes.

But we must all consider and reconsider these vital questions. How much control should the citizens of a community have over what the schools teach? How much selection should they do? How far from the beliefs of those citizens should the school stray? How much should the school, in fact, conflict with those beliefs? Should teachers see their roles as missionaries bringing the truth (by which is meant *their* truth) to benighted people? Society sees the schools as preserving and improving on the cultural heritage, inspiring students to success and reasonable virtue. It does not, I think, see the schools as attacking fundamental beliefs, even if those beliefs might, in fact, be seen as prejudices by many professional educators.

The Educational Dimension

"Why study literature in high school?" How that question devils English teachers: enjoyment, insights into self and others, broadening of horizons, etc. Currently, the cultural refinement goals of literature study are not very fashionable among "with it" English educators. Passing on the cultural heritage, exposure to the great creations of the literary art, improving taste, making students into cultured ladies and gentlemen, contact with the great thoughts—these are rarely spoken of with favor these days when individual response, relevance to life, having a good time, and something to talk about seem to be the reasons given for bringing literary works into the classroom. Yet we should not fool ourselves. There is not general agreement that the purpose of literary study in the schools should be to provoke questioning of values, to cause students to think about their lives, other people, and life in general, and to have students enjoy themselves. Many parents, in fact, may not see any excuse for literature study in school. It is something for them that somehow seems to have to go with those things of practical value such as training in reading well, writing well, and speaking well. Most of those parents who do see a reason for literature study, however, probably to a very large extent see it as making cultured people of their children.

Consequently, when teachers or textbook editors use as their criteria for selection the fact that a particular work provokes response or stimulates critical thought or is relevant to the students' lives, they really should not be too surprised that that purpose conflicts with the educational purpose believe in by parents. Nor should they be surprised that this conflict in purpose results in a conflict in fact. More than any other single piece of evidence used by critics to condemn certain contemporary literature textbooks has been the comments by the editors that the selections

(a) are not all great works;
(b) do not illustrate a literary tradition;
(c) raise questions but do not necessarily answer them, especially as many questions may not have answers;
(d) challenge accepted notions;
(e) are not all meant to be liked by everyone; and
(f) were chosen because they are about adolescent concerns.

Now, you and I might not see any problem with these six standards. But they are exactly the opposite of both the historical and, as far as many citizens are concerned, the current reasons for selecting works of literature for school study. Most parents would, I feel sure, maintain that all the literature used in school should

(a) be great works;
(b) represent the (largely Western) literary tradition;
(c) provide the answers to human questions found by the great minds;
(d) support accepted American social, cultural, and moral values;
(e) result in improved taste so that students come to like all these great selections; and
(f) be mature thoughts about mature concerns.

What we have here is a clear and probably unresolvable clash of ideas. Sometimes we act as if our opinions about the values of literature study are true and these others false; but we must remember that by rejecting cultural heritage for critical thinking, greatness for relevance, *the* truth for each reader's truth, answers for questions, we reject the main reasons why society has put us there to do what we do.

In addition, when censors condemn some literary works as morally corrupting, we often treat those claims with ridicule. No one was ever corrupted by a curse word, we say. Just because that story contains a character's argument against the existence of God doesn't mean students will stop believing. A story about sex doesn't provoke students to sexual activity. Is that right? Can we be the same people who maintain that literature can give readers insights into life? That literature can change people's lives? That the pen is mightier than the sword? We have been caught in our own inconsistencies and should admit it. It makes no sense to believe that literature can make people better but that it cannot make them worse. Either it has power, or it does not. And if it does have power, then it is to be feared as well as admired.

We have led parents—our former students, after all—to believe that great works contain great truths and that masterpieces are such because of their power to influence. Why should it now be so surprising that parents, discovering curse words, scenes of sexual relations, arguments against the current American social order, questions about the existence of God, believe that we are now pushing those ideas as we formerly pushed the ideas in *Silas Marner* and *Julius Caesar*?

The Human Dimension

We have usually tended to react to censorship efforts by treating the people involved as if they were either foolish or evil or both— that is, to misunderstand the human dimension. It is all too easy to dismiss the censors as strange and isolated "kooks" causing trouble way out of proportion to their numbers. Such a situation is certainly not true in my part of the country. Indeed, wherever I go I meet people—polite, reasonable people—who, finding that I have tried on several occasions to defend literature books which are under attack, reveal themselves to be disturbed by material which they have discovered to be in those texts. Such people speak from a genuine concern for their children, but they also speak from a deep frustration. And we must respect their frustration as we do that of blacks or native Americans hostile to what America has done to them.

In his book, *Future Shock,* Alvin Toffler pictures the depression and frustration that result from a society which is changing more rapidly than many of its people can adjust to. Where wholesome integration of the schools has taken place against the wishes of many parents, for example, racial hostilities and a sense of powerlessness in the face of governmental force do produce frustration. When the textbooks used in English classes contain works written by minority authors and in a form of English containing, as a casual part of the dialect, words and expressions considered blasphemous or obscene by many parents, a target is produced for those parents' frustrations.

Other conditions also produce frustration, of course, and thus a climate for censorship of school texts. Peaceful, rural areas have turned into suburban and urban areas in recent times, and with this change has come a rapid creation of new social and environmental problems. For people thus caught in a trap between life the way they want it to stay and a rapidly developing situation radically different from their wishes, the intrusion by the real world into the schools, particularly in the concrete form of materials in a textbook, can become a target which is both clear and unambiguous.

Then, too, many people look around America and see and read reports of people earning large incomes, leading exciting lives, and possessing power, fame, and prestige. Their own lives they see as much less, and much less than they may have hoped for when younger. Bored with the dullness of a repetitious job and a limited style of life, such people may turn to an attack on textbooks as a way of attacking those who write and publish such texts—those who are seen as representing a sort of social and economic elite of the successful. An editorial in the *Wall Street Journal* sympathetically analyzed this point of view:

> The deeper motive of the protestors seems to be resentment—against the schools, the bureaucrats, the upper classes in general. "Even hillbillies have civil rights," read one sign. The immediate protest was aroused by what appeared to them as an especially condescending attempt to revise their cultural outlook—by what was, in fact, an unconscious and thus all the more condescending attempt to revise their cultural outlook (7 October 1974, p. 20).

Most important, that sign, "Even hillbillies have civil rights," should shake us out of our narrow view of the people whose protests have caused current censorship crises. As I have written elsewhere,

> The dissatisfaction of the Appalachian protestor is no less than the dissatisfaction of the civil rights militant. The Appalachian protestor is no less proud and protective of his culture and way of life than are members of ethnic minorities. The Appalachian protestor may at times give way to extreme statements and violent actions, as have members of other groups asserting their rights. While condemning the violence, the bigotry, and the foolish remarks, we must give the Appalachian protestor's basic beliefs and feelings the same respect we now seem willing to give those of other protest groups. Modern experience makes clear that, if we do not, there will be more Kanawha Counties. Worse, it is easy to predict that, in the end, the schools will suffer the most (*English Journal* 65 [March 1976]:19).

When Charles Silberman blamed the flaws of American education on "mindlessness," he meant many things; but it is clear that our approach to textbook censorship efforts contains an element of the mindless. We have generally failed to try to understand it in its more complex, abstract, and philosophical dimensions and have concentrated instead on the immediate (the specific dimension), the popular (the freedom dimension), and the self-respecting (the professional dimension).

Thus it is that resolutions are made and passed condemning censorship with almost no understanding that protesting citizens are to a very considerable extent fulfilling the role assigned to them by the historical development of the American school. Thus it is that English teachers argue for the free selection of literature for reading and study in school without knowing why or examining the assumptions implicit in the reasons they may give. Finally, teachers who regularly maintain that books can change lives reverse themselves seemingly without realizing and maintain that no one was ever corrupted by a word or a scene in a book.

What happens, it seems to me, when we emphasize the specific, the freedom, and the professional aspects of censorship is that we concentrate not merely on parts of the problem, but on parts that give a false appearance to that problem. By examining the silly actions of censors, their foolish charges, their misunderstandings, their violence, we are led to conclude that there is nothing of substance in what they say. We decide that they are merely stupid or self-serving. By concentrating on the issue of freedom, we envelop ourselves in self-righteousness while twisting the protective attitude of parents into Hitlerite book burning. Finally, by looking exclusively at our professional rights, we lose track of who we are and what we are for. These three dimensions have in common the fact that they do not include the world beyond the school and the duty of the school to that world. Without the historical and social, the educational, and the human dimensions, censorship efforts aimed at the school appear to result from the folly and evil of the human race; with these other dimensions added, they become something else entirely, they become a part of the great philosophical debate about the purpose of education which began before today's crisis and will go on long after it is forgotten.

5 Obscenity and the Chill Factor: Court Decisions about Obscenity and Their Relationships to School Censorship

Kenneth L. Donelson
Arizona State University

This article may alert some teachers, librarians, and administrators to a few of the basic issues and problems involved in definitions of obscenity and their relationship to school censorship. Sketching briefly over the history of meanings and tests of obscenity evolved through more than two hundred years of court decisions and the influences these decisions have had and may have on censorship problems in the schools will suggest some interrelationships. These two matters, court decisions and school censorship, are not always directly related, but neither are they totally separable, and they are more and more intertwined today.

We will surely be on the path to madness if we attempt to determine some unambiguous meaning or meanings of "obscenity" through recourse to court decisions. And that path to madness becomes more crooked and certainly far more tangled by both verbiage and emotions when we compare the many court definitions with state statutes or with various lawyers' understandings and lawyers' applications or with laymen's understandings and laymen's applications.

As William Lockhart and Robert McClure wrote in 1954:

> No one seems to know what obscenity is. Many writers have discussed the obscene, but few can agree upon even its essential nature. Some find the key to it in the sense of shame; whatever violates the community's sense of shame is obscene. The obscene in this sense usually lies in the exposure of sexual matters, though it may also lie in the exposure of the excremental as well. Similarly, Havelock Ellis found the obscene in whatever is "off the scene" and not openly shown on the stage of life. The obscene in this sense also lies in the public exposure of the naturalistic aspects of sexual and excremental processes. Some have found a quite different kind of obscenity that lacks sexual and excremental exhibitionism. Termed critical obscenity, it attacks accepted moral standards and for this reason is held to be obscene.

> Others, however, have taken an entirely different approach; to them the obscene is that which arouses the 'lower passions or indulges in sensuality.' But most writers have found the term hopelessly subjective and lacking in any definite or acceptable meaning. ("Literature, the Law of Obscenity, and the Constitution," *Minnesota Law Review* 38 [March 1954]:320-21).

The imprecision noted by Lockhart and McClure twenty years ago remains very much with us. Whatever its modern application to violence or brutality or power or inhumanity or racism, "obscenity" in legal parlance has for many years referred almost exclusively to sexual matters.

The Evolution of the Legal Definition of Obscenity

The first case to involve some problem of obscenity took place in 1708 in *Regina v. Read,* 88 Eng. Rep. 953 (K.B. 1708). The defendant was charged in criminal court with publication of *Fifteen Plagues of a Maidenhead,* but the court held that the book was "no offence at common law," punishable only in the Ecclesiastical Courts. Judge Powell believed that a law against this kind of book was needed, but he did not act to create law on the matter.

In 1727, Edmund Curll, at best a highly controversial printer, was charged with printing *Venus in the Cloister: Or, the Nun in Her Smock.* In the resulting trial, *Dominus Rex v. Curll,* 93 Eng. Rep. 849 (K.B. 1727), the Attorney General argued that:

> Destroying that [morality] is destroying the peace of the Government, for government is no more than publick order, which is morality. My Lord Chief Justice Hale used to say, Christianity is part of the law, and why not morality too? I do not insist that every immoral act is indictable, such as telling a lie, or the like; but if it is destructive of morality in general, if it does, or may, affect all the King's subjects, it then is an offence of a publick nature.

While Justice Fortescue argued that "I own this is a great offence, but I know of no law by which we can punish it. Common law is common usage and where there is no law there can be no transgression," the other two justices accepted the Attorney General's argument and found for the state and against Curll.

The Queen v. Hicklin, 3 Q.B. 359, decision in 1867 was certainly the first major legal effort to devise a test of obscenity, and the ruling by Judge Cockburn set precedent that was to be with the law and the public for nearly 100 years. Henry Scott, a member of an anti-Catholic group, had sold copies of a pamphlet entitled *The Confessional Unmasked: Showing the Depravity of the Romish*

Priesthood, the Iniquity of the Confessional, and the Questions Put to Females in Confession. In his ruling against Scott, Judge Cockburn announced:

> It is quite clear that the publishing of an obscene book is an offence against the law of the land . . . and I think the test of obscenity is this, whether the tendency of the matter charged as obscenity is to deprave and corrupt those whose minds are open to such immoral influences, and into whose hands a publication of this sort might fall.

More than forty years later, Mitchell Kennerly published Daniel Carson Goodman's *Hagar Revelly,* a cautious, even restrained novel about vice in the big city. Reviews may have been generally good, but stalwart censor Anthony Comstock was not impressed, viewing the whole book as immoral and rotten. Comstock led a force of United States marshals into Kennerly's offices to arrest the publisher. Judge Learned Hand heard the case of *United States v. Kennerly,* 209 Fed. 119 (S.D. N.Y. 1913), and ruled for the state on the basis of the Cockburn decision because it had long been accepted by lower federal courts and it would be "no longer proper for me to disregard it." More important were the words he added to his finding. He said:

> I hope it is not improper for me to say that the rule as laid down, however consonant it may be with mid-Victorian morals, does not seem to me to answer to the understanding and morality of the present time, as conveyed by the words, 'obscene, lewd, or lascivious.' I question whether in the end men will regard that as obscene which is honestly relevant to the adequate expression of innocent ideas, and whether they will not believe that truth and beauty are too precious to society at large to be mutilated in the interest of those most likely to pervert them to base uses. Indeed, it seems hardly likely that we are even today so lukewarm in our interest in letters or serious discussion as to be content to reduce our treatment of sex to the standard of a child's library in the supposed interest of a salacious few, or that shame will for long prevent us from adequate portrayal of some of the most serious and beautiful sides of human nature.

The first groundbreaking decisions about obscenity viewed the book as a whole, arguing that excerpts alone were not sufficient to establish obscenity, notably in *United States v. One Book Called Ulysses,* 5 F. Supp. 182 (S.D. N.Y. 1933), with Judge Woolsey and in *United States v. One Book Entitled Ulysses,* 72 F. 2d 705 (2d Cir. 1933), with Judge Augustus Hand, both in 1933, for later decisions suggested that modern interpretations and tests of obscenity were hardly accepted by all judges. In a 1945 Massachusetts decision, Judge Qua speaking of the selling of Lillian Smith's *Strange Fruit* (*Commonwealth v. Isenstadt*, 62 N.E. 2d. 840) remarked,

> ... it contains much that even in this post-Victorian era, would tend to promote lascivious thoughts and to arouse lustful desire in the minds of substantial numbers of that public into whose hands this book, obviously intended for general sale, is likely to fall ... we are of the opinion that an honest and reasonable judge or jury could find beyond a reasonable doubt that this book 'manifestly tends to corrupt the morals of youth.'

But only four years later in *Commonwealth v. Gordon et al.*, 66 D.&C. 101 (1949), Judge Curtis Bok was called to judge the presumed obscenity in several modern books, Farrell's *The Studs Lonigan Trilogy* and *A World I Never Made*, Faulkner's *Sanctuary* and *Wild Palms*, Caldwell's *God's Little Acre*, Willingham's *End As a Man*, and Robbins' *Never Love a Stranger*. After reviewing past obscenity cases and decisions, Judge Bok wrote:

> From all these cases, the modern rule is that obscenity is measured by the erotic allurement upon the average modern reader; that the erotic allurement of a book is measured by whether it is sexually impure—i.e., pornographic, 'dirt for dirt's sake,' a calculated indictment to sexual desire—or whether it reveals an effort to reflect life, including its dirt, with reasonable accuracy and balance; and that mere coarseness or vulgarity is not obscenity.

Something of a change in obscenity definitions came in *Besig v. United States*, 208 F. 2d. 142 (9th Cir. 1953). Besig, owner of copies of Henry Miller's *Tropic of Cancer* and *Tropic of Capricorn*, appealed a U.S. customs decision to confiscate the books. In the decision, Judge Stephens noted in part, "Dirty word description of the sweet and sublime, especially that of the mystery of sex and procreation, is the ultimate of obscenity." But only four years later in *Butler v. The State of Michigan*, 352 U.S. 380 2d 412 (1957), Judge Frankfurter restored some semblance of sanity to the courts. Butler had appealed a Michigan statute which made illegal the dissemination or availability of any book for the general reading public which might have a potentially deleterious influence upon youth. Frankfurter wrote,

> The state insists that, by thus quarantining the general reading public against books not too rugged for grown men and women in order to shield juvenile innocence, it is exercising its power to promote the general welfare. Surely, this is to burn the house to roast the pig. . . . We have before us legislation not unreasonably restricted to the evil with which it is said to deal. The incidence of this enactment is to reduce the adult population of Michigan to reading only what is fit for children.

The case of *Roth v. United States,* 354 U.S. 467 (1957), opened the modern era of the U.S. Supreme Court definitions and tests of obscenity. The *Roth* test was "whether to the average person, applying contemporary community standards, the dominant theme of the material taken as a whole appeals to prurient interest." The Court rejected the Hicklin test of Judge Cockburn and further noted that "sex and obscenity are not synonymous. Obscene material is material which deals with sex in a manner appealing to prurient interest." Further they held that "obscenity is not within the area of constitutionally protected speech or press." A remark by Justice Brennan delivering the majority opinion was to prove significant in a later decision and would become highly controversial in view of the Burger majority in even more recent cases. Commenting on the questionable status of obscenity as constitutionally protected, Brennan noted, "But implicit in the history of the First Amendment is the rejection of obscenity as *utterly without redeeming social importance.*" (author's italics)

In 1964, *Jacobellis v. Ohio,* 378 U.S. 184, further underlined the Court's faith in the Roth standard for obscenity, although Justice Brennan in announcing the judgment of the Court noted that:

> Recognizing that the test for obscenity enunciated there . . . is not perfect, we think any substitute would raise equally difficult problems. . . . We would reiterate, however, our recognition in Roth that obscenity is excluded from the constitutional protection only because it is 'utterly without redeeming social importance.'

Brennan further clarified the meaning of 'contemporary community standards' by attacking the notion of local definitions of 'community' and concluded,

> We thus reaffirm the position taken in Roth to the effect that the constitutional status of an allegedly obscene work must be determined on the basis of a national standard. It is, after all, a national Constitution we are expounding.

In his dissent Chief Justice Warren clearly disagreed with Justice Brennan's reading of "community" saying:

> It is my belief that when the Court said in Roth that obscenity is to be defined by reference to 'community standards,' it meant community standards—not a national standard, as is sometimes argued. I believe that there is no provable 'national standard,' and perhaps there should be none. At all events, this Court has not been able to enunciate one, and it would be unreasonable to expect local courts to divine one. It is said that such a 'community'

approach may well result in material being proscribed as obscene in one community but not in another, and, in all probability, that is true. But communities throughout the Nation are in fact diverse, and it must be remembered that, in cases such as this one, the Court is confronted with the task of reconciling conflicting rights of the diverse communities within our society and of individuals.

In 1966, the three-fold test of obscenity that had been evolving for several years was coalesced and enunciated clearly in *A Book Named 'John Cleland's Memoirs of a Woman of Pleasure' v. Attorney General of the Commonwealth of Massachusetts,* 383 U.S. 413. Announcing the judgment of the Court, Justice Brennan said:

> Under this definition [Roth], as elaborated in subsequent cases, three elements must coalesce: it must be established that (a) the dominant theme of the material taken as a whole appeals to a prurient interest in sex; (b) the material is patently offensive because it affronts contemporary community standards relating to the description or representation of sexual matters; and (c) the material is utterly without redeeming social value.

Brennan further spelled out that last point slightly later in the decision:

> The Supreme Judicial Court erred in holding that a book need not be 'unqualifiedly worthless before it can be deemed obscene.' A book cannot be proscribed unless it is found to be *utterly* without redeeming social value. This is so even though the book is found to possess the requisite prurient appeal and to be patently offensive. Each of the federal constitutional criteria is to be applied independently; the social value of the book can neither be weighed against nor canceled by its prurient appeal or patent offensiveness. Hence, even on the view of the court below that *Memoirs* possessed only a modicum of social value, its judgment must be reversed as being founded on an erroneous interpretation of a federal constitutional standard.

Such was the law of the land until the 1973 *Miller v. California,* 93 S.Ct. 2607, Burger court finding. In *Miller,* Chief Justice Burger delivering the majority opinion repudiated the "*utterly* without redeeming social value" test and the use of national community standards. The three-fold guidelines for the trier of fact (jury or judge) announced in *Miller* were:

> (a) whether 'the average person, applying contemporary community standards' would find that the work, taken as a whole, appeals to the prurient interest, (b) whether the work depicts or describes, in a patently offensive way, sexual conduct specifically defined by the applicable state law, and (c) whether the work, taken as a whole, lacks serious literary, artistic, political, or scientific value.

The Chief Justice went on to underscore his view of contemporary community standards.

> Nothing in the First Amendment requires that a jury must consider hypothetical and unascertainable 'national standards' when attempting to determine whether certain materials are obscene as a matter of fact. . . . It is neither realistic nor constitutionally sound to read the First Amendment as requiring that the people of Maine or Mississippi accept the public depiction of conduct found tolerable in Las Vegas or New York City. . . . People in different States vary in their tastes and attitudes, and this diversity is not to be strangled by the absolutism of imposed uniformity.

In another decision announced the same day as *Miller*, Justice Brennan dissented in the case of *Paris Adult Theatre 1 et al. v. Slaton*, 93 S.Ct. 2628 (1973), and wrote, "The problem is, rather, that one cannot say with certainty that material is obscene until at least five members of this Court, applying inevitably obscure standards, have pronounced it so."

Brennan's prophecy proved well founded, for only a few days after *Miller* had been announced, the Georgia Supreme Court found the film *Carnal Knowledge* obscene. So the appeal came to the Court and in June 1974 in *Jenkins v. Georgia*, 94 S.Ct. 2750, Justice Rehnquist attempted to show why contemporary community standards did indeed mean local communities but apparently not all the time. Rehnquist wrote:

> Even though questions of appeal to the 'prurient interest' or of patent offensiveness are 'essentially questions of fact,' it would be a serious misreading of *Miller* to conclude that juries have unbridled discretion in determining what is 'patently offensive.'

Then having noted that the *Miller* catalog of examples of what states could specifically describe as obscene was not an exhaustive list, Rehnquist commented upon the viewing of the film by the Court.

> Our own view of the film satisfies us that *Carnal Knowledge* could not be found under the *Miller* standards to depict sexual conduct in a patently offensive way. Nothing in the movie falls within either of the two examples given in *Miller* of material which may constitutionally be found to meet the 'patently offensive' element of those standards, nor is there anything sufficiently similar to such material to justify similar treatment.

No matter how one reads *Jenkins*, the conclusion must be that 'obscenity' and 'community standards' are tough words to define, and Supreme Court Justices have as much trouble, possibly more, as other intelligent citizens defining them. The legal problem of defining obscenity and then applying some test or standard is unquestionably serious, but the Supreme Court has helped Americans understand the meaning of 'obscenity' very little in the last few years. Indeed, the degree of confusion and even obfuscation introduced by the Court has added some humor to the American scene, but very little light.

Indirect Effects of Recent Obscenity Decisions on Schools

The intent of these recent Supreme Court decisions was to attack hardcore pornography, to distinguish it legally from non-hardcore materials, and to lend assistance to state and local officials attempting to do away with the hardcore. Unhappily, the consequent efforts have not fared well. Burt Pines, Los Angeles City Attorney, noted in "War on Obscenity: A Wasteful Effort" (*Los Angeles Times,* 1 September 1974, pp. VI-1, 4), that "Los Angeles spent a quarter of a million dollars in unsuccessfully trying to stop the showing of *Deep Throat*" when the trial resulted in a hung jury. His recommendation, that litigation about hardcore pornography could bankrupt a community, is shared by some prosecutors, though hardly all.

The author was shocked when he read in the *New York Times,* 26 November 1974, pp. 1, 24, that his small home town, Clarinda, Iowa, permitted the showing of X-rated movies. The *Times* author wrote:

> In Clarinda, Iowa, a town one might expect television's Apple family to live in, *The Devil in Miss Jones,* a sex movie, was shown for a few days this fall across the street from the county fairgrounds. Residents appeared to be tolerant. Nobody complained. 'I didn't even know it was here,' said J. C. Irvin, County Attorney.

If hardcore pornography is relatively safe from attack in Clarinda, Iowa, then it must be relatively free from successful attack almost anywhere in the United States.

In his dissent in *Paris Adult Theater 1 et al. v. Slaton,* Justice Brennan referred to "chilling protected speech" and "the chill on protected expression" as a likely consequence of obscenity definitions and tests so obscure or so ambiguous as to lead to potential, perhaps even likely, censorship. To what degree that chilling effect has been felt by wholesale and retail purveyors of "adult bookstore" material is open to question, although most people have seen no perceptible diminution and newspapers have recently carried stories indicating that more and more towns are open territory for "adult" bookstores even if sales do seem to be falling. There may be a little chill felt by purveyors of this "literature."

But if hardcore pornography is relatively safe in many communities, the attention of those communities has been turned elsewhere towards textbooks and old favorites of the censor, *Brave New World, 1984, The Grapes of Wrath, The Catcher in the Rye, The Bible,* and *Soul on Ice.* The attention and the subsequent attacks on these books, clearly non-hardcore, may reflect a community's frustration. Unable to rid itself of hardcore pornography, X-rated movies, "adult" bookstores, or objectionable television programs, a community may turn to stopping what it can easily and safely and inexpensively stop, the right of young people to read freely.

School Censorship

But the chilling effect has been felt in schools—most obviously and publicly in Drake, North Dakota; Ridgefield, Connecticut; and Kanawha County, West Virginia, the past few years. That chilling effect can be felt in many English classrooms and in many libraries in selecting both textbooks and trade books. The chill may not destroy schools or teachers but it has worked harm, both in chilling the spirits of teachers and students and in placing some books in the deep freeze, at least temporarily.

Some parents may object to certain books in English classes or libraries. These parents are also likely to suggest that there are better books, less obscene, less controversial, that could be found. Recently, a friend received a letter from a parent objecting to a book—it little matters the specific title—a letter so typical it deserves quoting almost in its entirety. Many teachers or librarians or administrators have received such letters or know someone who has.

> Why do our decent children have foul-mouthed obscene trash like _____ when the purpose of reading is to provide wholesome and uplifting material for children? How can we expect young people who read _____ with all its base elements and vile actions and filthy words and suggestive situations to emerge morally unscathed? Isn't the purpose of English teaching to provide moral, clean, good, and happy literature to our children? Where are all the classics of the great past? Shouldn't you be whetting students' appetites with books which provide fine character building qualities? As parents, my husband and I can't stop all the evil from the outside world from coming to the

attention of our children, but we can protect our children from filthy books. Our home is a good, clean, Christian home. I expect you to help us keep it that way by providing unobjectionable literature rather than the obscenity of _____.

The problem is that a continuum of literature exists between the most outrageous and offensive volume in an "adult" bookstore and the most innocuous and inoffensive and noncontroversial book on the shelves of the most antiseptic library or English classroom. Presumably, there are gaps in that continuum, but those gaps exist for us largely because we are ignorant of many books, and the more reading we do, the more the gaps begin to fill in. Presumably, we could demonstrate to English teachers and librarians (although not necessarily to some parents) that from the most outrageous and offensive book we could move upward on some tentative or proposed continuum to Miller's *Tropic of Capricorn* to Ginsberg's "Howl" to Cleaver's *Soul on Ice* to Salinger's *The Catcher in the Rye* to Brautigan's *The Hawkline Monster* to Steinbeck's *Of Mice and Men* to Raucher's *Summer of '42* to Cormier's *The Chocolate War* to Frank's *Diary of a Young Girl* to Mitchell's *Gone with the Wind* and from there several steps onward to that most innocent of all possible books. English teachers are most unlikely to use the most outrageous book from the "adult" bookstore in secondary school, and it is almost as unlikely that they would use either of Miller's *Tropics*. But given a sensitive and intelligent and mature class, secondary English teachers might consider using "Howl" or Cleaver's *Soul on Ice* and the likelihood increases as we move up the continuum to Salinger's *Catcher* or any number of Steinbeck's works.

The good teacher would first select material appropriate to a class and its maturity and intelligence and sensitivity, and second, select material keeping in mind the contemporary local community standards. But second is not first. The teacher is not employed solely to reflect contemporary local community standards. The teacher is there to help make students more sensitive to and aware of their own immediate world and the outside world which more and more impinges upon even the most remote of communities. In a book (*The Sociology of Teaching*), still all too little known though it was published first in 1932, Willard Waller wrote, "Teachers are paid agents of cultural diffusion. They are hired to carry light into dark places. . . . Not only must the teacher know enough to teach the youngsters in the schools competently according to the standards of the community, but he must, usually, be a little beyond his community."

Clearly, the teacher must learn to gauge contemporary local community standards to stand any chance of survival. At the same time, teachers *know* that the community deserves far better than students indoctrinated into community standards which can prepare students only for permanent residence in a specific town permanently fixed in 1976, or whatever magic wondrous year the community feels it would like to lock itself into. Teachers *know* that students may leave their immediate community, at least temporarily, and students must face the reality of the world today and tomorrow, neither one nor the other but both.

Teachers may come under attack, and charges, official legal charges or unofficial rumor-mongering charges, are lodged because teachers have used something someone, someplace, sometime called obscene, or controversial, pornographic, filthy, leering, suggestive, objectionable, dirty, or any widely used synonym. The case may never appear in any official courtroom, but the book is likely to be lost, and the teacher and students and community lose any real possibility of anything bordering on education. These censors, parents or teachers or administrators or laymen or librarians, will almost never operate under any definitions or tests of obscenity the Supreme Court or any other court would recognize, but their interpretations of obscenity are operationally effective for their purposes. The definitions and applications may reveal little reasoning about, less reflection on, and no reading of a work taken as a whole, but the censorial definitions and tests have far more practical and immediate import and impact upon teachers than any philosophical or legalistic ruminations of Supreme Court justices. The definitions and tests applied to classroom teachers may be arbitrary and capricious, but the applications lead to a speedy trial and in many cases to an even speedier verdict. The extralegal trial tends not to be cluttered with trivia like accuracy or reasoning or fairness or justice.

That books in libraries and in English classes have and do and will come under attack for being "obscene" is no fiction for teachers or librarians. That both books and teachers using them can be lost to the profession is not at all uncommon. That the books cannot fight for themselves and that the teachers all too rarely fight is also true. Happily, the teacher faced with censorship may be tempted to fight back, but unhappily, a rapid survey of the experiences of friends in similar straits and the terrifying track record of teachers willing to go to court will often put a damper on the urge to respond to censorship through legal means. A couple of years ago, the author was one of two expert witnesses at a U.S. District Court trial involving a young English teacher quite obviously fired for using Albee's *Zoo Story* and Hemingway's *For Whom the Bell Tolls*. Although virtually everyone in the courtroom from the most casual observer to the judge knew precisely what the issue was—the School Board had been unquestionably unprofessional in getting rid of the teacher—the judge found for the young man, not with any official or legal regard to the censorship but rather with regard to the lack of due process accorded the teacher at his dismissal. Judges have been understandably reluctant to establish legal precedent in suits involving school censorship since no judge wishes to create precedent which may be reversed upon appeal. Teachers are also understandably reluctant to get involved in such suits since the teacher who gets publicity in this way is likely to have great difficulty finding any employment in teaching for years to come.

Teachers and librarians can debate endlessly about the priorities of their professions. Redefining professional needs, enlivening local or state organizations, and making teachers more proficient in teaching reading are important, but all these are insignificant to the one paramount priority of our teaching profession: protecting teachers against the attacks of censors. Some censors can make a valid case, and we would be wise to consider cases before running to the defense of every teacher. Many censors have little justification but much popular appeal, and for those censors we must be prepared. If teachers and librarians are coerced or forced or seduced into using only clean, unobjectionable, antiseptic, noncontroversial, uplifting works and in the process avoiding ideas which in the minds of many laymen seem controversial or irreligious or socialist or subversive or un-American, then it matters not one whit what teachers or librarians want or believe. If teachers and librarians do not have the intellectual freedom to explore the many visions of humanity and truth in their own private lives and with students in classes, then nothing remotely approaching *education* for anyone, teacher or student or community or society at large, is possible. The kind and degree of indoctrination being imposed by a society of school censors, passive or active, may vary from community to community, but indoctrination and not education is all that is possible in such a society. To pretend that *Miller* or *Paris Adult Theatre* is the major or the sole cause underlying the current emotionally charged climate in secondary schools is unwarranted and simplistic. *Real* problems are seldom easy to diagnose or remedy. But Justice Brennan's warning about the *chilling* effect that follows the repression of freedom should be taken personally and seriously by all teachers and librarians.

There is a chill in the air. Teachers who have not yet sensed the chill have apparently not recently gone outside. Either that, or the teachers cannot feel the chill because fear or vacillation or pressure have already frozen their professional souls, and they are dead or sterile and do not know it. Their students do, but these teachers do not.

The coming of the next ice age is not yet in sight. No record-breaking blizzard has been forecast, and major snowstorms may never occur, but in North Dakota the temperature dropped, in Connecticut there was a distinct coldsnap, and in West Virginia the mercury fell and the north wind blew. The chill factor is going to get worse. The winter of the intellect may be coming, and no one knows how long it may last or how ruthless or oppressive it may be. Winter is not yet here, but we do know the temperature outside is falling, falling, falling every day.

6 Legal Decisions and Censorship: A Game of Chance

Robert T. Rhode
Indiana University

Today, America may be experiencing one of the worst waves of censorship this country has known. Well-meaning parents often are disturbed by textbooks or by teaching methods that they feel are anti-American or anti-Christian. They ask that objectionable texts be removed from schools, that controversial teaching methods be discontinued, and that offensive books be removed from school library shelves. The courts have logged a confusing record of decisions regarding parental intervention in the operation of the schools. A review of these decisions indicates that a few courts have upheld parental rights to intercede for their children while other courts have supported teachers' claims to have academic freedom—to teach what they decided to teach.

A look at previous court cases, combined with speculation about future court cases, can resemble a game of chance in which a teacher may or may not win. Let us take a few moments to play this risky game.

Round One

Situation. You are a teacher in a junior or senior high school. One day a parent group complains that the textbook you are using is obscene and does not uphold the virtues of America. What can you do? Choose Card A, Card B, or Card C.

Card A. You tell the parent group that, according to existing law, "Whatever the agency which is given authority in a particular jurisdiction to select textbooks, the action of the agency designated is conclusive, so that the pupil and his parent or guardian have no voice in the matter" ("Schools," *American Jurisprudence 2d* 68 [1973]:607). You refer them to the 1877 case, *Trustees of Schools v. People,* 87 Ill. 303, which set that precedent. Then you argue that the textbook you are using was selected according to the approved method for your state; therefore, the parent group has no legal right to complain.

Card B. You argue that the U.S. Supreme Court has upheld a First and Fourteenth Amendment guarantee for an American's right to know. You explain to the parent group that the students in the school have a constitutional right to hear views to which their parents may be opposed. You cite the U.S. Supreme Court case, *Kleindienst v. Mandel,* 408 U.S. 753 (1972), to back up your point. (In that case, the U.S. Supreme Court said that an alien without a visa had to be allowed into the country because citizens had a right to hear him.) You conclude that the textbooks cannot be removed because students would be denied their constitutional right to know.

Card C. You contend that you, as the teacher, have academic freedom to decide what you will teach and how you will teach it. You cite two recent federal decisions which have upheld academic freedom. The first case, *Keefe v. Geanakos,* 418 F. 2d 359 (1969), held that "The Young and the Old," an article in *Atlantic Monthly,* was not obscene and that the teacher who had used the article in class did so for educational reasons that could be demonstrated. The second case, *Parducci v. Rutland,* 316 F. Supp. 352 (1970), held that "Welcome to the Monkey House," a short story by Kurt Vonnegut, Jr., was not obscene. The court applied the test formulated in the case, *Tinker v. Des Moines Independent Community School District,* 393 U.S. 503 (1969), that, when no disturbance is caused, teachers and students have First Amendment rights to freedom of speech. Applying the Tinker test, the court in Parducci decided that, in the absence of a disturbance, the teacher had academic freedom to teach whatever she decided to teach. You conclude that your textbook has not caused any substantial disruption to the normal operation of your school; you explain to the parent group that you have, therefore, an academic right to be free to teach from the textbook.

Results. If you chose Card A, you may have chosen a weak argument. Parents have a legally recognized political right to interfere after textbooks have been duly adopted. Parents have the right to bring pressure to bear against curricula, teaching methodology, and other educational systems or policies. Stephen R. Goldstein, in "The Asserted Constitutional Right of Public School Teachers to Determine What They Teach," *University of Pennsylvania Law Review* 124 (June 1976):1293-357, has said, "Moreover, in a democratic society it would seem desirable that politically responsive groups have the power to effect the public will concerning the structure and content of public education" (p. 1356). There are a number of court decisions (cited in footnote 94 in the Goldstein article) to back up this parental political right to complain. Furthermore, in the case, *President's Council, District 25 v. Community School Bd. No. 25,* 457 F. 2d 289 (1972), the U.S. Supreme Court, in denying certiorari in November 1972, held that there was no obvious court precedent for refusing, on constitutional ground, to remove books from a library. In other words, any parental group complaining of library books could have them removed by school authorities (thus exercising their political right to pressure school authorities). Translating that into the classroom, your textbook can be removed by school authorities reacting to parental pressure. Legislatures in some states have recognized a parental right to affect school policy decisions. These states have statutes permitting parents to serve on local textbook adoption committees. The 1877 Illinois case that you cited, while still on the books, is not a vital precedent anymore; it is being ignored by present-day courts.

If you chose Card B, again you may have chosen a weak argument, although no specific court cases have outlined beyond the shadow of a doubt whether or not teachers have a constitutional right to academic freedom. You may have that freedom. However, Goldstein (above) has said:

> The freedom of expression justification for teacher control is premised on an analytical model of education which views school as a marketplace of ideas. There is no historical or precedential basis, however, for concluding that the marketplace of ideas model is constitutionally compelled over the traditional value inculcation model. Thus, in the final analysis, teachers' constitutional rights, in and out of the classroom, do not extend beyond the first amendment rights of all citizens (p. 1356).

Case law backs up Goldstein's point. A student's presumed right to know is bound up in freedom of speech doctrine. If the teacher is perceived as teaching values which are objectionable to students or to parents, then that teacher may have no constitutional protection for what he or she is teaching. On the other hand, applying the Tinker test (above), the teacher may be within his or her rights so long as no disturbance results. The area of law surrounding academic freedom is so nebulous that it would be difficult to decide whether you have a viable argument, once you claim a constitutional right to academic freedom.

If you chose Card C, you may have a viable argument for the same reason as in Card B—no court has said you do *not* have academic freedom. However, your argument may be weakened by the decisions you cite. In the Keefe case, the court never explained the "grounds on which a teacher's curricular decisions take precedence over those of the school board or other school authorities superior to the teacher under state law" (Goldstein, p. 1321). If the parent group in your situation would enjoin the school board from putting into effect any offensive policy decision, then the Keefe decision would no longer hold precedent. The Keefe decision did not look at the chain of command—from school board to teacher, with the teacher at the bottom. You might be in danger of being fired, if your school board were not solidly supportive of its teachers and if enough pressure (such as "enjoining") were brought upon the school board by the parent group. Goldstein points out many flaws of reasoning in your other case—Parducci. With the flaws that Goldstein indicates, a court today might not consider the Parducci case to be a firm precedent. Another case may be more to the point. *Mailloux v. Kiley,* 436 F. 2d 565 (1st Cir.), after dismissal, 323 F. Supp. 1387 (D. Mass), aff'd, 448 F. 2d 1242 (1st Cir. 1971), limited academic freedom to the "tests" already set forth in Keefe and Parducci. In other words, the Mailloux case would not go beyond Keefe and Parducci to state an undeniable constitutional guarantee of academic freedom. Rather, the court concluded that academic freedom is more an "interest" than it is a "right," as Goldstein points out.

Some of your arguments in Round One might hold up in a court proceeding; however, these are muddy areas of law, and you might get stuck.

Round Two

Situation. The parent group brings pressure on the school board to remove from the library the textbook objected to in Round One. The school board agrees to remove the offensive textbook as well as two or three other books that the parent group also has found to be objectionable. The school board has ordered you to stop using the textbook in your classes. You want to preserve your right to teach what you decide to teach. What can you do? Choose Card D or Card E.

Card D. You decide to go against the school board's order, and you continue to use the disputed textbook in your classes. Your argument is that you have the academic freedom to use the duly adopted textbook which has been found objectionable by parents who are not professional educators. Also, you urge the librarian to keep the textbook shelved in the school library, along with the other "offensive" books. You instruct the librarian to respond to parental attacks by citing the recent Ohio case, *Minarcini v. Strongsville City School District,* 541 F. 2d 577 (6th Cir. 1976). In that case, the court decided that books could not be removed from the library simply because someone found the books to be offensive. The court reaffirmed U.S. Supreme Court opinions which held that students have a constitutional right to know and to hear opposing points of view. This right to know would be denied by removal of books from a library.

Card E. You argue that the textbook is not obscene and does not conflict with the Judaeo-Christian morals and values of the community. You go against the school board order and continue to teach from the disputed textbook. You also talk the librarian into keeping the textbook shelved in the school library, along with the other objectionable books. You and the librarian decide to use as your argument "academic freedom."

Results. If you chose Card D, you may have chosen an unwise course of action, although your argument involving the Minarcini case may be one of the best arguments available to teachers today. The school board is enjoined by the parent group to back up its order to remove the book from the curriculum and from the library (as well as the other "offensive" books). Despite your references to legal precedents that have stated that textbooks, after being duly adopted, must be used and cannot be discontinued ("Schools and School Districts," *Corpus Juris Secumdum,* 79 [1952]:433; and "Schools," *American Jurisprudence 2d,* 68 [1973]:607), the court decides that old laws are not precedential in this case, and it gives the decision to the parent group. The school board has the right to remove objectionable textbooks, according to the court. The court follows the thinking of Goldstein; that is, academic freedom is a constitutional interest but not a guaranteed right, particularly in cases where a teacher can teach objectionable material to impressionable young minds, thus violating the students' rights. Furthermore, the court holds that the books should be removed from the library. The court refers to the decision in *President's Council, District 25 v. Community School Bd. No. 25,* (cited above), wherein the court said that books could indeed be removed from the library. The foregoing is one path the court might take.

Legal Decisions and Censorship 81

On the other hand, the court might accept the Minarcini argument and award you the decision. The court in the Minarcini case upheld the students' right to know. The court said, "Here, the court is concerned with the right of students to receive information that they and their teachers desire them to have. Recent Supreme Court opinions firmly establish both the First Amendment right to know involved in this case and the standing of the students to raise the issue." The Minarcini case may be one of your strongest cards.

The court might take yet another path in this situation. First, you might be in danger of being fired, particularly if your school board is not solidly behind its teachers. Your refusal to acknowledge the school board's order to stop using the disputed textbook could be read as insubordination. Secondly, if you signed a group contract when you began to teach at your school, then you may have signed away your rights to academic freedom. Many group contracts have clauses that sign away a teacher's right to academic freedom. In the case, *Bob Cary, David Nykerk, Glenn Reed, Laurel Stonbraker and Lee Bridgeman v. Board of Education of the Adams-Arapahoe School District 28-J, Aurora, Colorado*, discussed in an article by Claire Cooper in the March 5, 1977, edition of *The Rocky Mountain News*, a district court judge said that teachers could surrender their academic freedom through group contracts.

Also, in your situation, the board might decide to fire the librarian. As Robert M. O'Neil has pointed out in *Human Rights* 4 (Summer 1975):295-312 and in *University of Cincinnati Law Review* 42 (1973):209-52, the librarian is caught between several legal constraints. Had the librarian removed the book (as the school board ordered), other parents in the community might have complained. A librarian's rights have not been clearly spelled out, and it is difficult to predict the consequences of a librarian's actions.

If you chose Card E, you may have arrived at a sound argument. The parent group may have received advice from Educational Research Analysts, the nonprofit public foundation of Mel and Norma Gabler of Longview, Texas. You may have glanced through a book about the Gablers, called *Textbooks on Trial*, by James C. Hefley (Wheaton, Ill.: Victor Books, 1976). You may have realized that the Gablers have long concluded that America was founded on Christian principles, which your textbook allegedly rejects. You may have decided to look into an 1890s case referred to in Appendix 10 (p. 209) in the book about the Gablers. The case the Gablers refer to may be *Holy Trinity Church v. United States,* 143 U.S. 457 (1891); the Gablers contend that this 1890s case stated that America was founded on Christian principles. You may have discovered that the case states that America is a "religious" country—not necessarily a fundamentalist Christian country. You explain this to the parent group, and they have no argument. You may also have a right to academic freedom (as discussed in the Results to Round One).

In Round Two you have fared somewhat better. You have developed a strong argument against removal of library books, based on the Minarcini case. You have also made a plea for academic freedom, which may be a constitutional right (as long as you have not signed a group contract waiving that right). Also, you may have been able to argue rationally with the parent group by contradicting statements in *Textbooks on Trial.*

Round Three

Situation. The parent group gets a great deal of newspaper space to attack textbooks, library books, and teaching methods in your school. The parents also secure radio air time and television commercials for the purpose of attacking offensive books and methods. The attacks are filled with references to "secular humanism," a religion being taught by the teachers in the school—a religion contradicting the Christian principles on which this country is based. The ads and commercials point to two U.S. Supreme Court decisions which held that secular humanism is a religion. Therefore, with separation of Church and State in this country, secular humanism cannot be taught. What can you do? Choose Card F, Card G, or Card H.

Card F. You decide to research the U.S. Supreme Court decisions making secular humanism a religion. You discover that the Court, in *Torcaso v. Watkins, Clerk,* 367 U.S. 488 (1961), referred to the religion of secular humanism in a footnote to that decision. In addition, you find that the case, *United States v. Seeger,* 380 U.S. 163 (1965), never mentioned the term "secular humanism"; rather, the case footnoted the Torcaso decision. The research you are doing leads you to the case, *Fellowship of Humanity v. County of Alameda,* 153 Cal. App. 2d 673 (1957). In that California Appeals Court case, the court discussed secular humanism—a religion that met at regular intervals, much like other denominations. After searching in the *New Catholic Encyclopedia* and other books on

American religions, you discover that a religion of secular humanism does exist; but you are far from being a member of that religion. You *do* have a belief in a Supreme Deity (secular humanists do not, ordinarily), and you are not on the membership roster of any church of "humanity." Suddenly you realize what is happening; the parent group is confusing the religion of secular humanism (which cannot be taught in the schools, due to separation of Church and State) with "humanism"—a philosophy of teaching—or with humanities programs. You decide to counter the parent group arguments with an explanation of what constitutes secular humanism, followed by a denial that you are a member of a secular humanist church.

Card G. You go to your department head and ask that a philosophy of what you are teaching be prepared at once and put into writing. You speak to your school administrators to see whether they will back you up. Then you organize a group of parents and teachers (parents not in alliance with the complaining parent group) to hold regular meetings and to publish reports in local papers, thus airing your side of the argument.

Card H. You do nothing and wait for the storm to blow over.

Results. By your clear demonstration that humanism, the educational philosophy detailed by such writers as Carl R. Rogers and Carl Weinberg, and secular humanism, the religion or movement allegedly begun by Dr. John H. Dietrich, Unitarian pastor (Charles Samuel Braden, *These Also Believe* [New York: Macmillan Company, 1963], p. 468) are two different philosophies, you have taken the main force out of the parent group's argument. In this situation, one of your best defenses may be to define accurately the differences between secular humanism and the words that sound like that—humanism, or humanities program, for example. Card F is a good choice of cards.

If you chose Card G, you may have made a wise move—but you are a little late. Before a controversy ever arises in your community, you must have a written philosophy for what you are teaching. And you should know in advance of any disturbance whether or not your administrators will back you up. The idea to use the tactics of the parent group—getting newspaper space, and so on—is a sound idea. Fight their fire with logical argument and try to get equal coverage.

If you chose Card H, you chose a poor card. You should not think that the storm will blow over. In times of national distress, such as the Watergate dilemma and inflation, people become frustrated. They would like to complain to Washington, D.C., but that place seems far away and unreachable. The schools often become the target for criticism. It is true that the pendulum may swing back; parents may gradually cease to object to textbooks and to teaching methods as the national sociopolitical climate changes. But keeping an alert mind is to be preferred over waiting for things to change. Be prepared to act. Know your cards and how to play them.

There is hope for teachers, but there are dangerous pitfalls as well. One such pitfall would be to assume your opposition is uneducated or kooky. As you can see from this game of chance, the parent group depicted here is well organized and willing to work hard for its goals. To dismiss complaining parents as kooks is to lose the game. The game is risky, but it can be won.

II Issues and Pressures

In many ways the second section is an extension of the first, but with a more specific focus on issues and pressures that are influencing teaching generally and especially influencing the teaching of English language arts. Hogan cites the inflamed rhetoric with which censorship battles are currently being fought and proceeds to paint an emphatic picture of the censor. He shows that in many of our anti-censorship activities we simply further alienate the already alienated. He considers ways in which we are all censors and ends by suggesting that English teachers become more involved in the community, including the media of the community. Park's article focuses on right wing groups and concludes that a new right wing coalition is emerging which may be politically very influential. Jenkinson's article concerns what some view as the ultimate in pro-censorship groups—the Gablers. He shows how organized censors combat textbooks they deem objectionable all over the country. He also delineates what they object to. Rhode attempts to explain secular humanism, as it is defined by certain groups and individuals who oppose it. Even though these groups have confused humanism with secular humanism, they are causing problems for teachers who espouse humanistic approaches. He encourages teachers to write rationales for everything they teach and to improve their communication with local communities. Berger's essay explores further the problem of defining obscenity, especially of applying community standards. She summarizes landmark legal decisions and the difficulties many of them have caused. Beach's article on research into the effects of and response to reading points out that at the heart of most censorship is the assumption that reading certain works has a negative influence on the reader. As might be expected, the research Beach surveys does not give definitive answers, but it does provide counter-evidence against claims about reading experiences that appear to justify censorship.

7 Some Thoughts on Censorship in the Schools

Robert F. Hogan
National Council of Teachers of English

I

In these tense times we often fight our battles with rhetoric. Whichever side calls the other the strongest name and invokes the highest principles in defense of its position lives with the illusion that it is winning the battle. Consider the rhetoric of the book opponents in recent times: they are fighting against *atheism, godless communism, filth, corruption,* and *social and familial disintegration.* And they are motivated by their commitment to a belief in *God, democracy,* the *family, law and order, fundamental Christian values,* private as well as public *decency and purity,* and *clean language.*

We teachers are in no place to throw stones. If our houses aren't made chiefly of glass, most of the newer school buildings seem to be. We invoke the First Amendment, often without having read the text of it; we shrill about academic freedom in a case in which a teacher seems to have exercised academic license. We strain to make a parallel between book burnings in Nazi Germany and the effort of parents to remove a book they regard a direct subversion if not violation of one or more of the Ten Commandments. A not uncommon question among educators these days is "Censorship: What is the nature of the Beast we are facing?" *Beast*—now that's a strong word. It ought to be worth at least six points in the contest. But let's consider one emanation of this Beast.

He's a blue-collar father and if he graduated from high school, it was a small one that wasn't very good academically and has since been consolidated with others to make a large high school, probably integrated culturally and racially. His children are or soon will be in that high school. He clings to fundamentalist religion and conservative morality in an increasingly pluralistic and secular world.

He knows (or believes, and that's about the same thing operationally) from what he hears in church and reads or views in the media that juvenile crime is up; that, except among girls who are on the pill, teenage pregnancy is up; that among all adolescents, venereal disease is approaching epidemic proportions and society's response to that is the condom; that use of marijuana and alcohol by adolescents is up; that opportunities to go wrong are up. He also knows that the Supreme Court has banned from the public schools those religious or other devotional exercises that might reinforce what he tries to teach at home.

Now he's told by someone he respects—either by his minister, or by someone his minister vouches for, or by a public official he has voted for—that there is a movement afoot in the schools called "secular humanism" or "scientific humanism" which is designed to (1) destroy any belief in the God he believes in; (2) undermine parental authority; and (3) call to question and thus erode those moral and ethical values he has been hoping to inculcate in his children.

Is it any wonder he panics? His panic troubles us, but would we be reasonable to expect any other response? Wouldn't it actually surprise us if he shrugged all this off, saying, "Well—what the hell—times are changing, I guess"?

If he or any of his friends gets in touch with the school to complain about what's happening, they learn there's a complaint form they have to fill out in order to have their complaint acknowledged and acted upon. Then he learns that in order to fill out the form, he has to read all the books that trouble him. The problem is not only that he has to read books he is already convinced are harmful, but he knows he doesn't read easily or well. It's not that he doesn't value some kinds of reading: he reads maps, blueprints, instructions, headlines. But he reads mostly to "find out"; he doesn't read to "read."

Maybe because he simply doesn't understand, he mistrusts those who do; he feels threatened by those who do, by those who read to "read." Besides, if his children sit around reading to "read," when will they get their chores done? Before we make a middle-class judgment about that concern over chores, let's remind ourselves that in many marginal-income, blue-collar families, chores do not signify what they do in our homes. In his home, chores are not a set of tasks to make the child learn "industry" and "responsibility." They are a set of tasks which, only if they are performed, will keep the family from tripping over the poverty line.

But that's not the end of it. When he has read all the books and filled out all the forms, the next step is the confrontation. It's the hearing with a group of college-graduated, verbal educators who seem always to pepper their talk with phrases like "anticipatory socialization." Yes, after the reading and the writing, there is the talking. And that doesn't come easy either, not with us as antagonists. Is it any wonder he seeks some other channel through which to express his concern? Are there some new ways for relating to this parent? Can we find any human relationship other than intimidation for dealing with this honest, confused, scared, caring father?

Behold the beast!

II

The uncomfortable truth is that we are all censors. The difference is that when English teachers practice censorship, we call it "book selection." We are protected by skimpy budgets from directly confronting that uncomfortable fact. When we make selections for classroom use or recommendations for library acquisitions, we take several variables into account. We think about (1) the budget, the available funds; (2) the level of difficulty and/or sophistication of the materials ("Are they *right* for our students?"); (3) the accuracy, the scholarly and professional respectability of the materials; (4) the narrowness of focus vs. the breadth of appeal; (5) the transactional relationship that obtains between our schools and the communities that support the schools.

Let's try some of these considerations on for size. *Budget:* As intrigued as I am by the *Compact Edition of the Oxford English Dictionary,* in a tight year I couldn't recommend its purchase by the department or library. There are too many other ways of distributing $90. *Level:* Even though some teachers of English and language arts are worried about what they regard as the deterioration of the language, it would be impossible to justify the purchase of an expensive, hard-to-find, durable copy of *Webster's Second International Dictionary* (as an antitoxin for the more liberal third edition) for the library in an elementary school. *Focus:* If I were recommending some special-interest, supplementary periodicals for school libraries in southeastern Ohio, I would be hard pressed to justify a subscription to a periodical concerned with surfing or skin diving. And so it goes. But we escape any, or much, sense of the other considerations because, by the time we get to them, we are usually out of money.

But let me bare my soul. If someone gave me $1,000,000 to be spent entirely in getting books to supplement the school library and my classroom library, I'd have to confront my censorious self. Even if money were no object, I still would not purchase the complete works of the Marquis de Sade, nor the *Kama Sutra,* nor the American update of that second title—*The Joy of Sex.* Nor would I subscribe to *Penthouse* or other magazines like it. It would not be just because I was confident the community might rise up in storm, although it probably would. I would avoid those publications because *I* think they're inappropriate for a public school library. What else is there to say: I am a censor.

If someone willed his or her entire library to me for inclusion in the school library or as a classroom library and accompanied that gift with funds sufficient to catalogue and shelve the books, I would still go through the collection title by title, volume by volume, sorting, selecting, and—yes—censoring. If I really believed in the universal application of the First Amendment, I'd put the entire collection on the shelves without checking any of the titles.

I can conclude only that I believe in censorship and the only difference between me and the censor—the one I'd brand as "censor"—is that his or her stack of rejects would be higher than mine. When I look at my choices, I concentrate on the ones I mean to include in the library; when I look at the other person's stack, I focus on the books he or she wants to keep out of the library. I select; they censor. Our criteria blend: the books I reject are ones I don't think the children are ready for; the ones they censor are books they don't think their children are ready for.

III

With respect to the rising frequency and intensity of censorship, the profession asks, "Why is this happening to us? What have we done to deserve this?" To be sure, external forces beyond our control and influence have helped create the situation. But we have helped, too, and in a variety of ways.

First, we have unionized, collectivized, and insisted on binding arbitration in disputes over salary increases, reduced class loads, and better working conditions. We had depended for so long on our own individual authority, on what only we knew with confidence, real or pretended: the six acceptable ways of spelling "parakeet"; the correct form of "whoever" and "whomever"; the distinction between trash and literature; how *Moby Dick* finally turned out (hardly anyone else ever finished it). When we found ourselves at the limits of our authority and still underpaid, we set aside our particular authority and banded together with other teachers also willing to set aside their particular authority—the table of elements, the distinction between rocket propulsion and jet propulsion, the formula for solving quadratic equations, etc. We all banded together and set out to exert power that would *force* where authority could no longer persuade.

Don't misunderstand: I know what salaries are like in places where teachers still choose to or have to depend on their scholastic authority. But what some of us didn't foresee clearly was the consequence of that shift. Authority depends on—and when it's well applied, it evokes—respect. Exerting power elicits antagonism. It assumes or creates an adversary relationship. To be sure, the successful exertion of power elicits a kind of respect (Nobody messes around with or otherwise takes lightly Albert Shanker!), but it's a different kind of respect.

What I, at least, failed to foresee was the inevitable consequence of teachers' collectivizing. It's happened: parents have collectivized. They've gone national, too. The frameworks were there already: fundamentalist churches, ethnic special-interest organizations, political special-interest groups. All that concerned lay people had to do was take advantage of the channels that had already been dug and levied. This stunning truth came home to me when the National Council of Teachers of English met in New Orleans in 1974: teachers I'd worked with in a workshop at the University of Alaska in 1973 told me that parents in Kanawha County, West Virginia, were in regular phone contact and correspondence with parents in Anchorage, Alaska.

One of Woody Allen's zaniest lines is that "Albert Shanker has 'the bomb.'" Like it or not, we have to accept the fact that the parents now have it, too.

Second, we English teachers have asserted our "rights" faster and further than we have prepared the rest of the community to accept. Again, this has been an exercise of power. Our position— in fact, NCTE's official policy—is that English teachers are the experts. We know children and how they develop; we know literature and the choices available; we know what it is that children need to know. Therefore, *we* are in the best position to choose the books. That's our right. When we moved from "The Lady of the Lake" to *Slaughterhouse-Five*, we didn't lay any groundwork in the community. After all, it was within our rights to do that. We were the experts. We found ourselves out on a limb and our first line of defense was our "authority." We forgot that we had yielded our authority and found ourselves caught in a power struggle. When our authority failed and our power proved insufficient, we retreated to our possessive pronouns—this is *my* subject, these are *our* classrooms, these are *our* students. The trouble is, *our* students are *their* children.

According to Hugh Prather, I think (but it could have been someone else), there is an oriental language which doesn't accept the construction "my children" or "my dog." That kind or degree of possessiveness doesn't "compute" in the language. One has to say something like "the children who live with me" or "the dog who stays at the house I live in." The more tightly the *my*ness is affirmed, the more control the affirmer claims; the less circumscribed is his or her authority. The thing is: if I say "English is *my* subject" and "these children are *my* students" and "this is *my* classroom," and if the parents say, "yes but these children are *my* children," we've retreated to the American West and to disputes over mine claims. The heavy question is this: Which ones, the parents or the teachers, are claim jumping?

They're both claim jumping. Neither side "owns" the children. But the parents think they do and the teachers often assume *they* do. Our problem is to work out a strategy that genuinely persuades parents that while we are teaching the children that live in their houses, we are not jumping their claim, a strategy that might ever so gently lead them to wonder if they have a claim, either, or make them less likely to assert that claim if they think they have one.

Third, we have failed to take into responsible account the rest of the media. As a profession we have consistently, if not unanimously, supported the more generous interpretations of the perimeters of the First Amendment. We have not with equal responsibility supported the constraints which properly ought to accompany increased liberalization. The more we advocate freedom of access, the more we should advocate protection from affront. We have argued that consenting adults should be free to read or view anything they want to read or view. By the covers and contents of recent periodicals and motion pictures, we might assume that we— and others whom we have joined in supporting this position—have been more or less successful, but more rather than less. Movies and the magazines are "dirtier" than they used to be. But we haven't taken, so far as I know, a single stand with respect to the blatant advertising and display of those products which invade the attention of nonconsenting adults. Even though some of us are nonconsenting adults, we've taken no professional stance. Consequently, by default we have aligned ourselves with the libertarians.

Frightened parents don't see subtle distinctions we see. The language of *The Catcher in the Rye,* the visual content of *Deep Throat,* and the window displays of the typical "adult" bookstore seem, to frightened parents, all of a single piece. To them, these are simply different fragments of the same mosaic. We haven't done enough collectively, except defensively, to clearly distinguish between the first, second, and third. *The Catcher in the Rye* is defensible not despite its language, but because of its language. The "dirty" bookstore is defensible not because of its window display, but in spite of it.

IV

Since we have committed ourselves to a power struggle and since the "other side" has also seized power, it's too late to abandon that state of affairs. In matters of salary and working conditions, we probably have no choice but to stay committed to or become committed to national and local unions (the American Federation of Teachers or the National Education Association). In matters peculiarly related to English, we have no choice but to stay committed to or become committed to NCTE and its affiliates.

A healthy NCTE means continued publication of annotated book lists, so that an individual teacher or librarian, questioned about the recommendation of a particular book, can argue and document that the choice was not just an individual one, that the book has been recommended and endorsed by a committee of professionals from across the country. NCTE can continue to provide, as it has provided, tailored letters in moral and professional support of teachers caught up in individual situations. NCTE can continue to cooperate with such groups as the Office for Intellectual Freedom of the American Library Association, the National Ad Hoc Committee Against Censorship, and the Freedom to Read Committee of the Association of American Publishers, etc., in coordinated national efforts to counter censorship. NCTE can continue to recommend genuinely professional procedures for book selection. NCTE can continue, through official resolutions and individual publications, to illuminate the problem and call for help from other segments of communites who oppose censorship. But none of this by itself is sufficient.

So far I have been dealing in the past and the present, in case history and diagnosis. That's useful and necessary, but not by itself ultimately productive. As we deal with our troubles and our agonies and their roots, we are tempted to wish things had been different before and were different now. That's thinking in the subjunctive mode. The lesson of the moment is that the subjunctive has no future, either grammatically or operationally.

Our resolutions and solutions must be posited in the future, in our responses to three questions: (1) What do we want to happen? (2) What will it take to make that happen? (3) What and/or how much are we prepared to pay to make that happen—to pay in money, time and effort, and sharing of sovereignty? If our answer to the third question is "not very much," we might as well stop fussing and accept the present dreary state of affairs. If we concentrate on how we wish things were, instead of how we *want* them to be different and what we are *willing* to do to make them different, we are mired in the subjunctive. We're stuck in a mode that keeps us from dealing in any responsible way with the future.

Obviously, what we want to happen is that the community will accept our selections of books and nonprint works for basic texts, supplementary texts, library acquisitions, and supplementary reading and viewing lists. What will that require? Heightened credibility and confidence in *us* and, therefore, in the choices we make. As I noted above, we have—however unthinkingly—yielded our authority. Maybe we didn't mean to, but we did. It's too late to say, "Oh, but we didn't mean that. . . ." We did it, and probably for understandable if not always conscious reasons. Moreover, in the present climate, the exercise of power won't work. "They" have it, too. We are at a standoff. So, what's left as a means for gaining heightened credibility and confidence? And are we willing to pay for them?

It may seem, at first glance, ridiculous to suggest that English teachers are members of the privileged class. But we share at least one advantage with the privileged members of this society. We have moved into social and intellectual ghettos of our own making. These ghettos are not like those of Spanish Harlem, Black Harlem, or the barrios of Los Angeles and the Southwest. Our ghettos are not places where society has consigned us to live. They are more like medieval walled cities, meant not to keep people in, but to keep "the others" out. We live less and less under the scrutiny of the community. We have moved farther and farther from living under the constraints that surrounded Caesar's wife. We may not enjoy Caesar's status yet, but at least we don't have to be above all suspicion. Well, maybe that's not quite right; but at least we are no longer under a limelight. If what we do is suspicious, fewer people see it and suspect.

What we must do now is come out of our closets, to come out from hiding, to renegotiate our social contract with the community. Our heightened credibility lies in personal diplomacy. In rapidly increasing numbers we must join and take an active part in community groups; invite parents to sit in on book selection committees; organize speaker bureaus for community and civic groups, and not just on censorship (and if we're short of good speakers, let's first agonize over and then do something about our poverty); establish stronger links with public librarians; meet the press (like coming up with one extra brown bag lunch for a local editor to join the English department for lunch); go to church (unless that would be hypocritical, in which case—for God's true sake, stay home); write a short, clear letter to an editor. It's shuttle diplomacy, to be sure, and we're all on the bus. Let's just sort out the best stop for each of us.

I know, I know. This all takes time and we don't have extra time. But what will it profit English teachers if they get all the papers marked, but lose the books? Or worse, their subject.

Part of our plight stems from the fact that, in protecting our ghettos, only under pressure do some of us admit our profession. And it comes out in the end as a confession. Let's resolve never again to confess our profession. Rather, let's proclaim it from the outset. If people ask of us, "What do you do?" let's say it right out: "I teach English," or "I'm an English teacher." No cop-outs. Never again, "I'm an educator," or "I'm a high school teacher," or "I'm 'into' education." *No,* and for one very good reason. The inquisition won't stop there. They'll want to know what we teach. Even if we sidestep and say, "Eighth grade" or "Mostly juniors and seniors" they'll bore in. "But *what* do you teach?" All that prior evasion drives us inescapably into confessional cowering. However we word it, the message comes out, "Please accept/tolerate/forgive me, for I teach English."

Let's brave it out. At the very beginning, before ever running for cover, let's tell the truth. Then, when we hear the stock response, "Well, I guess I'd better watch my grammar," let's reply in fundamental truth, "Look, if you promise not to watch your grammar, I won't have to watch mine. Why don't we talk, not watch?"

The last line of our defense under present circumstances may become, in time, the first line of our offense. It won't be the First Amendment. It won't be the fortress of a profession. It won't be the wall of a discipline. It won't be the fence around "our" classrooms. It will rest on your credibility and mine. What it will probably be is an open door. Through the door the parent will come and ask, "Why did you let or ask my son or daughter to read this story or poem?" And the one of us who's asked will say, "Do you really wonder why? Then I'm glad you asked. Let me tell you. . . ."

If the parent feels free to ask *us* and not a national wire service, and if we feel confident about the answer, we're all home free. If they won't or we don't, it will come to be Kanawha County on a national scale.

8 Clouds on the Right: A Review of Pending Pressures against Education

J. Charles Park
University of Wisconsin—Whitewater

Fed by increased taxes, union militancy, liberals in power, and godlessness in the public schools, a number of ultraconservative, far-right, and fundamentalist groups are showing remarkable success in developing a grassroots political structure designed to restrict social legislation, reduce spending, elect like-minded persons to public office, and turn America back to the basics. During a time of distrust of government, public apathy at the polls, and conflicting results of educational programs, the conditions are ripe for a well-organized group of true believers to exert influence far beyond their numbers.

As of this early 1978 writing, it appears a new right-wing coalition is emerging in American politics: a coalition led by seasoned political ultraconservatives with sufficient funds and grassroots support to influence the 1978 Congressional election. Widespread apathy, on one hand, and deep-seated dissatisfaction with the social advances of American education, on the other, can be expected to move some citizens to support the growing campaign to elect ultraconservatives. Whether we like it or not, American education can never be entirely removed from the political process. Educational support is a function of public opinion, and we are caught in the web of changing, diverse, and conflicting debate about the future.

Ultraconservatives and the New Right

Evidence of the growing organizational support for ultraconservative politics may be found in a recent report from the National Committee for an Effective Congress.[1] It notes that unlike campaigns of the past, the new evil is not a communist conspiracy; the new evil is liberalism. It also calls attention to the ability of the New Right to influence public opinion and sees this as constituting a source of concern for educators and for the future of public schools. A partial list of the more significant New Right organizations includes the following.

The Committee for Survival of a Free Congress (CSFC), established through the money of ultraconservative Joseph Coors, and now headed by Paul Weyrich, past president of the conservative Heritage Foundation. The Committee plans to raise over three million dollars to elect ultraconservatives to Congress in 1978. In 1976 the organization spent over two million dollars to elect ultraconservatives.

The National Conservative Political Action Committee (NCPAC), associated with the growing influence of Richard Viguerie, political fund raiser and coordinator of the Wallace campaign, hopes to spend over four million dollars for the election in 1978.

The Gun Owners of America, headed by John Birch leader H. H. Richardson, plans to support candidates opposing gun legislation but in practice supports only arch-conservatives.

The Council for National Defense, a new entry from the far right, plans to defeat senators and congressmen who "believe we should take our national defense dollars and spend them on social-welfare programs."

The Conservative Caucus (TCC), director Howard Phillips claims, is "going after people on the basis of their Hot Buttons."[2] The hot buttons Phillips describes include, among others, gun control, capital punishment, Panama Canal, ERA, and taxes. TCC is credited with offering assistance to Anita Bryant in helping her campaign go national.

Key figures behind the New Right appear to be Richard Viguerie, Ronald Reagan, Joseph Coors, and Phyllis Schlafly.

Richard Viguerie, a major engineer of the New Right complex and fund raiser for a number of conservative and far-right groups including the Wallace presidential campaign, claims, "There is new strength in the conservative movement, a strength that comes from single issue organizations joining forces with broader conservative groups to defeat legislation. A coalition politics, as practiced by conservatives for the first time in recent memory, is having a profound impact on the Congress, the press and the country."[3] Viguerie estimates his organization has collected between twenty-five to thirty million dollars to support ultraconservatives through 1977 and predicts his organization will yield over forty million during 1978.[4] Out of distrust of the liberal media, Viguerie has embarked upon a massive direct mail campaign. Viguerie's headquarters near Falls Church, Virginia, contains 3,100 computerized mailing lists from conservative and right-wing contributors. It is estimated that Viguerie sends out an average of five million pieces of mail a month.[5] Terence Smith, in the *New York Times*, reports that leaders of the New Right regularly meet with Viguerie to coordinate and forge an effective far-right coalition. Unlike campaigns of the past, the New Right is prepared to accept partial victories that the old right would have rejected. Viguerie's target in 1978 ". . . is to replace as many liberals of both parties as possible with 'leverage conservatives,' men who can influence policy and help elect other conservatives."[6]

Ronald Reagan supporters, and ultraconservatives to the right of the traditional Republican party, are pressing to establish a continuing base for political power. Reagan's Citizens for the Republic continues to provide money to defeat candidates for the House and Senate and to elect those supporting his program of conservatism. Supported by a radio show and newspaper column, the Citizens for the Republic have been receiving funds at the reported rate of $100,000 per month and have access to over one million dollars from the last presidential campaign. During an off-year election when traditional voter turnout has tended to be light and the Republican party is at a forty year low in membership, it would appear we are in the beginning stages of an interesting political development.

At a meeting of moderate Republicans called by Michigan Governor William G. Millikan to discuss fighting the takeover of the party by the New Right, Congressman John B. Anderson, the third-ranking leader of the Republicans in the House, charged that "extremist Fringe elements who claim membership in our party seek to expel the rest of us from the GOP using their own arbitrary philosophical purgative."[7] Saul Friedman, a writer for the Knight-Ridder papers, has observed "in legislative battles in Congress, in political fund raising, in mobilizing support on controversial issues throughout the country, in winning key off-year elections, and in sheer intellectual energy and talent, the New Right has overwhelmed the traditional Republican establishment."

Underscoring the strength of the New Right is the list of legislative winners in the John Birch Society voting index for this session of Congress. In the House: Steven Symms, George Hansen, James Collins, Robert Stump, Robert Bauman, Eldon Rudd, and Phillip Crane and Larry McDonald, a member of the Birch Council, have scored 100 percent. In the Senate: Orrin Hatch, Paul Laxalt and Jesse Helms along with Carl Curtis and Jake Garn are given high scores of from 100 to 96 percent. Such conservative influence and support of rightist principles would have been undreamed of ten years ago when Birch headlines drew strong opposition from conservatives such as William F. Buckley and Russell Kirk.

Joseph Coors, an ultraconservative multi-millionaire, was appointed to the Board of the Corporation for Public Broadcasting the day before President Nixon resigned.[8] He was not confirmed, due in part to a conflict of interest resulting from his Television News Service, which was reportedly designed to counter the liberal media.[9] Coors is reported to have financed, or contributed to, a number of conservative and right-wing causes such as the John Birch Society,[10] Americans for Agnew, and the Committee for the Survival of a Free Congress (CSFC).[11] The CSFC was designed to defeat liberal candidates at the national level and the prime mover was Paul M. Weyrich, "Coors' man in Washington," an aide to Senator Carl Curtis.[12] With the assistance of Richard Viguerie, a top political organizer for the Wallace campaign, funds were directed to such ultraconservative candidates as C. R. Lewis, a member of the Council of the John Birch Society, who tried unsuccessfully to defeat Alaska's Senator Mike Gravel. Although Coors' TV news has folded, it appears that Coors is experiencing success in a new and potentially significant organization designed to sell ultraconservatism to the American public.

The Heritage Foundation, created and funded by Coors,[13] was formed in 1973 as a tax-exempt Washington-based think tank to support conservative ideology, free enterprise, individual liberty, limited government, and strong national defense.[14] Paul M. Weyrich, the Foundation's first president, reports initial internal correspondence was routinely packed and sent to Coors for review.[15] During the last few years the Heritage Foundation has grown significantly in funding sources and influence, comprising over thirty full-time staff members, ten research assistants, and an annual budget of over one million dollars.[16] Principal activities of the Heritage Foundation include:

> Resource Bank . . . to assist like-minded groups in developing issues and timing for impact on national legislation.
>
> Communication Network . . . a speakers bureau which includes ideology from conservative to far right. Lawrence McDonald, of the Birch Council, and Phyllis Schlafly, have been advertised as speakers.[17]
>
> Washington Briefing series . . . designed to inform legislators of key matters before Congress.

Model Citizens Program . . . designed to assist persons in their local community to study their local school board, legislature, etc.

Education Update . . . newsletter to individuals and organizations reporting current issues in education.[18]

Education Update, edited by Dr. Onalee McGraw, appears designed to establish communication between conservative and fundamentalist private school organizations regarding funding, curriculum content, and educational issues at the state, local, and national levels. McGraw, an active opponent of the Mondale-Brademas Child Care Bill and *Man: A Course of Study* (MACOS),[19] and an endorser of the Conlan Amendment, which would have denied federal funds to support so-called atheistic secular humanism in public schools, is the coordinator for the National Coalition for Children.[20] Her booklet *Secular Humanism in the Schools: An Issue Whose Time Has Come,* published by the Heritage Foundation, argues that the cause for the precipitous deterioration of learning achievement in our schools is humanistic education.

> Children are . . . being taught at school that moral and social beliefs and behavior are not necessarily based upon Judeo-Christian principles being taught by most families at home, but should be fashioned instead to suit the wishes and convenience of the majority of society as a whole.[21]

The Heritage Foundation will be remembered by some educators for its active support of school critics in Kanawha County.[22] However, later developments suggest their influence will become more pervasive; the Board of Advisors and staff are politically experienced and capable of influencing issues. Examples of the emerging style can be found in its campaign to stop big labor, launched by a fund-raising letter signed by Senator Jake Garn of Utah. And, in *Education Update,* the names and addresses of committees reviewing federal funds for education were circulated to subscribers in an effort to reduce federal funds for educational projects. With a current mailing list of over 70,000, the Heritage Foundation program and political expertise should continue to be a source of educational interest.

The American Legislative Exchange Council (ALEC), whose board of directors includes the last three presidents of the Heritage Foundation,[23] publishes a booklet intended for conservative state legislators throughout the nation. The booklet includes, word for word, legislative bills that can be introduced on a number of topics, including education.[24] Among the bills affecting education, the 1977 edition of *Suggested State Legislation* included items on free enterprise, parental rights, teacher proficiency, school discipline, and a bill prohibiting forced busing. A quote from Onalee McGraw, whose degree is in government, is included in the booklet's introduction to legislation on values of education claiming that:

> Humanistic education is the latest manifestation of the 'so-called progressive life adjustment philosophy' that has dominated our schools and teacher education for decades. Humanistic education 'places all' emphasis on the child's social and psychological growth, 'instead' of on the learning of basic reading, writing, thinking, communicating skills, and factual knowledge.[25]

In June of 1977, ALEC invited conservative legislators to submit bills to be included in the next edition of *Suggested State Legislation*. The chairperson of the evaluation committee for review of bills to be included in the 1978 booklet is Donna J. Carlson,[26] a member of the Arizona legislature and of the American Opinion Speakers Bureau, which promotes a John Birch Society viewpoint. It is likely that the results of ALEC's booklet will have an impact on state legislators and education.

Phyllis Schlafly and the campaign against the Equal Rights Amendment continues to gain headlines and impact in state legislatures across the country. Phyllis Schlafly, a frequent speaker at a number of conservative and right-wing gatherings including the John Birch Society, includes a potentially significant feature in her organization's membership leaflet, the *Eagle Forum*. In the statement of purposes is a reference to education which declares a belief in the right of parents to insist that schools permit voluntary prayer, teach the precepts of holy scriptures, use textbooks that do not offend the religious and moral views of parents, permit children to attend schools of their neighborhood, and use textbooks that honor families in which the woman's role as wife and mother is primary.[27]

In December of 1976, the *Phyllis Schlafly Report* circulated an address by Jo-Ann Abrigg, president of the Committee for Positive Education, in which she claimed, "We parents are indeed paying taxes to school systems that hire teachers and purchase educational programs that fill our children's minds with garbage and utilize psychological techniques to condition our children to antichristian judeo philosophy and religion."[28]

If, as some suggest, the ERA movement is doomed to failure, it is quite possible that the opposition political organizations and grassroots systems created through Phyllis Schlafly will find education an attractive target.

The Evangelical Right

During the last few years significant growth has occurred among religious fundamentalists, estimated as high as forty million voters.[29] Some segments are clearly associated with far-right interests in opposing public education and establishing private schools devoted to a return to basics. The growth of fundamentalism and private fundamentalist schools should raise serious questions regarding increased pressure on public school financing and curricula.

The Institute for Creation Research, Inc. (ICR) is devoted to "a revival of belief in special creation as the true explanation of the origin of the world."[30] ICR will send free materials to any person who will present them formally to their school board.[31] Among the publications that have generated controversy is *Biology: A Search for Order in Complexity*.[32] In Indiana, Texas, Arkansas, Tennessee, and California the text has raised debate.[33] In Indiana, the text was adopted by the state textbook committee, but later ordered removed by Judge Michael T. Duggan, who asserted, "The book's claim that it presents a balanced view is a sham that breaches the separation between church and state voiced by Thomas Jefferson."[34] ICR has grown considerably as a result of renewed interest in evangelical fundamentalism. The implications for future growth and influence upon school curriculum and financing should not go unnoticed.

Third Century Publishers offer materials designed to mobilize a conservative Christian political base. The materials, written for the most part by Rus Walton, a former campaigner for Barry Goldwater and Ronald Reagan,[35] include *One Nation under God*.[36] Walton's thesis suggests, among other things, that God is an ultraconservative who is against coercing persons into joining unions, against having to pay for public school material that is offensive, and against forcing children to attend school.[37] Chapter 6, "Are Public Schools Ruining Our Children?" suggests the root evils are compulsory education, curriculum, and financing (taxation).[38] In the study guide, Walton's students are asked to "consider the parents in Kanawha County, W. Va., and other school districts. Are there similar problems in your area?" Later they are asked, "Have you audited the materials used in your local school?"[39] In its *In the Spirit of 76: the Citizens Guide to Politics,* Third Century Publishers provides details on how to organize a political campaign.[40]

Third Century Publishers should not be easily dismissed. This publishing company has been closely linked to Bill Bright of the Christian Embassy and Campus Crusade for Christ.[41] Ultraconservative interests are aware of the potential. Richard Viguerie has been quoted as saying, "The next real major area of growth for the conservative ideology and (political) philosophy is among evangelical people. I would not be surprised if in the next year you did not see a massive effort to involve them, utilizing direct mail and other techniques."[42]

The Old Right

The John Birch Society includes a speakers bureau, a publishing company, and a number of front groups capable of exerting pressure through some four thousand Birch chapters controlled and directed by Robert Welch.[43] In March of 1977 Welch called for a major effort to establish five hundred Tax Reform Immediately (TRIM) Committees in each congressional district to lower taxes through less government.[44] "We are confident," writes Welch, "that pressure will continue to grow if thousands of TRIM bulletins are distributed throughout each and every congressional district."[45]

Birch involvement in the anti-ERA movement appears to be much stronger than the general public may recognize. In a series of close state decisions, it appears the Birch influence has in some cases made the difference. "We wish we had space," wrote William Dunham of the Birch staff, "to describe in detail the fantastic effort put forth by so many Birchers."[46] An example from North Carolina, where the ERA bill was defeated by one vote, is instructive. A Birch section leader comments, "Though the JBS was never publicly mentioned, the leadership positions were filled, and the movement's success was made possible by our people, and I am sure the enemy knows it."[47]

Birch effectiveness in influencing public issues and candidates has, in some instances, been crucial. Referring to the election to Congress of Birch Council member Lawrence McDonald, Welch writes, ". . . as early as we could, in 1975, we assigned an excellent full-time coordinator to work in that [Georgia] Congressional district alone."[48] And, in the Birch petition drive to get the United States out of the United Nations, more than eight million signatures were submitted to selected congressmen in 1976.[49]

Should the Birch efforts to influence the growing anti-tax movement be successful, educators can anticipate a move to reduce funds for public education at the local, state, and national levels.

Liberty Lobby, a Washington-based organization with several publications, front groups, and their own publishing firm, has devoted considerable attention to the anti-tax movement. The circulation of *The Spotlight,* a major lobby publication, has grown from 40,000 in 1975 to over 100,000 and is actively advertising the aims of similar groups across the country.[50] Martin A. Larson, a staff writer, has published a number of books encouraging persons to refrain from paying their income tax. One such book, *How to Defend Yourself against the IRS,* includes the promotional remark, "If several million taxpayers would follow the advice and techniques offered in my manual, IRS operations would soon become impossible."[51] Audie McBrearty, indicted by a federal grand jury for tax evasion, received the Lobby's Liberty Award, as head of the United States Taxpayers Union.[52] Citizens, including some members of congress, will feel the influence of Liberty Lobby. The radio message of Liberty Lobby is heard on 340 stations daily.[53]

Conclusion

The climate for a resurgence of political ultraconservatism is reflected in recent polls of American public opinion. In one Gallup public opinion poll, some 47 percent of the respondents described themselves as "right of center," 32 percent as "left of center," and only 10 percent as "middle of the road."[54] Although the figures can be variously interpreted, it is clear that ultraconservatives hope to draw strength from the prevailing mood of discontent. At a time when the traditional coalition for social legislation composed of the civil rights, labor, and liberal Democrats appears to be dissolving, the chances are good that the next election will be a key factor in determining the future direction of state and national programs.

The future of public education is a function of public opinion. As such, we are well advised to consider the recent strength of the new right and consider the probable consequences for education. If, as seems predictable, we are on the verge of another round of ultraconservative pressure, what might educators expect for the future?

Although it may be too early to predict the specific issues that may surface in education, it would appear that taxes, progressive social curricula in the area of human relations, busing, and federal funding for educational projects will become prime targets. So too, we might expect to see increased concern regarding program development in the area of women's treatment in textbooks, specifically, a review of text materials related to the traditional role of women. Such a review has already been suggested by Phyllis Schlafly to anti-ERA groups across the country. A related matter regarding godlessness in the school can be expected to surface as we witness the growth of fundamentalist organizations, some of which are quick to accept the claims of the far right. It is likely this pressure will occur under the guise of attacks on secular humanism in the schools.

At issue here is not the right of persons within society to express their views regarding public education. Rather, at issue is the capability of educators to effectively respond to organized pressure from the New Right.[55] To be competitive in the marketplace of ideas requires tools and strategies that are effective in molding public opinion. In this regard, a significant element in recent moves by the New Right is the organized ability to influence public opinion using organizational tools that most educational organizations cannot match at present.

Today a disparate but growing grassroots support system is ripe for coalescing into a politically effective campaign against public education costs, curriculum development, and liberal education. During a time of public apathy at the polls and withdrawal from concern with social problems, the climate is very favorable for right-wing, ultraconservative, and evangelical rightists to influence legislation, funding, and curriculum. "The New Right is moving," claims Viguerie. "They're organized, they've got talent in spades, and they're going to have an impact."[56]

Educators would be wise to consider the warning clouds; we could be in for a major storm.

Notes

1. "Guess Who's Running for Congress?" The National Committee for an Effective Congress, 10 East 39th St., New York, N.Y., October 1977.

2. Bill Sievert, "Collision Course: New Right vs. Gay Rights," *Capital Times* (Madison, Wisconsin), 1 August 1977.

3. *Conservative Digest*, September 1977.

4. "The New Right's Strong Ambition Is Fueled by Huge Mail Campaign," *New York Times*, 4 December 1977, p. 73.

5. David Gelman, et al., "Is America Turning Right?" *Newsweek*, 7 November 1977, pp. 34–44.

6. Terence Smith, "Opinion in U.S. Swinging to Right, Pollsters and Politicians Believe," *New York Times*, 4 December 1977, p. 73. See also "The New Right's Strong Ambition Is Fueled by Huge Mail Campaign," *New York Times*, 4 December 1977, p. 73.

7. *New York Times*, 19 September 1977, p. 26.

8. "Hearings Scheduled on Coors Nomination," *Denver Post*, 11 June 1975, p. 35.

9. See Stephen Isaacs, "Coors Bucks Network 'Bias'," *Washington Post*, 5 May 1975. Also, Stanhope Gould, "Coors Brews the News," *Columbia Journalism Review* 13 (March 1975):17-29.

10. Stephen Isaacs, "Coors Beer—and Politics—Move East," *Washington Post*, 4 May 1975, p. A1.

11. Charles R. Baker, "Coors on Tap, September 9-10," *Homefront* (September 1975):36.

12. Ibid.

13. Isaacs, "Coors Beer—and Politics—Move East," p. A1.

14. Leaflet: "The Heritage Foundation: Introduction," The Heritage Foundation, 513 C St. N.E., Washington, D.C. 20002.

15. Stephen Isaacs, "Coors' Capital Connection," *Washington Post*, 7 May 1975, p. A5.

16. Leaflet: "Heritage Foundation vs. . . . Brookings Institute and Big Labor." The Heritage Foundation, 513 C St. N.E., Washington, D.C. 20002.

17. Baker, "Coors on Tap, September 9-10," p. 38.

18. Leaflet: "The Heritage Foundation: Introduction."

19. *Group Research Report*, 23 November 1976, p. 39. Contact Wesley McCuen, 419 New Jersey S.E., Washington, D.C. 20003.

20. John Conlan, "MACOS: The Push for a Uniform National Curriculum," *Social Education* 39 (October 1975):390-92.

21. Onalee McGraw, *Secular Humanism and the Schools: The Issue Whose Time Has Come* (Washington, D.C.: The Heritage Foundation, 1976), p. 5.

22. Isaacs, "Coors' Capital Connection," p. A5.

23. Edwin J. Feulner, Executive Director, Republican Study Committee and President, Heritage Foundation, 1977. Paul M. Weyrich, Executive Director, Committee for Survival of a Free Congress, and Past President, Heritage Foundation. Frank J. Walton, Past President, Heritage Foundation.

24. *1977 Suggested State Legislation*. American Legislative Exchange Council, 600 Pennsylvania Ave. S.E., Washington, D.C. 20003, 1977.

25. Ibid., p. 51.

26. Letter distributed June 1977. American Legislative Council, 600 Pennsylvania Ave. S.E., Washington, D.C. 20003.

27. Membership Leaflet: *Eagle Forum: The Alternative to Women's Lib.*, Box 618, Alton, Ill. 62002.

28. Jo-Ann Abrigg, "In the Name of Education," *The Phyllis Schlafly Report* (December 1976).

29. Robert Sherrill, "Elmer Gantry for President," *Playboy* 22 (March 1975):170.

30. Brochure: *Books—Textbooks—Audio Visuals*. Institute for Creation Research, 2716 Madison Ave., San Diego, Calif. 92116, p. 1.

31. *Acts and Facts* (March 1977).

32. John N. Moore and Harold S. Slusher, *Biology: A Search for Order in Complexity*. Institute for Creation Research, 2716 Madison Ave., San Diego, Calif. 92116, p. 596.

33. "Biology Text Banned," *Church and State* 30 (June 1977):17-18.

34. Ibid., p. 17.

35. Jim Wallis and Wes Michaelson, "The Plan to Save America," *Sojourners Magazine* (April 1976). Reprinted in *The Humanist* 36 (September/October 1976):13-14.

36. Rus Walton, *One Nation Under God* (Washington, D.C.: Third Century Publishers, 1975).

37. Ibid., pp. 67-68.

38. Ibid., p. 129.

39. Rus Walton, *"Study Plan and Leader's Guide: One Nation Under God"* (Washington, D.C.: Third Century Publishers, 1975), p. 27.

40. *In the Spirit of '76: The Citizen's Guide to Politics* (Washington, D.C.: Third Century Publishers, 1975).

41. Wallis and Michaelson, "The Plan to Save America."

42. Ibid.

43. *The John Birch Society Bulletin* (January 1977):12.

44. Ibid.

45. Ibid. (March 1977):13.

46. Ibid. (May 1977):15.

47. Ibid., p. 18.

48. Ibid. (January 1977):14.

49. George Lardner, Jr., "The John Birch Society: Fighting Reds and Red Ink," *Washington Post*, 19 September 1976, p. C4.

50. "Big-City Papers Lose Readers as Credibility Plunges," *Spotlight*, 21 March 1977, p. 15.

51. Martin A. Larson, "Our World in Conflict," *Spotlight*, 16 April 1977, p. 17.

52. "Scare Stunts Aim for Tax Deadline," *Spotlight*, 18 April 1977, p. 11.

53. "Liberty Lobby Progress Report: Legislative Efforts Intense, New People Reached—Dall," *Spotlight*, 19 December 1977, p. 3.

54. Terence Smith, "Opinion in U.S. Swinging to Right, Pollsters and Politicians Believe," *New York Times*, 4 December 1977, p. 73. See also, "The New Right's Strong Ambition Is Fueled by Huge Mail Campaign," *New York Times*, 4 December 1977, p. 73.

55. Some excellent resource materials discussing the nature of political extremism are: Daniel Bell, ed., *The Radical Right* (Garden City, N.Y.: Anchor Books, 1964); S. M. Lipset and Earl Raab, *The Politics of Unreason* (New York: Harper and Row, 1970); Harry and Bonaro Overstreet, *The Strange Tactics of Extremism* (New York: W. W. Norton & Co., 1964); and Mary Anne Raywid, *The Ax-Grinders: Critics of Our Public Schools* (New York: Macmillan Co., 1962).

56. "The New Right's Strong Ambition Is Fueled by Huge Mail Campaign," *New York Times*, 4 December 1977, p. 73.

9 How the Mel Gablers Have Put Textbooks on Trial

Edward B. Jenkinson
Indiana University

Norma and Mel Gabler have turned their Texas home in Longview into "the nation's largest textbook review clearing house."[1] As the founders of Educational Research Analysts, they "help the 'educationally underprivileged.' As a service organization we are dedicated to *helping parents* who are concerned about what their children are being taught."[2]

In the mimeographed and printed materials made available to concerned parents by Educational Research Analysts, the Gablers make statements like the following:

> *Until textbooks are changed,* there is no possibility that crime, violence, VD, and abortion rates will do anything but continue to climb.[3]

> *Textbooks* mold *nations* because textbooks largely determine *how* a nation votes, *what* it becomes and *where* it goes![4]

Since they started reviewing textbooks in 1961 and protesting what they consider to be objectionable content, the Gablers' efforts have paid dividends. For example, in one of the printed sheets they distributed to interested parents in 1977, they noted that last year "God gave parents a number of victories. In Texas alone, the State Textbook Committee did a good job of selecting the best of the available books. Then, the State Commissioner of Education removed 10 books, including the dictionaries with vulgar language and unreasonable definitions."[5]

According to a printed sheet distributed by Educational Research Analysts in November 1977, the success of the Gablers has not been limited to Texas. "Mrs. Gabler has travelled much this year, including six weeks by invitation in New Zealand and Australia during July and August. A nationwide impact has been felt in New Zealand because of her visit, and a similar impact was made in one of the largest states of Australia."[6]

The Gablers' "ongoing battle to oust objectionable textbooks from public schools—and to urge publishers to produce better ones"[7] has been reported in *Textbooks on Trial*.[8] James C. Hefley's account of the Gablers, which was first published late in 1976, was in its fourth printing by early 1978, and it was the June 1977 selection of the Conservative Book Club. The Gablers now distribute the book through Educational Research Analysts, their nonprofit organization.[9]

Through Educational Research Analysts, the Gablers have made available "thousands of textbook reviews—their own, plus reviews from many other states. Most are by page, paragraph, and line, prepared by parents for parents, and consider the age level and knowledge of the student. They concentrate on pointing out 'questionable' content. . . ."[10]

A concerned parent who requests a set of reviews receives this advice:

> There is *much* that you as a parent or concerned teacher can do, but you *must* observe some important "do's" and "don'ts." Among them, *never* protest any textbook until *you* have personally examined the "questioned" portions in the book (or books) involved. To do this, our reviews can be of great help to you.
>
> *Always* try to make your case to key area leaders and one or more board members *before* confronting your school or making a public protest. To educators you are an "outsider" who is "infringing" in "their" area when you question, or even examine, school subject matter. Thus, because of professional pride, even good, concerned educators will feel professionally bound to defend what they are using.[11]

Included in the packet of reviews that one concerned parent received from Educational Research Analysts is a copy of a twenty-seven-page letter from the Gablers to the Texas State Commissioner of Education.[12] Dated August 9, 1974, the letter requested the Commissioner not to accept the Ginn 360 Reading Series for use in Texas. The Gablers made 163 objections to ten of the readers for grades seven and eight. In their letter, which they provide to parents who request reviews of the Ginn series, the Gablers cite specific paragraphs and page numbers in the student's or teacher's edition and quote the questionable passage before giving their objections. Here are thirteen representative objections grouped according to the title of the book in the series:

Conflicts

P. 77, question 3, "What are some other commonplace experiences that cause fear in people? How might people deal with them? Choose one of these experiences and tell how you think you would deal with it."
Objection: Invasion of privacy.

P. 128, question 1, "What is the meaning of long hair to those adults who might object to it? What do you think might be the reason for this? What does long hair mean to you?"
Objection: Puts adults in bad light.

Awakenings

P. 60, par. 8, lines 5 and 7, "Oh, God."
P. 61, par. 3, "Oh, God."
Objection: Not showing respect to God. Profanity.

P. 67, par. 2, last sent., "School was such a bore."
Objection: Depreciates school.

P. 69, par. 6, lines 4-5, "It was so false, so pointless. How could they sing of the land of the free, when there was still racial discrimination?"
Objection: Majority of people are free. Only people in jail are not free.

Pp. 67-75, story titled "The Fan Club," relates girl's struggle to be accepted by the artificial, cruel in-crowd. Is accepted at the expense of another girl's dignity.
Objection: Vicious, cruel, demeaning story. Not suitable for 7th graders. The teacher is pictured as intolerant.

P. 78, poem, "Corners on the Curving Sky," lines 2-5, ". . . that means that you and I can hold completely different points of view and both be right."
Objection: No definite standards—situation ethics.

Pp. 81-86, title, "What Are the Doldrums?"
Objection: This story is silly and a waste of time except for pure amusement.

Changes

P. 17, par. 4, line 3, ". . . the day apricots were ripe enough to steal. . . ."
Objection: Implies that there is nothing wrong with stealing.

P. 48, last par., "But it was always China that we were taught was home. In those days we were all *immigrants*. Whether we were born in America or not, we were all immigrants."
Objection: This does not foster patriotism toward America and is somewhat of a derogatory statement about our country.

Failures

P. 19, par. 3, lines 2-3, "Besides Aunt Mo's too dang nosey."
Objection: Implies profanity.

Speculations

P. 39, question 3, "Munro asks, 'Can an instrument have "second sight" or respond to forces that are beyond our reckoning?' What answer would you give. . . ? Do you think that the events in this story could happen in real life?"
Objection: What does this have to do with literature?

Questions

P. 57, first teacher's note: "The title (Luther) has allusive force, recalling Martin Luther and Martin Luther King, Jr., both reformers."
Objection: These two men should not be put in the same category. Martin Luther was a religiously-dedicated, non-violent man.

The Gablers' objections do not go unnoticed in Texas. According to stamped comments[13] on the copy of the letter of objections, 26 of the 163 objections were honored by the Texas State Commissioner of Education. The twenty-six objectionable passages or offensive words were deleted, or an entire story or poem was replaced in the Texas version of the Ginn series.

The Gablers do not write all of the textbook reviews they distribute through Educational Research Analysts. Instead, they invite concerned parents to write reviews for them. To provide a degree of uniformity in the reviews, the Gablers send their followers a three-page outline that lists these ten categories the reviewers should use for summarizing objectionable content in textbooks: (1) Attacks on Values, (2) Distorted Content, (3) Negative Thinking, (4) Violence, (5) Academic Unexcellence, (6) Isms Fostered (Communism, Socialism, Internationalism), (7) Invasions of Privacy, (8) Behavioral Modification, (9) Humanism, Occult, and other Religions Encouraged, and (10) Other important Educational Aspects.[14]

After reading and rereading the reviews that the Gablers mailed to a concerned parent who was interested in the Ginn 360 Reading Series, I followed the outline to find representative objections. Ten typical objections are recorded below as they appear in the reviews. If an objectionable passage is cited by the reviewer, that is noted here. The objections are also recorded according to subheadings in the outline.

Attack on Family, Home, and Adults

In Ginn 360, stories are presented which depict parents as stupid and idiotic, such as in "The Reluctant Dragon" (Level 12), where the son knows more than the parents; and, again, in the story "Curtains for Joey" (Level 12), where the antics of the children save the parents from looking stupid. To further have children doubting parents, stories where children solve adult problems are presented, such as "The New Fence" (Level 6) in which the objective is clearly stated: "Understanding that children can help adults solve problems."[15]

Attack on Bible and Christianity

P. 138 (of *Man the Myth-maker*), question 1, "How is Deirdre like Pandora and Eve? . . ."

Objection: This last comparison between Pandora and Eve misleads the student into erroneous beliefs that Eve's story was mythical.[16]

Attack on Morality—Stealing

T.E. (of *To Turn A Stone*) p. 300, col. 2, #6, "There are some people who would censor the tales of Robin Hood, for they do seem to support an outlaw and make the life of crime seem glamorous. It is shown in this story, however, that Robin Hood felt he did not have recourse to justice. . . ."

Objection: Stealing and highway robbery is [sic] wrong any way you look at it. The end does not always justify the means.[17]

Attack on Fixed Values Censored—
Questions with no firm answer

P. 39 (of *Speculations*), topic 2, "Plan a panel discussion based on the following topic: Computers are incapable of creative thinking and cannot replace man."

Objection: Infers [sic] that there can be more than one answer.[18]

Distorted Content—Errors of fact

P. 224 (of *Man the Myth-maker*), SE (student edition), bottom, " 'No one I've ever known is what he appears to be on the surface.' Could Charlie's statement suggest that life consists of many kinds of metamorphoses?"

Textbooks on Trial 113

Objection: The text is trying to stress change as being the major thing in life. This is not true. Change has no reliability; it cause [sic] the personality to be shattered. Remember that the word used in this assignment is "metamorphoses."[19]

Negative Thinking—Prejudicial

Student Textbook—page 72, "There was a riot on our block, and there were a lot of whites doing most of the shooting. Sometimes some blacks would come by with guns, but not often; they mostly had clubs."

Objection: Infers [sic] that whites are bad and blacks are good. Talk about discrimination! There is no story in this series that depicts the reverse![20]

Negative Thinking—Skeptical

T.E. (of *To Turn a Stone*) p. 106, col. 1, para. 4, lines 1-2, " 'There's a sucker born every minute.' "

Objection: The P. T. Barnum philosophy is sceptical [sic]. This is a depressing thought.[21]

Academic Unexcellence—
Inappropriate content and pictures

P. 21-29 (of *Questions*), pictures

Objection: Pictures with no identification. This is an eighth grade reader; not just pictures.[22]

Isms Fostered—Communism not treated
realistically (too favorable)

T.E. (of *To Turn a Stone*) p. 187, ". . . Of An Organization" concentrates on the promotion of UNICEF.

Objection: UNICEF is a known Communist front. See "Fact Finder," Oct. 16, 1969. Vol. 27 Number 23 from Phoenix, Arizona.[23]

Humanism

Teacher's Manual—Page 147 (for *On the Edge*) Part II, 4. "*Humanism* is an attitude about life that centers on human values."

Objection: Constantly, thoughout the stories, situation ethics which is the morality of the religion of Humanism is offered. Now we even find the definition of Humanism. Nowhere is the definition of Christianity given. What ever happened to "equality"?[24]

The nearly two hundred pages of reviews that I examined contain many more objections that could be classified according to the outline's subheadings and that I did not use in listing sample objections. However, additional sample objections would not provide any more insight into the nature of the complaints about literature textbooks and basal readers.

In a one page announcement in which they call themselves "your consumer advocates for education," the Gablers urge their supporters to "exchange and share reviews." They note that they "need a copy of every review possible. We welcome textbook reviews primarily, but also reviews of films and library books. Rest assured that your reviews will be sent nationwide to help others."[25]

Shortly after I accepted the chair of the National Council of Teachers of English Committee against Censorship, I learned that the Gabler reviews are indeed sent nationwide. Their reviews and/or other materials about objectionable textbooks or courses have obviously been used by concerned parents in attempts at censoring schoolbooks or courses in at least this third of the fifty states: California, Colorado, Florida, Illinois, Indiana, Iowa, Minnesota, Missouri, Ohio, Oklahoma, Pennsylvania, Texas, Vermont, Virginia, Washington, West Virginia, and Wisconsin.

The Gabler-distributed reviews of *Man: A Course of Study* (MACOS) have been used by a number of citizens' groups to protest that social studies program, which was developed with funds from the National Science Foundation. Reviews, comments, reprinted editorials, and suggested petitions from Educational Research Analysts have also been used to challenge courses and specific textbooks that deal with values clarification, the new math, science courses (especially those that do not include the creationist theory), role playing, sensitivity training, sex education, and nearly all innovative educational programs. Finally, the Gablers distribute a great deal of information on secular humanism, the religion that they believe is being taught in the schools. They obviously hope that their work to rid the textbooks and the schools of secular humanism will pay dividends.

In the meantime, they continue to fight for basic education. As Norma notes in *Textbooks on Trial*, "I think the pendulum is swinging our way. If the movement keeps gaining strength, we'll be going back to the basics—learning skills, traditional math, phonics, morality, patriotism, history that is really history, science that is science, and fair play for free enterprise economics."[26]

The Gablers are obviously convinced that they know what is best for America's children, and they have the dedication, the drive, and the spirit to achieve their goal. Apparently they have hundreds of dedicated followers, too, since the number of censorship incidents in which Gabler-distributed materials are used is on the rise.

There is little question that the Gablers and their followers have put public education on trial. The question facing public education now is this: Can teachers and administrators throughout the country unite long enough to put the Gabler thinking on trial?

Notes

1. See printed sheet entitled, "The Mel Gablers Educational Research Analysts," November 1977. The sheet was included with a packet of materials that the Gablers sent to a concerned parent.
2. See green printed sheet distributed by the Gablers entitled, "The Mel Gablers—Consumer Advocates for Education."
3. See mimeographed sheet distributed by the Gablers entitled, "For Your Consideration. . . ."
4. See note 3.
5. See note 2.
6. See note 1.
7. See dust jacket of James C. Hefley's *Textbooks on Trial* (Wheaton, Ill.: Victor Books, 1976).
8. Hefley, *Textbooks on Trial*.
9. See note 1.
10. Hefley, *Textbooks on Trial*, p. 205.
11. See mimeographed strip of paper included by the Gablers in their packet sent to a concerned parent.
12. Letter dated August 9, 1974, to Dr. M. L. Brockette, Texas Education Agency, Capitol Station, Austin, Texas, from the Mel Gablers. A mimeographed copy of the letter was included in the packet that the Gablers mailed to a concerned parent when he requested reviews of the Ginn 360 Reading Series.
13. Specific objections in the mimeographed letter have been stamped "This Section replaced in Texas adoption" or "Deleted or changed for Texas adoption."
14. Mimeographed outline entitled, "Textbook Reviewing by Categories." The outline was included in the packet that the Gablers sent to a concerned parent.
15. Mimeographed review distributed by the Gablers entitled, "The Ginn 360 Reading Series—A Critical Analysis," by Mrs. Evelyn Parise, C.P.F. member from Winterville, Ohio, p. 3.
16. Mimeographed review distributed by the Gablers entitled, "*Man the Myth-Maker*/Literature, Uses of the Imagination/Harcourt/1973/High School/Student's Edition/Review by Mosby," p. 15.
17. Mimeographed review distributed by the Gablers entitled, "*To Turn a Stone*/Ginn and Company/1970/Reading/6th Grade," p. 8.
18. See note 12, p. 15.
19. See note 16, p. 24.

20. Mimeographed review distributed by the Gablers entitled, "Specific Objections to Ginn 360," p. 16.
21. See note 17, p. 4.
22. See note 12, p. 20.
23. See note 17, p. 6.
24. See note 20, p. 14.
25. See note 1.
26. Hefley, *Textbooks on Trial,* p. 188.

10 Is Secular Humanism the Religion of the Public Schools?

Robert T. Rhode
Indiana University

"What do you mean by 'secular humanism'?" the principal asked. He looked bewildered.

"A religion that teachers in this school are teaching to our children," replied the spokesman for Parents Watching the Schools (PWS), a local organization whose goal is to rid the public school of objectionable textbooks. "Your teachers are Secular Humanists who are causing our children to become anti-God, anti-Christian, and anti-American."

"You have to be kidding," the principal said with a smile.

"Not at all!" shouted a member of PWS. "Have you looked at the books used in your school? Take the English books, for instance. The stories in them are violent, filthy, completely lacking in morals...."

"Stop teaching from these Humanist books," another PWS member demanded. "Don't our children have any rights? Situation ethics cause our children to believe there are no absolute morals."

The PWS spokesman said, "Get rid of this false religion."

"But what is 'secular humanism'?" the principal asked, looking from face to face in the crowd of PWS members.

Parent groups, like PWS, and special interest groups dissatisfied with the public schools for a variety of reasons, are calling many teachers "secular humanists," particularly those teachers who teach within humanities departments or who follow the educational philosophy of humanism. These highly organized groups apparently are confusing terms which sound alike but actually have widely different meanings. "Humanities" sounds like "humanistic education," and both sound like "secular humanism," which one critic of education defines as a religion that "believes man is God and rejects biblical standards of living."[1] In spite of the confusion of sound-alike terms, the parent groups and special interest groups can make the label of secular humanist stick—at least long enough to tie up schools, school boards, and administrators in a series of time-consuming confrontations.

Teachers within the field of humanities are not the only targets for attack. In one state, the schools of many cities and towns around a large metropolitan area came under widespread attack in the following areas: sex education, sociology, values clarification, science fiction, science courses with emphases on evolutionary theory, and, of course, humanities. The complainants called all of these areas examples of secular humanism.

State and national groups are spreading their literature across the country. Their books, brochures, pamphlets, and letters seem to include nearly all public school teachers under the label of secular humanist. Apparently these groups have money and power, and they are willing to launch a full-scale attack on the schools.

The following is a partial listing of state, national, and local organizations or periodicals concerned with school textbooks and teaching methods:

America's Future, Inc.
542 Main Street
New Rochelle, N.Y. 10802

The John Birch
　Society Bulletin
395 Concord Avenue
Belmont, Massachusetts 02178

Church League of America
422 N. Prospect Street
Wheaton, Illinois 60187

Citizens Coalition
P.O. Box 1765
Albany, New York 12201

The Citizens Committee
　of California, Inc.
1110 S. Pomona Avenue
Fullerton, California 92632

Educational Research
　Analysts, Inc.
P.O. Box 7518
Longview, Texas 75601

Firm Foundation
P.O. Box 610
Austin, Texas 78767

Frederick County
　Civic Federation
Frederick, Maryland 21701

The Heritage Foundation
513 C Street N.E.
Washington, D.C. 20002

Let's Improve Today's
　Education (LITE)
9340 W. Peoria Avenue
Peoria, Arizona 85345

The Barbara M. Morris Report
P.O. Box 416
Ellicott City, Maryland 21043

The National Educator
P.O. Box 333
Fullerton, California 92632

The Network of Patriotic
　Letter Writers
Box 2003D
Pasadena, California 91105

Parents of Minnesota, Inc.
P.O. Box 118
St. Paul Park, Minn. 55071

Parents Rights, Inc.
12571 Northwinds Drive
St. Louis, Missouri 63141

Santa Clara County Citizens
　Action Committee Opposing
　FLE (Family Life Education)
San Jose, California 95125

The Phyllis Schlafly Report
Box 618
Alton, Illinois 62002

TAX FAX
The Independent American
P.O. Box 636
Littleton, Colorado 80120

The Truth, Inc.
3400 W. Michigan
Milwaukee, Wisconsin 53208

Young Parents Alert
P.O. Box 15
Lake Elmo, Minnesota 55042

Apparently, critics of the schools feel that secular humanism leads to an increase in authoritarianism. They seem to fear that the family unit will be destroyed if secular humanism is rampant in the schools. The *Barbara M. Morris Report,* June 1974, states,

> Based on the philosophy of Godless Secular Humanism, Humanistic education is designed to promote and inculcate the principles of Humanism. . . . The Humanistic child rejects his Christian heritage, his Christian parents, Christian belief and our Judeo-Christian ethic.[2]

According to the above quotation, secular humanism causes children to become anti-Christian; they no longer believe in God after they have been exposed to secular humanism in the schools.

According to The Heritage Foundation, organized groups of complainants are seeking an end to the teaching of secular humanism, which is considered a religion, by urging that both the courts and statutory laws be used against it.

> Parents, teachers, and citizens across the nation, concerned with the drift in the tax-supported schools toward humanistic education and academic decline, are confronting the question in their local communities, in the Courts, and in the halls of Congress. The public is growing more aware of the inequity of using tax dollars for the support of nontheistic religion. Secular humanism in the schools is indeed an issue whose time has come.[3]

It seems that parent groups and special interest groups are ready and willing to fight against secular humanism, which is often made synonymous with "atheism." In *A Christian Mother's View of the Values Clarification Program,* a concerned parent writes,

> This article is a call to battle, to bring it out in the open that all who love God may realize it is fight now or forever lose the opportunity to save their children and this nation from going irretrievably the route of atheistic, one-world collectivism toward which the government, psychologists, and educators are pushing them.

> Now the public school is making a frontal attack on Protestant ethics. And they make their attack by using our children; the young are grist for their mills, and the young come from us. They use our children to form a secular-humanist America.[4]

The above quotations seem to indict the public schools with waging an "attack" on Christianity.

If all of these quotations are taken together, and if the bulk of material circulated by organized groups is consulted, then a definition of secular humanism—as critics of education define it—can be formed. According to state and national groups decrying the teaching of secular humanism in the schools, a secular humanist is:

> Anti-God. The secular humanist wants to tear God down from His throne and make Man the sovereign of the universe.
>
> Anti-democracy. The secular humanist hopes to do away with present governments and make the world one huge, totalitarian state.
>
> Anti-family. The secular humanist undermines the family concept, denies Christian values that are taught in the home, and preaches to the youth of America that there are no absolute morals.
>
> Anti-Christian. The secular humanist preaches the religion of Secular Humanism through textbooks and by means of the following teaching techniques: values clarification, moral education, human development, family life and human relations, affective education, and psychosocial learning, to name a few.

That is the nature of the label that is being applied to teachers, librarians, administrators, and publishers across the United States today. That is what is meant by being branded a Secular Humanist; the person so branded is anti-God, anti-democracy, anti-family, and anti-Christian.

The literature frequently refers to the terrifying effects that secular humanists have on children. An example from *The Barbara M. Morris Report,* June 1974:

> The "success" of Humanistic Education can be seen in the product—young people who are alienated, confused, skeptical, cynical, aimless, suicidal and just plain unhappy.[5]

How do teachers allegedly produce such "unhappy" young people? By teaching values clarification, situation ethics, family life and human relations, and so on. All of these subjects are bound together in the package labeled secular humanism. Secular humanism takes many forms, from humanities to sociology, from health classes to all of affective education.

The complainants at all levels of organization are particularly antagonized by values clarification and situation ethics. One critic of education expresses concern that secular humanism in the form of situation ethics may lead children to reject Christianity.

> Christian children are constantly bombarded with stories of situation ethics (it's all right in certain circumstances; or, in other words, the Humanist philosophy that any ethic must be looked at and decided upon by the "situation" from which that ethic is viewed). How long will it be, under this kind of bombardment (from the textbook and the teacher's manual) before children begin first to question and then to doubt the very foundation of his own Christian-Judeo morality—the Ten Commandments.

The same source then concludes:

> Christianity is based on a belief in God and His absolute laws, the Ten Commandments, are the moral code by which to live. On the other hand, secular Humanism states that there is no God and bases its morality on situation ethics, thus denying that there is a right or a wrong or any absolutes.[6]

According to the above quotations, situation ethics is helping to erode the Christian beliefs of children. Secular humanism seems to deny the absolute authority of God.

What recourse is available to teachers under attack? Are teachers to blame for the attacks? The second question has a definite answer: teachers have brought several of these attacks on themselves. The problem begins in a lack of communication; teachers frequently have not made it clear why they were teaching something or what it was that they were teaching. Teachers have not always communicated effectively with students or with parents, and the lack of dialogue has produced misunderstandings of mountainous proportions.

The first question, "What recourse is available to teachers under attack?" is more difficult to answer. Once misunderstandings between teachers, students, and parents have reached the altercation stage, it may be difficult to solve the problem. There are, however, ways to prepare for an eventual confrontation. One way is for departments within a school to develop written philosophies for what those departments teach. An English department, for example, should have a written philosophy that answers the question, "Why teach literature?" Also, schools should develop a written set of procedures for dealing with complaints. Thus, every complaint directed against a school could be handled along clearly delineated channels of communication. Also, departments within a school should write rationales for the books those departments use. It is not enough, however, to have philosophies, procedures, and rationales in hand; teachers and administrators must also be able to explain those rationales to any parent or concerned citizen. Teachers must have good reasons for what they teach. After all, academic freedom may soon be a thing of the past. Already, in some instances, the shield of academic freedom has been pierced by victorious opponents of certain textbooks and teaching techniques.

A teacher under attack could explain that he or she is not a secular humanist. If one traces the origin of the term "secular humanist," one finds that it is the name of a specific religion, but that religion is not defined as critics of education define it. Only by a rather large stretch of the imagination can one assume that nearly all teachers are actual secular humanists. The literature from state and national organizations that are critical of the schools often cites a U.S. Supreme Court decision that proclaimed secular humanism a separate religion. In June of 1961, the high court, in the case *Torcaso v. Watkins,* 367 U.S. 488 (1961), termed "secular humanism" a religion—*but only in a footnote to that decision.* The footnote referred to a decision by the First District Court of Appeals of California. There is indeed a church of secular humanists, and one congregation was involved in litigation in California. This church is rather Unitarian in outlook and does not deny God's existence; the church simply does not deal with God in an overt way. Rather, the church focuses on human life at the present moment.

To say that all, or nearly all, teachers are members of this church is to say that teachers are not Protestants, Catholics, Jews, or members of any of the large number of religions that are allowed freedom to worship in this country by virtue of the Bill of Rights. Clearly, the definition of secular humanism, a specific religion, is not the definition that critics of public education are using. These groups have seized upon a term that sounds like "humanities" and "humanistic education," and they are bent upon labeling teachers across the country with a term defined by their own standards.

How did critics of public education arrive at their definition of secular humanism? In 1933, the famous educator John Dewey signed the "Humanist Manifesto I"—a document that looked optimistically toward America's future and tried to project what life would be like then. In 1973, the famous educator B. F. Skinner signed the "Humanist Manifesto II"—a document that, like the 1933 version, gives projections about America's future. The critics of public education see a link between these "humanist" documents and the religion of secular humanism, as they define it.

A number of the critics of public education assume that nearly all teachers are followers of Dewey and Skinner, and they feel that these men (and others like them) are representatives of secular humanism:

> Under the influence of such ardent advocates of humanistic education as John Dewey, Jean Piaget, Carl Rogers, Lawrence Kohlberg, Abraham Maslow, William Glassner, Jerome Bruner, and others, professional educators have made "socialization" of the child the main purpose of education.[7]

The above quotation points out another misunderstanding on the part of state and national groups organized to rid schools of secular humanism. They confuse the terms "secular humanism" and "humanistic education." If teachers are advocates of an educational philosophy of humanism, then they appear to critics of education to be dyed-in-the-wool, card-carrying secular humanists.

Thus, the definition of secular humanism—as critics of education have defined it—differs widely from the definition of the specific religion of secular humanism. The critics have applied the term to nearly all teachers by an ingenious method of confusing sound-alike terms, and their censorship of textbooks and teaching techniques affects nearly all areas of the school, from English to health, from sociology to home economics.

It is time for teachers, administrators, librarians, and publishers to become fully informed of the threat of being labeled secular humanists. Also, it is time for schools to improve their communication with local communities. Again, it is time for schools to develop written rationales for what they teach. Armed with effective communication and written rationales, the schools should be better able to defend against the attacks that are to come.

Notes

1. Untitled mimeograph sheet distributed by Educational Research Analysts of Longview, Texas.

2. Barbara M. Morris, *The Barbara M. Morris Report* 5:3 (1974):1.

3. Onalee McGraw, "Secular Humanism and the Schools: The Issue Whose Time Has Come," *Critical Issues Series 2* (Washington, D.C.: The Heritage Foundation, 1976), pp. 19-20.

4. Georgine Schreiber, "A Christian Mother's View of the Values Clarification Program" (Typewritten. Concerned Citizens and Taxpayers for Decent School Books, Baton Rouge, 1975), p. 1.

5. Morris, *The Barbara Morris Report*, p. 1.

6. Evelyn Parise, "The Ginn 360 Reading Series—A Critical Analysis" (Typewritten. Committee for Positive Education, Youngstown, Ohio, 1976), p. 2.

7. McGraw, "Secular Humanism," p. 4.

11 Hester Prynne and Linda Lovelace, Pure or Prurient

Gertrude Berger
Brooklyn College

The June 21, 1973, Supreme Court decisions on obscenity, *Miller* and *Paris Adult Theatre,* placed the two heroines, Hester Prynne and Linda Lovelace, in equal jeopardy. In both cases, the decision as to who is pure or prurient rests in the hands of "contemporary community standards." There are communities where the vehicles in which the two superstars are featured have been declared obscene. According to Ken Donelson in "Censorship and Arizona Schools: 1966-1968," (*Arizona English Bulletin* 2 [February 1969]:13-22), two complaints were recorded against *The Scarlet Letter.* In both cases, the book was judged "filthy." The school principal in one case asked the English teachers in his school to refrain from using it since the book arouses controversy, and in the other case, the book was retained. As for the film *Deep Throat,* Linda Lovelace plays the role of a woman, unable to achieve sexual pleasure through the normal course of anatomical events, who searches for fulfillment. In a ruling handed down by the Criminal Court of the City of New York, Judge Joel J. Tyler in the *People of the State of New York Against Mature Enterprises* banned the film from public viewing. Judge Tyler, describing the explicit scenes involving many and varied forms of sexual activity, concluded with these words, "Justice Jackson says he knows hard core pornography when he merely sees it (*Jacobellis v. Ohio,* 378 U.S. 184). We have seen it in *Deep Throat* and this is one throat that deserves to be cut. I readily perform this operation in finding the defendant guilty as charged. . . ." In this act, Judge Tyler, in order to preserve public morals, is surgeon, judge, film critic, and arbiter of community taste.

When the Supreme Court used the word "contemporary" in describing community standards, it recognized that the passage of time is a significant factor in the determination of obscenity.

The sins of Hester Prynne have passed into respectability as well as obscurity, but Ms. Lovelace's transgressions are, at the present moment in history, unforgivable.

In 1933, the United States Customs authorities sought to exclude James Joyce's *Ulysses* from importation because of pornographic content and the use of four-letter words. In order to make a test case of the book, which was being smuggled openly into the country, Bennett Cerf of Random House arranged for the book to be seized by the port authorities. Morris L. Ernst, counsel for Random House, argued the case. He said:

> Judge, as to the word "fuck," one etymological dictionary gives its derivation as from *facere,* to make—The farmer fucked the seed into the soil. This, your honor, has more integrity than a euphemism used every day in every modern novel to describe precisely the same event.

The case was decided by Judge Woolsey who rendered the decision in an eloquent example of fine literary criticism.

> In writing *Ulysses* Joyce sought to make a serious experiment in a new, if not wholly novel, literary genre. He takes persons of the lower middle class living in Dublin in 1904 and seeks, not only to describe what they did on a certain day early in June of that year as they went about the city bent on their usual occupations, but also to tell what many of them thought about the while.
>
> Joyce had attempted—it seems to me, with astonishing success —to show how the screen of consciousness with its ever-shifting kaleidoscopic impressions carries, as it were on a plastic palimpsest, not only what is in the focus of each man's observation of the actual things about him, but also in a penumbral zone residual of past impressions, some recent and some drawn up by association from the domain of the subconscious. He shows how each of these impressions affects the life and behavior of the character which he is describing.
>
> What he seeks to get is not unlike the result of a double or, if that is possible, a multiple exposure on a cinema film, which would give a clear foreground with a background visible but somewhat blurred and out of focus in varying degrees.

Judge Woolsey declared that *Ulysses* could be admitted into the United States because reading the book in its entirety "did not tend to excite sexual impulses or lustful thoughts, but that its net effect on them was only that of a somewhat tragic and very powerful commentary on the inner lives of men and women." *United States v. One Book Called "Ulysses,"* 5 F. Supp. 182 (S.D. N.Y. 1933).

Since the courts act for the public good, it is well to see if the public has been served by legal actions against obscenity. Judge Tyler, in March of 1973, removed *Deep Throat* from circulation in order to prevent impinging on the privacy of any adult willing or unwilling to pay the five dollar admission price. Has the banning of the film deprived any consenting adult with such cultural proclivities from finding an object for his or her fancy? According to a survey conducted by the *New York Times* in October of 1973, four months after the Supreme Court ruling in June, it was still possible to see blue movies and purchase graphically explicit books in all major cities, including Washington, D.C., where there were six theaters showing hardcore films. However, while the Supreme Court decision has not diminished the production of pornography, it has influenced reputable book publishers, movie makers, librarians, and teachers in schools and universities.

The burning of novels and short story anthologies by a North Dakota school board was reported in the *New York Times,* 11 November 1973. When a sophomore student complained about the language in Kurt Vonnegut, Jr.'s novel *Slaughterhouse-Five,* the five-member school board of Drake, North Dakota, met and agreed that the book was profane. They ordered all thirty-two copies burned. Other books scheduled to be withdrawn or burned were *Deliverance,* by James Dickey, and *Short Story Masterpieces,* an anthology which included short stories by Ernest Hemingway, William Faulkner, and John Steinbeck. An English teacher at the school said in defense of the books, and the four-letter words used in them, "All I can say is, the author is trying to tell his story like it is, using language as it is being used today out there in the real world." None of the school board members had read the books in their entirety that they had ordered destroyed.

Was the North Dakota school board acting under the mandate given it by the June 21, 1973, Supreme Court decision which places the determination of what is or is not obscene in the hands of the "community"? If contemporary community standards appear to be the criteria for such a determination, does "community" mean state, city, neighborhood, or a local school board? The courts have made no decision on this matter, and the effect has been a struggle between vocal groups concerned with pornography and its alleged ability to provoke antisocial acts, and teachers, librarians, publishers, and movie makers concerned with the First Amendment guarantees of free speech and free expression.

This was the struggle in School District 25 in Queens, New York, when the local school board banned the book *Down These Mean Streets,* by Piri Thomas. Those members of the school board who voted for removing the book from the library shelves—and it was not a unanimous vote—objected to the language and depiction of deviant sexual behavior.

District 25's Local School Board believes, as do all anti-obscenity groups in the country, in a causal relationship between exposure to pornography and the onset of antisocial acts. There is a clear unwillingness of the Supreme Court to confront this behavioral connection. The courts contend that, in the absence of clear proof, States have the right to assume that there is a causal connection between crimes of a sexual nature and exposure to pornography.

In 1967, President Nixon and the Ninetieth Congress authorized a Commission on Obscenity and Pornography and empowered it to study the effect of pornography upon the public and its relationship to crime and to recommend legislative action. The findings of the Commission Task Force took three years to develop and when published were publicly rejected by the President and many members of Congress. Senator Eastland of Mississippi funded and authorized a subcommittee to investigate the sources of information used by the Task Force. What were the conclusions rejected? Among the forms of obscenity, the Task Force cited advertising to which all citizens were a captive audience: ". . . even more serious than the overt sexuality in advertising is its ability to exploit the psychology of subliminal perception." It appears accurate to those who view airline and stocking advertisements that a message on television need not be overly pornographic to carry an erotic message to viewers. In addition, the Task Force rejected a punitive and narrow approach to the elimination of obscenity. The report reads, "Consumption of obscenity is really a symptom of social ills that have become endemic in our society." Ills such as unemployment, welfare, and poor housing are mentioned. The Ninetieth Congress was not exuberant at hearing that the problem of pornography was tied to programs supporting job training, a welfare program that does not contribute to social disorganization, and a greater commitment to a federal housing program. Those who desired a less complex, "law and order" approach were greeted with a sociological explanation which they promptly rejected.

However, the Task Force did support the establishment of local juries to assess each allegedly obscene book, film, or play. The idea was attributed to Senator Everett Dirksen and was highly recommended by the Task Force.

While communities may be granted jurisdiction in obscenity rulings, the courts have given them a test to be applied which itself has proven capricious and impossible to apply. The test is pruriency. Does the average person, applying contemporary community standards, find that the interest in the material as a whole is prurient? Matter appealing to prurient interest arouses sexual desire or impure thoughts. Judge Brennan in *Roth v. United States,* 354 U.S. 467 (1957), cites a dictionary definition of "prurient" as "itching, longing, uneasy with desire." The result of such an elastic definition is that not only are both *The Scarlet Letter* and *Deep Throat* open to such a charge, but so is virtually any other literary work as well (there are individuals who can even be aroused by turning the pages of a profusely illustrated seed catalogue).

Because of the lack of clarity in the legal definition of obscenity, the Supreme Court has spent a considerable amount of time viewing allegedly pornographic films and reading allegedly hardcore books. The Court has wondered whether their frequent deliberations in this area have been fruitful. The public may wonder whether they are served by having nine robed male judges retire for a private viewing of a film and then emerge with a decision. The Court has never revealed whether they wait for Judge Brennan's "itch" to come upon them as a sign that a prurient interest is present. Does the age of the viewer determine susceptibility to such visceral reactions? Certainly the sex of the viewer will alter the reaction. Since all of the decisions rendered by the Supreme Court on obscenity have been arrived at by males, it is possible to question whether one half of the contemporary community standard—the female half—has been fairly represented. In the June 21, 1973, decision, Judge Burger says, "Woman is degraded." Since no woman has ever participated in a decision involving the higher court judgments on obscenity, such a statement can be viewed as paternalistic. The Court has never posed the question of prurience by applying the test to women as well as men. The fact is that, whatever the decisions made by the Supreme Court, they were made on the assumption that what is of prurient interest to men can be assumed to be of prurient interest to women as well.

To summarize, the Supreme Court in its June 21, 1973, ruling yields jurisdiction in matters of obscenity to communities. Communities will now have to make decisions on questions of morality in sexual behavior, standards of what is art and what is pornography, and judgments about the relationship of books and films to behavior.

There are clear indications throughout the country that an assault on intellectual freedom will accompany the search for the obscene.

12 Issues of Censorship and Research on Effects of and Response to Reading

Richard Beach
University of Minnesota

Demands for censorship of library books are based on the assumption that reading certain books has an undesirable effect on the reader. This survey of research on response to reading and the effects of reading examines the empirical evidence for the validity of this assumption.

Those research findings do not provide any definitive answers as to the need for censorship. Nor do the researchers pretend that they can empirically define what constitutes desirable or undesirable reading; those decisions are made by the advocates or critics of censorship based on their own beliefs and values. Even if empirical evidence were conclusive that reading has no undesirable effects on readers, such a finding would not lessen demands for censorship. Provocative writing always threatens established cultural values; as long as people strongly believe in certain values and the need to defend those values, censorship will exist.

What these research findings do provide is some degree of objectivity and common sense perspective as to the effects of the reading experience.

This survey will examine research in two general areas: research on response to reading and research on the effects of reading. Research on response to reading concerns the nature of the reader's experience with a work and the effects of reader characteristics on that experience. For example, a hypothetical study might find that readers become more emotionally involved with characters similar to themselves than they do with characters who are dissimilar. The research on the effects of reading concerns changes in the reader's attitudes, personality, values, or behavior as a result of reading. For example, as a result of reading books depicting violence, a reader may commit violent acts.

131

A reader's response to a work may or may not be related to the manner in which he is affected by the work. A reader may be emotionally moved by a work, but that does not necessarily mean that the experience changes his attitude or behavior. The work is not simply a stimulus that causes an effect on a passive reader; the nature of the reader's experience with the work is influenced by the reader's personality, reading ability, values, attitude, and reason for reading.

Extensive empirical research in both of these areas has been done only in the last two decades. Research in response to literature, summarized in Purves and Beach (1972) and Monson and Peltola (1976), grew out of a shift in the theory of literature instruction in the 1960s from emphasis on teaching literary critical analysis towards the need for students to express their own responses to their reading. One of the assumptions of previous literature instruction was that there was one "correct meaning" of a work residing within the context of the work itself. An increased interest in the reader's response to a work is based on the assumption that there is no one "correct meaning," but that the meaning of a work evolves from an interplay of reader and work. Thus, a work may mean different things to different readers.

While the research on the effects of reading dates back to the beginning of the century, the research on the effects of reading material considered as obscene or erotic was sketchy until the formation of the Commission on Obscenity and Pornography (1970), which funded two million dollars worth of research. Much of that research concerned effects of visual material, and the subjects were generally college age and older. However, some of the research on effects of reading funded by the Commission is applicable to this review, particularly the survey research on related areas such as public opinion about sexual materials, amount of exposure to sexual materials, and some studies on response to sexual materials.

The findings of this research are applicable to a number of assumptions underlying arguments in school library censorship cases.

A person's objection to a particular book frequently rests on the assumption that because he responded in a particular manner to that book, others reading the book will respond in the same manner. Or, even if the person did not read the book, he assumes that because the book contains certain subject matter or language, he can predict the responses to that book. However, the research on response to reading indicates that: (1) readers respond in a highly unique manner to works; (2) the same reader responds differently to different works; and (3) differences in readers' responses are due to differences in readers' personality, sex, literary training, age, reading ability, cognitive development and other characteristics. If responses are unique and relative to the reader's own characteristics, then predictions as to how others may respond are often invalid.

A third assumption is that reading changes people. While the research on the effects of reading is somewhat inconclusive, the trend in the findings indicates that reading does not have much short term effect on readers' attitudes or behavior. This suggests that readers' attitudes or behavior are symptomatic of stable aspects of personality which are influenced more by parents, peers, schooling, and cultural socialization than by reading.

While the research findings may be used to question these three assumptions, some of the research on response to literature may also be used to justify the value of certain experiences with a work. In cases of challenges to a book, the librarian must not only argue against various charges against reading the book, but also must be able to justify the value of reading that book. Such justifications are often based on the assumption that reading changes people, and is vulnerable to the countercharge that if a book changes readers in a positive manner, it may also change them in a negative manner. Or, that what a librarian regards as a positive change, a parent may regard as a negative change.

An optional justification is that given a certain reader, a book provides certain experiences of value to that reader, regardless of any effects on the reader. For example, the fact that a reader with certain developmental problems can vicariously respond to a character coping with the same problems may not change that reader but may provide an experience that is intrinsically rewarding. Such justifications are most successful on a case-by-case basis in which the makeup of an individual reader is known. This does not preclude certain generalizations about readers' experiences based on categories of age, sex, personality, reading ability, or developmental needs—many research findings on response are reported according to these general categories. But the general statement, "This book is worthwhile reading because junior high girls can identify with the main character's problems," is more difficult to document than the statement, "Student X was able to identify with the main character's problems."

All of this leads to a fourth assumption, that not allowing a student access to a book, i.e., censoring the book, will deter a student's interest in the content portrayed in the book and his desire to read such a book. In fact, there is some research indicating that censorship itself enhances the desire for a book.

Problems of Definition, Methodology, Measurement

It should be emphasized that any empirical research in an area as subjective, ineffable, and relative as a reader reading a book poses certain problems to researchers. One of these problems is that, in research on reading "obscenity," individuals or groups vary considerably in their definitions of "obscene."

Many legal definitions of obscenity are based on the assumption that certain persons who are reasonable, rational, and unbiased could judge works as obscene. As Clor (1969) argues:

> It is . . . impossible to be absolutely certain that the average reader will 'infallibly' respond one way or another. But obscenity statutes do not rest upon such an assumption of unfailing mechanical cause and effect. They assume that a book which is designed to produce a certain effect will ordinarily produce that effect in the average reader, or reader for whom it is intended, in average circumstances.

Because researchers obviously cannot produce "average readers" with "average sexuality" or duplicate "average circumstances" or generalize from one set of "community standards" to another, their findings do not necessarily solve legal disputes over censorship. The situation is further complicated because researchers themselves often have difficulty in controlling or accounting for all of the variables that impinge on a single reader's response. Even the circumstances in which a book is read evokes different responses. As Hein (1971) notes, "A passage that is sexually arousing when read luxuriantly of an evening by the fire might be coldly neutral when parsed and analyzed at a desk or by the blackboard." One study (Kammann, 1966) compared ratings of poems read for discussion by a professor with poems read for discussion with friends and found significant differences in the ratings due simply to the reasons for the reading.

Another problem is that measures (open-ended verbal response, questionnaires, rating scales) of response to reading may not be a valid measure of the reader's actual covert experience. Similarly, physiological measures of a reader's response may not provide a valid measure of a reader's emotional or psychological experience.

A third problem is that survey or descriptive study results indicating relationships (significant correlations) between variables are sometimes confused with experimental study results indicating a cause and effect relationship between an independent variable and a dependent variable. For example, much of the survey research finds a strong relationship between the amount of exposure to obscenity and sexual activity. That does not necessarily mean that reading obscenity causes sexual activity. In order to determine that, a researcher would typically employ an experimental design in which one group is given a treatment (extensive exposure to obscenity) and another group is given a different treatment (non-obscene books) or no treatment, and the effects of extensive exposure are measured by comparing pre- and post-measures of amount of sexual activity of both groups. Unfortunately, because of the difficulty in controlling all of the variables which could be influencing a dependent variable, experimental research on effects of reading is fraught with problems.

There are also a number of methodological problems associated with studying the response to, or effects of, erotica. While there is considerable survey research on pre-college-age adolescents' experiences with erotica, most of the experimental research on the effects of erotica exclude pre-college adolescents, for obvious ethical reasons. Thus, the few studies reported in this survey on effects of reading erotica were conducted with college students (studies with adults are excluded). College students may not be representative of the larger population, because sex is a highly salient and uncertain experience for many college students (Amoroso and Brown, 1973). Another problem in both response and effects studies with erotica is that self-report measures of arousal are often inaccurate when compared with physiological measures. Females are often more inaccurate in detecting arousal than males (Heiman, 1975), and physiological devices for females have been unreliable, which may have biased results towards higher arousal with erotica for males than females. Devices used to measure physiological response may themselves distort findings. Amoroso and Brown cite their study in which subjects "hooked up" to devices rated slides as more stimulating and pornographic than subjects not "hooked up."

Research on Response to Reading

The research on response to reading attempts to define the nature of readers' experiences with a work and the characteristics of the reader that influence that experience. This review is limited to analysis of those characteristics of the reader most often cited in censorship debates—personality, values, sex, and previous experience with reading. While the influence of each of these is examined separately, they all coalesce differently within the reader.

Personality and Response

Much of the recent research on response to reading suggests that readers project their own unique personality or identity style onto a work, thereby deriving different meanings from the same work. For example, a reader with high achievement orientation will react positively to characters with similar personality traits. Petrosky (1975) studied the relationship between some of the many variables that influence response and found that the three variables carrying the most weight were identity themes (personality patterns), level of cognitive thought processes, and past experience of the reader. Other studies indicate that the reader's self-concept strongly influences the semantic meanings attributed to main characters (Kingston and White, 1967); that readers judge most favorably those characters most like themselves (Stout, 1964); ascribe to liked characters those traits considered likable (Thayer and Pronko, 1959); impute values to characters not contained in a story (McCaul, 1944); and form mental pictures of characters even though no physical descriptions are given (Thayer and Pronko, 1958).

Based on their extensive case-study research, Holland (1973, 1975) and Bleich (1969, 1971) conclude that a reader's identity style is the most important determinant of differences in response. Holland (1974) defines "identity style" as "the sameness and continuity we sense in ourself and other human beings, and it can be expressed as a centering 'identity theme'. . . . Readers re-create what the writer has written in terms of their own identity theme."

Readers also differ in response according to personality development. As adolescents develop more tolerant, flexible, and complex personalities, they attribute more complexity to characters (Beach and Brunetti, in press).

Differences in personality also influence attitudes toward and responses to obscenity. Wallace's survey (1973) of adults' conceptions of obscenity indicated that persons who were highly religious rated erotic material as always obscene. The more authoritarian a reader, the more likely he is to judge erotica as pornographic. Subjects high in sex-guilt inhibited sexual fantasy while reading (Clark, 1952) and reported significantly greater increase in guilt level after reading an erotic literary passage than those low in sex-guilt (Mosher and Greenberg, 1969). Readers also differ according to personality in the amount of anxiety evoked by erotic passages and their ability to cope with that anxiety.

This research suggests that a reader's personality strongly influences his response to reading, and that because readers differ in personality, their responses to the same work are unique. Moreover, because personality tends to be relatively stable, the influence of personality on response may be stronger than any short-term changes in personality resulting from reading certain books (Byrne and Sheffield, 1965).

These findings suggest one justification for reading books with characters whose values differ considerably from community norms. Because adolescent readers do identify or empathize with such characters, they perceive themselves from a different perspective and a different set of values. For adolescents, many of whom are highly egocentric, the experience of assuming the perspectives of others, particularly perspectives that are radically different from their own, momentarily breaks them out of their egocentricity. Whether such experiences actually change the rate of their cognitive or role-taking development is doubtful.

Readers' Values and Response

Differences in personality also reflect differences in readers' cultural or social upbringing resulting in differences in values. As is the case with personality, readers' values remain relatively stable. They are, therefore, more likely to impose values on works than change their values as a result of reading certain works. Unfortunately, there is little research on the relationship between reader values and response; this relationship is often at the heart of censorship issues.

Differences in values strongly influence positive or negative judgments of erotic material. One representative study found that college students who judged materials as pornographic tended to be females, churchgoers, from small towns, sexually sheltered, and children of farmers, ministers, or blue collar workers (Reed and Reed, 1972).

The question arises as to whose values prevail in censorship decisions or whose values are best representative of "community standards." Zurcher, et al. (1973) found that antipornography groups had the political and rhetorical advantages in asserting their own values, even though their definitions of pornography were highly diverse and lacked focus, and 67 percent had never read anything that they would define as pornographic.

Zurcher's research suggests that regardless of the values espoused, given a particular community value system, those groups who employ arguments most appealing to the community are the groups whose position often prevails in censorship decisions. This suggests a need for further research on the socializing effects of various institutions on attitudes towards reading. For example, if increased amounts of education result in changes in attitudes towards controversial reading material, research could focus on those specific aspects of education or home experience that influence attitudes. Some research indicates that the home literary environment was the only significant variable contributing to fourth graders' attitudes toward reading (Hansen, 1969).

Sex-role and Response

The effects of values or cultural socialization on readers' responses is evident in studies on differences in sex. The research on reading interests indicates that, next to age, sex is the most important determinant of differences in reading interests: females differ from males in preferring romance, home life, and drama while males prefer sports, war, and science. These differences may shift as cultural values and the content of available books changes. While readers' sex-role values definitely influence their interests, there seems to be less influence of sex-role values on responses. Males and females do not differ significantly on *types* of response to reading; although, in response to erotica, one study found that males reported more arousal than females (Abelson et al., 1970), while another study (Kutsckinsky, 1970) found no differences according to sex. Females also experience more concurrent negative emotions in responding to erotica than males, except males high in sex guilt (Goldstein and Kant, 1973).

Research in this area takes on increasing importance given the recent concern with sex-role stereotyping in many books now on the library shelves. Reading such books, it is argued, reinforces sex-role stereotyping instilled by the culture, particularly writing that exploits the stereotype of woman as a sex object. Because the implication (rarely formulated) is that these books should not be made available to students, this issue touches on the larger issue of censorship.

It could be argued that not all students are reinforced by reading about stereotypes; that those with values or attitudes contrary to traditional sex-role stereotypes will respond critically while those with traditional sex-role stereotypes will respond positively. Unfortunately, while a number of studies have found that, in terms of preferences, boys prefer stereotyped males and girls prefer stereotyped females (Nelson, 1975; Beaven, 1972), there is little research on differences in readers' values (traditional versus nontraditional) and their response to stereotyped characters. In a study by this writer (Beach and Brunetti, in press), male and female high school and college students differed significantly in their conceptions of their own personality as measured by the *Adjective Check List*. However, they did not differ by sex in their conceptions of a male and female main character in two short stories. One reason that their conceptions of themselves were highly stereotyped and their conceptions of the characters were not stereotyped was that the characters, from the researchers' perspective, displayed highly non-stereotyped behaviors. This suggests that complex and/or non-stereotyped characterizations do not necessarily reinforce the readers' own values.

It is often assumed that males respond more positively than females to male-oriented content (most pornographic writing), while females respond more positively than males to romantic stories supposedly oriented towards females. The findings on differences by sex in response to pornographic/nonpornographic romance writing is highly inconclusive, but, as with characterization, the degree of stereotyping seems to have some effect on sharpening or reducing sex differences.

Drawing on some previous research, Schiller (1970) found that females were more aroused by romantic themes in books and romance magazines than were males. The degree to which sexual activity is placed in the context of a story line and is described in wish-fulfilling versus realistic language results in sex differences. Females rated wish-fulfilling descriptions of sexual activity with a story line as more interesting and arousing than did males, while males rated realistic portrayals of sexual activity with little or no story context as more arousing; although a replication of this study (Englar and Walker, 1973) found that both males and females rated wish-fulfilling descriptions with a story line as more arousing.

A recent study on response to specific types of erotic and romantic passages (Heiman, 1975) gives an even clearer picture of the effect of stereotyped content on response. Contrary to previous findings of female preference for romance, both males and females were most aroused by passages with explicit sexual description. One reason for this finding was that the explicit sexual descriptions included female-initiated, female-centered encounters, which female subjects rated as more arousing than did males. Thus, when the stereotyped nature of erotic, male-oriented material is changed, different response patterns emerge.

All of this points to the importance of examining the effects of cultural socialization influencing response to stereotyped/nonstereotyped materials. In their review of the research on response to erotica, Johnson and Goodchilds (1973) argue that much of the research has only studied population means which often mask the wide range of different value systems in society. Each value system influences readers' responses to erotica differently. For example, in some value systems, females are discouraged from being sexually assertive. Their responses to erotica therefore produce a conflict in them between assertiveness and nonassertiveness.

While censorship issues often focus on the nature of the response to content, they often fail to examine the different cultural values that shape the response and the natural tendency of adolescents to reject these values. Thus, if students respond positively to a portrayal of values contrary to what they consider to be their own stereotyped community values, then understanding the nature of that response requires careful examination of their perceptions of the community values. Adolescents may attach certain cultural meanings to erotica or books considered undesirable by a community, so that it is not only the content but also the symbolic function of such books within their peer group and within the community that is influencing their response.

Age, Literary Training, and Response

Readers also respond differently to works because of age differences and literary training. A number of studies find that American students' responses to reading show a progressive development from predominantly an emotional/engagement type of response in the elementary grades to increased description/retelling in the junior high grades to a decline in engagement and description and an increase in interpretation in the senior high school grades (Pollock, 1972; Thompson, 1973; National Assessment, 1973; Purves, 1973). This development towards more interpretative, analytic response reflects the type of literary/critical instruction characteristic of

American secondary education. In a study comparing the influence of literature instruction in ten countries on students' response in those countries, Purves (1973) found that students in each country tended to respond according to the critical approach emphasized in that country's curriculum (for example, British students responded with more evaluative response; Italian, with more biographical response); the older, senior-high-age students reflected greater curriculum influence than the younger, junior-high-age students.

Readers also respond differently to different works. In a study of thousands of secondary students' responses in ten countries, Purves (1973) found that readers differed considerably in their responses to different short stories, primarily due to differences in the content of the story. Secondary students differ in types of response according to the difficulty of short stories (Somers, 1972) or novels (Angellotti, 1972). Even within the context of a work, types of responses or attitudes towards characters vary at different points in the work (Angellotti, 1972; Squire, 1964; DeVries, 1967).

This research indicates that because of differences in works and in reader characteristics, responses are often highly unique. This casts some doubt on the validity of predictions that students will respond in certain ways. While someone may predict that a student will become emotionally involved with a character who is considered "undesirable," the student may respond to that character from a detached, analytic perspective.

This research also provides some justification for the use of adolescent "problem" novels that have occasionally been criticized and in some cases, censored for their realistic treatment of adolescent problems. Because adolescents, particularly those in grades eight, nine, and ten, are highly concerned with adolescent problems, they seek out such novels as a way of vicariously experiencing others coping with similar problems. Because these novels are written in a simple, uncomplicated form while dealing with psychological problems, adolescents can understand and interpret the experiences. In contrast, when they seek out adult novels dealing with adolescent problems, they often have difficulty in understanding the content, often responding with more perception/description responses than with interpretational response. For example, Angellotti (1972) compared responses of eighth graders to the adult novel *A Separate Peace* with responses to *Tuned Out,* an adolescent novel. The eighth graders responded primarily with descriptive response to *A Separate Peace* while responding primarily with interpretational response to *Tuned Out,* reflecting comprehension difficulties with the complexities of the adult novel versus the appropriate reading level of the adolescent novel.

One problem with questioning people about the nature of their previous experience is that they are likely to indicate that they themselves had experienced "socially desirable" or "neutral" effects while predicting "negative" effects on others (Abelson, et al., 1970). Abelson's survey found that persons with considerable recent experience with sexually explicit works were more likely than those with little or no recent experience to believe that sexual materials provided information and entertainment and less likely to believe that exposure leads to moral breakdown. Repeated exposure to obscenity leads to more positive judgments of obscenity (Eliasberg and Stuart, 1961) and a decrease in belief that there are potential detrimental effects from such exposure (Howard, et al., 1970).

One of the interesting ironies of demands for censorship is that those demanding censorship have often had little exposure to obscenity, perhaps due to their own reluctance to be exposed (Zurcher, et al., 1973). If increased familiarity leads to more positive judgments, then demands for censorship without knowledge of the material rest on a vicious circle between the poles of refusal to be exposed and familiarity—those who associate obscenity with negative emotional response do not become familiar with obscenity and thereby continue to believe that it has a negative emotional effect (Byrne and Lamberth, 1970).

Other variables—occupation, amount of education, and attitudes towards sex—enter into this relationship (Higgins and Katzman, 1969; Byrne and Lamberth, 1970).

Developing familiarity with erotica changes response or attitude because as the novelty of erotica diminishes, so does the emotional response. The positive or negative disposition of a person's emotional responses is a key variable in understanding his attitude towards censorship. Attitude towards censorship depends more on emotional response, positive or negative, than upon views towards the effects of reading erotica. Individuals responding with positive affect conceive of erotica as not pornographic and would not censor erotica (Byrne and Lamberth, 1970; Byrne, Fisher, Lamberth, Mitchell, 1974). If socialization predisposes readers to expect a negative emotional experience with initial exposure to obscenity, then these readers, particularly younger readers, respond just as much to the novelty of the experience as to the content.

Extensive exposure, which occurred in one experimental study (Howard, 1970), resulted in a satiation effect: subjects became bored with the extensive exposure and chose to read nonobscene material, although they developed more positive attitudes towards obscenity.

This research on what could be called the novelty and satiation effects is sketchy. Because censorship contributes to lack of, or delay of, exposure, it may create a novelty effect when readers are eventually exposed. If adolescents are negatively predisposed to obscenity, their delayed initial exposure may be negative, leading to a refusal of further exposure, resulting in the vicious circle previously mentioned. The various aspects of this process are extracted from separate studies and need to be combined in further research.

Response to Obscene Language

Censorship cases do not necessarily involve entire books. Objections often focus on specific parts of a book, particularly obscene language. While some readers view the use of obscene language as highly objectionable and others do not, there exists little research on reasons for differences in response to such language. Rogers (1973) suggests that readers respond differently to technical, poetic, and obscene words referring to the same concept due to differences in psychological or subconscious associations. Technical and obscene words appeal on a conscious level while poetic words appeal on both a conscious and subconscious level. "Technical terms are essentially neutral and are designed to be. Obscene words are generally hot, strong, raw verbiage and are meant to be. Because they are not controlling and containing, the muted words of poetry usually appear mild in their surface effects." Unfortunately, there exists no empirical evidence for such claims for certain psychological associations or for cultural taboos on obscenity.

There is little doubt that negative response to obscene words provokes demands for censorship. Donlan (1973) examined journal articles citing cases of censorship and found that obscene words were the predominant reason for complaints, even though many of the books containing the words were not about sex or violence. When Donlan elicited parents' responses to a list of obscene words, the parents reacted strongly. They objected more to children saying the words than reading them, more to reading words in school than out of school, and based their objections more on matters of taste and appropriate behavior in social contexts than on any adverse effects on behavior.

One of the difficulties in conducting research on response to language is that the meanings of words depend on the context in which they are used. An obscene word used in the context of an impersonal report means something quite different than when used in the context of an erotic story.

Research on the Effects of Reading

The research on response to reading indicates that readers respond in unique ways because of differences in personality, values, sex, age, literary training, and previous experience with reading. These findings set the stage for understanding the research on the effects of reading.

Because readers derive different meaning from their experience with the same work, the effects of that experience on readers' attitudes, values, or self-concept will differ considerably. The general trend of the research suggests that the relatively stable and defined characteristics of readers shape the experience with a work to a greater extent than the work affects characteristics of the reader. Reading is only one of many influences on a person. Adolescents report few if any models drawn from literature (Averill, 1950; Havighurst, Robinson, and Dorr, 1946).

A problem faced by researchers is that, in the typical experimental study comparing the effects of reading certain materials on one group compared to a group that did not read those materials, pre- and post-comparisons are made according to group means which mask the influence of certain individual differences in effects. Researchers also face the problem of positing or implying qualitative judgments about effects. If a researcher finds that reading certain books, for example, novels about politics, changes the political attitudes of adolescents to a more liberal political attitude, then the researcher may judge that change as a positive change. However, others may judge that change as an undesirable change.

An overriding problem is that most studies examine change in attitude or values over a short time period. This runs counter to much social science research indicating that people's values or attitudes change only gradually over a long term. Because they therefore impose a stable set of values onto their reading, readers respond positively to aspects of reading that reinforce their values and suppress aspects that threaten their values. Readers in one study (Thayer and Pronko, 1958) ascribed desirable traits to characters they liked and undesirable traits to characters they disliked; in another (Meckel, 1946), they did not identify with a character when that character's behavior was unacceptable.

When asked to cite effects of reading on long range change in attitudes, most readers have indicated positive changes in attitudes (Smith, 1933; Weingarten, 1954; Shirley, 1969). The self-reports reflect people's tendency to present themselves in a positive manner. There is some question as to individuals' awareness or ability to define a consistent set of values derived from reading. Half of high school students' responses to "value-laden generalizations" in anecdotes and incomplete plots were logically inconsistent (Snapper, 1958). There is also no method of retroactively testing the accuracy of these self-reports (Kimmel, 1970). Moreover, people's attitudes do change over time, but reading is only one of many variables influencing that change.

The nature of attitude change depends on subjects' own unique psychological orientation towards reading. A reader who is indifferent to reading is affected less than a reader who becomes highly involved with his reading. Shirley (1969) defined the attitudes towards reading of five subjects reporting high influence from reading and five subjects reporting little influence. No two students were influenced in the same manner. Shirley defined five types of readers who hold different attitudes: the indifferent, the observer, the participator, the synthesizer, and the decision-maker. The readers who were most influenced were the synthesizers who conceived of reading as resulting in a new or reinforced self-image. Unfortunately, there is little other research on readers' attitudes toward reading and the degree to which readers are affected by reading. Such research would be particularly helpful in understanding cultural attitudes toward reading versus watching television. In a culture in which people devote far more time to watching television (When given a choice between watching television and reading, the vast majority of lower socio-economic high school students chose television [Greenberg and Dervin, 1970]), positive attitudes towards television content as entertaining and non-threatening are developed. Concurrently, content in either television or reading that is not necessarily entertaining but threatening is viewed negatively and with increasing suspicion, enhancing demands for censorship.

A number of experimental studies, attempting to control certain variables influencing possible effects of readings, have generated somewhat inconclusive findings on the effects of reading on attitudes, values, self-concept or behavior. In most of these studies, one group of subjects read materials dealing with a certain topic while a control group did not read those materials. Pre- and post-measures were used to determine if the reading resulted in any change in attitudes, values, self-concept or behavior. The findings of these experimental studies lean towards the conclusion that reading has no short term effect on readers' attitudes, values, or self-concept. Many of the studies reporting no significant change from reading (Lodge, 1953; Bovyer, 1962; Ponder, 1968; Milgren, 1967; Holdsworth, 1968; Brandhorst, 1973; Harless, 1972; Wagener, 1971; Bazelak, 1973; Carter, 1974; Mattera, 1961) have more sophisticated designs and less susceptibility to the influence of researcher expectation than those reporting significant change (Feltman, 1954; Young, 1963; Fisher, 1965; Tauran, 1967; Hayes, 1969; Cooke, 1971; Kimoto, 1974; Frankel, 1972; Alsbrook, 1970). Most of the latter group of studies dealt with change in attitude towards minority groups. For example, children reading stories favorable to Eskimos (Tauran, 1967) or favorable to Indians (Fisher, 1965) developed positive attitudes towards Eskimos and Indians, respectively.

In an attempt to clarify reasons for influence or lack of influence, Harless (1972) defined three patterns of reader identification and resulting changes in attitude—entertainment/attraction, identification with context, and instrumental payoff in which the content allows for problem solving. He found no change in attitude; readers experienced two types of identification—they were entertained by the story and attracted to the characters. This supports Jahoda's (1954) finding that most readers' attitudes are not affected by reading because they are more interested in the entertainment value of the story than in attitudes portrayed.

Research on attitude change is highly susceptible to biases and lack of experimental control. Certain expectations as to the direction of attitude change can be subtly communicated to experimental group subjects. Attitude questionnaires may include leading questions which bias responses towards the researcher's expectations. In some studies, subjects are not randomly assigned to experimental or control groups. In the case of the Hayes study (1969), no control group was used.

Some attitude changes may be momentary or superficial. In an early study finding attitude change towards blacks, Jackson (1944) administered the same attitude test two weeks after the study and found no significant differences between the experimental and control groups; although Alsbrook (1970) found that attitude gains in ethnocentricity were retained after one month.

Another variable influencing change is discussion or activities conducted in addition to the reading. Sixth graders in Zucaro's study (1972) who read books about blacks with discussion experienced a greater change in attitude towards blacks than those who read the books without discussion.

Even if reading certain books does have an adverse effect on students, discussing such books may reduce the anxiety and negative feelings evoked by a book. For example, if a book heightens feelings of aggression, then discussing such feelings allows for their expression without anxiety, a cathartic release. It also allows for sharing of feelings with others who may also have experienced some anxiety, reducing the reader's concern that only he or she experienced such feelings. In a study comparing reading-and-discussion with simply reading short stories with aggression and nurturance themes (Lewis, 1967), elementary students who read without discussion experienced a significant increase in aggressive feelings and a decrease in nurturant feelings, while students who did discuss the stories experienced a reduction of aggressive feelings and increased feelings of nurturance.

When adults or peers conceive of certain books as undesirable, this often implies that open discussion about these books is taboo. Ironically, without such discussion, negative emotional effects may be heightened rather than reduced. An atmosphere conducive to open discussion also allows a student to develop a trust in his own ability to formulate responses and in his own critical standards for judging books.

Attitudes towards Sex and Violence

A major concern of censors is the effect of obscenity on attitudes towards sex. The survey research previously cited (Eliasberg and Stuart, 1961) noted that those persons with more exposure to, or experience with, obscenity had a more tolerant attitude towards obscenity—the greater their familiarity with obscenity, the more tolerant they were.

Most of the experimental research examining a direct cause and effect relationship between exposure to obscenity and change in attitudes towards sex consists of studies using adults and primarily visual material. Four of the major studies sponsored by the Commission (Howard et al., 1970; Kutschinsky, 1970; Mann et al., 1970; Mosher, 1970), with all but the Howard study employing visual stimuli, found no significant effect due to exposure on attitudes towards sex. In the Kutschinsky study, subjects experienced a decrease in interest in perverted sexual activity, had no wish for more access to similar material, and experienced boredom more frequently than strong emotional reactions.

Some critics justifiably charge that pornography portrays a calloused and exploitive attitude towards women. The experimental research on the effects of reading pornography on attitudes towards women is nonexistent. While male attitudes towards women as developed through cultural socialization affect their behavior (Mosher, 1970), viewing films did not change "sex-calloused" attitudes (Mosher and Katz, 1970).

Critics also charge that pornography has a general "corrupting influence" on character, particularly at a young, "impressionable" age. Davis and Braucht (1970) hypothesized that the earlier readers were exposed to pornography, the more detrimental the effect. They asked males, aged 18–30, representing a wide variety of social groups, to recall their experience with pornography and the earliest age of exposure. The "moral character" of subjects was measured using four different measures, in addition to peer ratings. The overall amount of exposure was negatively correlated with moral character. There was no evidence that the earlier the age of exposure, the more detrimental the effect.

Public concern has been expressed over the effects of violence in film and television, but there is little research on the effects of reading material with violent or aggressive acts on attitudes or behavior.

Self-censorship by the comic-book industry of violent content was highly influenced by Wertham's (1953) extensive case-study research leading to his conclusion that comic books triggered aggressive or violent behavioral effects in adolescents who were already maladjusted. More recent research with reading materials casts doubt on Wertham's contentions. Auerbach (1974) compared two groups of high school students' change in attitude towards violence. Subjects were distinguished as favorable, neutral, or unfavorable toward physical aggressiveness. Subjects read three stories containing violence and wrote responses. Attitudes toward physical aggressiveness were not related to the type or the intensity of response; there was no change in attitude due to reading the stories. In Dembo's study (1973), British boys were rated as aggressive or nonaggressive by peers. No significant differences between the aggressive and nonaggressive groups were found in the frequency of contact with various media or attraction to aggressive or sensational content in books, magazines, or comic books.

The majority of these studies find little or no attitude change. This may be due to the high stability of attitudes, which reading simply reinforces rather than changes. For example, Lancaster (1971) compared changes in prejudice from voluntary reading of childrens' books with positive racial attitudes for two groups of fifth graders, those high in prejudice and those low in prejudice. The more books the low prejudiced students read, the more positive their attitudes; the more books the prejudiced students read, the more prejudiced they became.

Thus, claims in censorship cases that certain books are themselves the cause of either favorable or unfavorable attitudes are questionable. However, because it is so difficult for researchers to cleanly separate out the effects of other influences—family, peers, community, schooling—from the effects of reading, the research on this topic remains inconclusive.

The Effect of Reading Obscenity on Sexual Behavior

One justification for censorship of books depicting sexual activities is that it influences sexual behavior, resulting in deviant sexual behavior and sex crimes. Survey research indicates that many adolescents are exposed to erotica at an early age (Wilson and Jacobs, 1970; Elias, 1970; Abelson, et al., 1970). There is also a high relationship between amount of exposure and sexual activity (Berger, et al., 1970; Davis and Braucht, 1970).

Experience with erotica seems to be a symptom of sexual behavior. With adults, a high frequency of established sexual activity predisposes individuals to more exposure than sexually inactive individuals. But also, to cite the Commission's conclusion, because patterns of sexual behavior are highly stable, they are not substantially altered by exposure (Report of the Commission on Obscenity and Pornography, 1970).

It is difficult to study the effects of exposure on activity without studying the social context. Both the amount of exposure and the amount of sexual activity are influenced by social norms or family and peer pressure. Deviant family and peer circumstances are significantly related to early age of exposure (Davis, et al., 1970; Abelson, 1970; Elias, 1970; Propper, 1970). Thus, experience with obscenity is a function of social context (Berger, et al., 1973) and social context influences sexual activity.

In some cases, social context influences certain types of sexual activity while obscenity influences other types. When Davis and Braucht (1970) examined the relationship of exposure and sexual activity, exposure was more strongly related to solitary sexual practice while peer pressure was more strongly related to heterosexual experience.

All of this suggests that reading about sex is a concomitant of an adolescent's sexual development and that it is related to sexual activity, primarily solitary. Whether reading about sex leads to deviant, illegal behavior is a different question.

Law enforcement officials have argued that exposure to pornography results in sex crimes and delinquency (Hoover, 1961), while testimony by psychiatrists and psychologists working with delinquent youths indicated no relationship (Wilson and Jacobs, 1970). In no other area is the research more conclusive than that indicating a lack of relationship between exposure and delinquency.

While the availability of erotica increased several fold from 1960 to 1970, the number of juvenile arrests for sex crimes decreased over the same time period by four percent (Kupperstein and Wilson, 1970). A number of studies comparing the amount of exposure of delinquent and nondelinquent youths found that delinquent youths had no more exposure to erotica than nondelinquent youths and, in some cases, less (Berninghausen and Faunce, 1965; Schiller, 1970; Johnson, et al., 1970; Walker, 1970; Gebhard, 1965). In not one of 1,000 cases of delinquency did erotica have any influence (Glueck and Glueck, 1950).

Some research suggests an interesting irony: lack of normal, healthy sex experience during adolescence involving some experience with erotica leads to later sexual deviancy or delinquency. Erotica may therefore contribute, among other things, to healthy sexual development. In a large-scale study of sexual deviancy, Goldstein (1973) found that sex-deviants experienced far less frequency of exposure to erotica than nondeviants. Deviants also came from homes with little parental tolerance for erotica (Goldstein), in which discussion of sexual subjects was tabooed (Hughes, 1970). Persons who had read more erotica were more at ease in interviews talking about sex than deviants with little exposure

(Kant and Goldstein, 1970). As Kvaraceus (1965) argued, reading material dealing with sex provides hard-to-get information about sex that adolescents often cannot acquire elsewhere. Erotica also provides adolescents with a vicarious substitute for actual sexual behavior, the so-called 'safety-valve theory' (Cairns, Paul, and Wishner, 1962; see also Clor, 1968, for a critique of that theory).

The Effects of Censorship

The research on adolescent experience with erotic material suggests that depriving some adolescents of this material normally accessible to others may be detrimental. This assumes that erotica is generally beneficial to adolescents' normal sexual development.

One problem in studying the effects of censorship is that it is obviously impossible to study the effects of reading nothing. The option is to study the effects of reading material that would otherwise not have been available, and then to generalize that depriving readers of such books deprives them of these effects, a risky inference.

A number of studies examining the relationship between availability of obscenity and sex crimes in Denmark suggests that increased availability without censorship is related to a decline in sex crimes. The Danish Parliament erased erotic literature from an obscenity statute in 1967 and in 1969 repealed that statute, allowing availability of sexually explicit material for persons 16 and older. Literary erotica had been easily available since 1965; there was a large increase in the number of erotic paperback novels available from 1960 to 1967. Despite this increase in availability, the sex crimes reported declined during this period, the sharpest decrease occurring from 1967 on, the year of the appeal (Ben-Veniste, 1970). Further analysis discovered that the decrease in sex crimes was not due to other reasons—changes in laws or law enforcement (Ben-Veniste) or changes in public attitude towards sex crimes or willingness to report crimes (Kutschinsky, 1970). However, because this is only a relationship, the findings do not mean that increased availability necessarily causes a decline in crime.

Fromkin and Brock (1973) argued that placing restrictions on reading increases the desirability of those materials. In an empirical test of this hypothesis (Zellinger, Fromkin, Speller, and Kohn, 1975), one group of college males was led to believe that a book was restricted to persons twenty-one years and older, while another group was given no information as to restriction. Some of the students were told that the book was pornographic; others were not told this. Students who had been told that the book was restricted expressed greater willingness to read the book, perceived the book as more desirable, and liked reading the book more than subjects given no information as to restriction. Restricting a book may therefore enhance the desirability of that book, provided a reader has some previous knowledge about that book, which is often not the case.

It could be argued that the effect of censorship depends upon individuals' own sense of guilt resulting from knowing that they would be or were reading material harmful to them. One study (Schill, Evans, Monroe, and Drain, 1975) examined the hypothesis that censorship would enhance attraction for reading an erotic magazine for low-guilt but not for high-guilt persons. Contrary to the prediction, the high-guilt subjects experienced greater attraction in the censorship conditions than the low-guilt subjects.

This research raises some doubt as to the effectiveness of censorship as consistent with its intent, to prevent exposure leading to change in attitudes or behavior and to deter availability to adolescents. If exposure does not lead to change in attitudes or behavior, then arguments for censorship must fall back on objections to the intrinsic characteristics of works—that "filth" is "filthy." However, if censorship of library books enhances their desirability and adolescents seek out such books elsewhere (Fersch, 1970), then arguments defining the undesirable intrinsic qualities may actually assist rather than hinder adolescents' search for reading content considered taboo.

Conclusions

The research surveyed here suggests several conclusions related to issues of censorship. As previously noted, these studies do not imply that censorship is valid or invalid. Rather, they provide evidence or counter-evidence for claims about reading experiences used to justify censorship. (1) Claims that books are undesirable are often made in the form of predictions that, given a certain book, a student or students will respond in a certain predicted manner. The research on response to reading indicates that readers' responses are highly unique and vary considerably from one book to another. Predictions as to the nature of readers' responses are therefore highly questionable. Similarly, (2) persons often assume that other readers will respond similarly to the same book—that if a book has undesirable meanings for them, it has undesirable meanings for all readers. The research indicates that differences in readers' age, personality, values, sex, literary training, and previous reading result in highly unique meanings for different readers. (3) Advocates of censorship often assume that reading certain books changes students' values or attitudes. While the findings of a large number of experimental studies on effects of reading are somewhat inconclusive, most of these studies indicate little short-term change in values or attitudes from reading certain books. Readers' values are determined by family, peers, schooling, and the media to a far greater extent than by reading. (4) Advocates of censorship also assume that reading certain books results in deviant behavior. There is little or no evidence of any relationship between reading and deviant behavior. (5) Claims are made that certain books, particularly those dealing with sex, are harmful to adolescent development. However, some research suggests that exposure to sexual material may be an integral part of normal adolescent sexual development, providing information about sex not available elsewhere. The research also suggests that adolescents deprived of such material do, in some cases, experience deviant sexual development. (6) Claims are made that censorship benefits students in that if books are not available, students will lose their interest in reading such books, choosing books considered more desirable. However, some research indicates that when a book is not available, desire for that book is not reduced, but enhanced. Moreover, the assumption that censorship deters interest in reading a book by appealing to a reader's sense of guilt is not borne out by the research.

References

Abelson, H., Cohen, R., Heaton, E., and Suder, C. Public attitudes toward and experience with erotic materials. *Technical reports of the Commission on Obscenity and Pornography.* Vol. 6. Washington, D.C.: U.S. Government Printing Office, 1970.

Alsbrook, E. Y. *Changes in the ethnocentrism of a select group of college students as a function of bibliotherapy.* Ed.D. Dissertation, University of Illinois, 1970.

Amoroso, D. M. and Brown, M. Problems in studying the effects of erotic material. *Journal of Sex Research,* 1973, *9,* 187-195.

Angellotti, M. L. *A comparison of elements in the written free responses of eighth graders to a junior novel and an adult novel.* Ph.D. Dissertation, The Florida State University, 1972.

Auerbach, L. *The interaction between social attitude and response to three short stories.* Ph.D. Dissertation, New York University, 1974.

Averill, L. The impact of a changing culture upon pubescent ideals. *School and Society,* 1950, *72,* 49-53.

Bazelak, L. P. *A content analysis of tenth-grade students' responses to black literature, including the effect of reading this literature on attitudes towards race.* Ed.D. Dissertation, Syracuse University, 1973.

Beach, R. and Brunetti, G. Differences between high school and university students in their conceptions of literary characters. *Research in the Teaching of English* (in press).

Beaven, M. H. Responses of adolescents to feminine characters in literature. *Research in the Teaching of English,* 1972, *6,* 48-68.

Ben-Veniste, R. Pornography and sex crime—the Danish experience. *Technical reports of the Commission on Obscenity and Pornography.* Vol. 7. Washington, D.C.: U.S. Government Printing Office, 1970.

Berger, A. S., Gagnon, J. H., and Simon, W. Pornography: High school and college years. *Technical reports of the Commission on Obscenity and Pornography.* Vol. 9. Washington, D.C.: U.S. Government Printing Office, 1970.

Berger, A. S., Simon, W., and Gagnon, J. H. Youth and pornography in social context. *Archives of Sexual Behavior,* 1973, *2,* 279-308.

Berninghausen, D. K. and Faunce, R. W. Some opinions on the relationships between obscene books and juvenile delinquency. Unpublished manuscript, University of Minnesota Graduate School, 1965.

Bleich, D. Emotional origins of literary meaning. *College English,* 1969, *31,* 30-40.

Bleich, D. Psychological bases of learning from literature. *College English,* 1971, *33,* 32-45.

Bovyer, G. G. Stories and children's concepts of sportsmanship in the fourth, fifth, and sixth grades. *Elementary English,* 1962, *39,* 762-765.

Brandhorst, A. R. *The effects of reading historical fiction on attitudes of high school students toward selected concepts.* Ph.D. Dissertation, University of Missouri—Columbia, 1973.

Byrne, D. and Lamberth, J. The effect of erotic stimuli on sex arousal evaluative responses, and subsequent behavior. *Technical reports of the Commission on Obscenity and Pornography.* Vol. 8. Washington, D.C.: U.S. Government Printing Office, 1970.

Byrne, D. and Sheffield, J. Response to sexually arousing stimuli as a function of repressing and sensitizing defenses. *Journal of Abnormal Psychology,* 1965, *70,* 114-118.

Byrne, D., Fisher, J. D., Lamberth, J., and Mitchell, H. E. Evaluations of erotica: Facts of feelings. *Journal of Personality and Social Psychology,* 1974, *29,* 111-116.

Cairns, R. B., Paul, J. C. N., and Wishner, J. Sex censorship: The assumptions of anti-obscenity laws and the empirical evidence. *Minnesota Law Review,* 1962, *46,* 1009-1041.

Carter, A. L. *An analysis of the use of contemporary black literature and music and its effects upon self-concept in group counseling procedures.* Ph.D. Dissertation, Purdue University, 1974.

Clark, R. A. The projective measurement of experimentally induced levels of sexual motivation. *Journal of Experimental Psychology,* 1952, *44,* 391-399.

Clor, H. M. *Obscenity and Public Morality.* Chicago: University of Chicago Press, 1969.

Cooke, G. J. *The effects of reading on students' attitudes.* Ph.D. Dissertation, The University of Connecticut, 1971.

Davis, K. E. and Braucht, G. N. Exposure to pornography, character, and sexual deviance: A retrospective survey. *Technical reports of the Commission on Obscenity and Pornography.* Vol. 7. Washington, D.C.: U.S. Goverment Printing Office, 1970.

Dembo, R. Gratification found in media by British teen-age boys. *Journalism Quarterly,* 1973, *50,* 517-526.

DeVries, J. H. D. *A statistical analysis of undergraduate readers' responses to selected characters in Shakespeare's "The Tempest."* Ph.D. Dissertation, University of Illinois, 1967.

Donlan, D. Parent versus teacher: The dirty word. *Diversity in Mature Reading: Theory and Research, 22nd Yearbook of National Reading Conference,* ed. Phil Nacke. Vol. 1. Boone, N.C.: National Reading Conference, 1973, 224-231.

Elias, J. E. Exposure to erotic materials in adolescence. *Technical reports of the Commission on Obscenity and Pornography.* Vol. 9. Washington, D.C.: U.S. Government Printing Office, 1970.

Eliasberg, W. G. and Stuart, I. R. Authoritarian personality and the obscenity threshold. *Journal of Social Psychology,* 1961, *55,* 143-151.

Englar, R. C. and Walker, C. E. Male and female reactions to erotic literature. *Psychological Reports,* 1973, *32,* 481-482.

Feltman, I. *Study of fiction as source material in vocational guidance.* Ph.D. Dissertation, University of Illinois, 1954.

Fersch, E. The relationship between students' experience with restricted access to erotic materials and their behaviorist attributes. Unpublished manuscript. *Commission on Obscenity and Pornography* files, 1970.

Fisher, F. L. *The influences of reading and discussion on attributes of fifth graders toward American Indians.* Ph.D. Dissertation, Berkeley, 1965.

Frankel, H. L. *The effects of reading "The Adventures of Huckleberry Finn" on the racial attitudes of selected ninth-grade boys.* Ed.D. Dissertation, Temple University, 1972.

Fromkin, H. L. and Brock, T. C. Erotic materials: A commodity theory analysis of the enhanced desirability that may accompany their unavailability. *Journal of Applied Social Psychology,* 1973, *3,* 219-231.

Gebhard, P. H., Gagnon, J. H., Pomeroy, W. B., and Christenson, C. V. *Sex offenders: An analysis of types.* New York: Harper & Row, 1965.

Glueck, S. and Glueck, E. *Unravelling juvenile delinquency.* Cambridge: Harvard University Press, 1950.

Goldstein, M. J. Exposure to erotic stimuli and sexual deviance. *Journal of Social Issues,* 1973, *29,* 197-219.

Goldstein, M. J. and Kant, H. S. *Pornography and sexual deviancy: A report of the legal and behaviorism institute.* Berkeley: University of California Press, 1973.

Greenberg, B. and Dervin, B. *Uses of the mass media by the urban poor.* New York: Praeger Publishing, 1970.

Hansen, H. The impact of the home literary environment on reading attitude. *Elementary English,* 1969, *46,* 17-24.

Harless, J. The impact of adventure fiction on readers: The tough guy type. *Journalism Quarterly,* 1972, *49,* 65-73.

Havighurst, R., Robinson, M. J., and Dorr, M. The development of the ideal self in childhood and adolescence. *Journal of Educational Research,* 1946, *40,* 241-257.

Hayes, M. T. *An investigation of the impact of reading on attitudes of racial prejudice.* Ed.D. Dissertation, Boston University, 1969.

Heiman, J. R. The physiology of erotica: Women's sexual arousal. *Psychology Today,* 1975, *8,* 91-94.

Hein, H. Obscenity, politics, and pornography. *Journal of Aesthetic Education,* 1971, *5,* 17-97.

Higgins, J. W. and Katzman, M. B. Determinants in the judgment of obscenity. *American Journal of Psychiatry,* 1969, *125,* 149.

Holdsworth, J. N. Vicarious experience of reading books in changing nursing students' attitudes. *Nursing Research,* 1968, *17,* 135-139.

Holland, N. H. *Poems in persons.* New York: W. W. Norton and Co., Inc., 1973.

Holland, N. H. *Five readers reading.* New Haven: Yale University Press, 1975.

Holland, N. H. "Poems in persons": A review and a reply. *Research in the Teaching of English,* 1974, *8,* 9-14.

Hoover, J. E. The fight against filth. *The American Legion Magazine,* 1961, *70,* 48-49.

Howard, J. L., Reifler, C. B., and Liptzin, M. B. Effects of exposure to pornography. *Technical reports of the Commission on Obscenity and Pornography.* Vol. 8. Washington, D.C.: U.S. Government Printing Office, 1970.

Hughes, D. A. *Perspectives on pornography.* New York: St. Martin's Press, 1970.

Jackson, E. P. Effects of reading upon attitudes toward the Negro race. *Library Quarterly,* 1944, *14,* 47-54.

Jahoda, M. *The impact of literature: A psychological discussion of some assumptions in the censorship debate.* New York: American Book Publishers Council, 1954.

Johnson, P. and Goodchilds, J. D. Comment: Pornography, sexuality, and social psychology. *Journal of Social Issues,* 1973, *29,* 231-238.

Johnson, W. T., Kupperstein, L., and Peters, J. Sex offenders' experience with erotica. *Technical reports of the Commission on Obscenity and Pornography.* Vol. 7. Washington, D.C.: U.S. Government Printing Office, 1970.

Kammann, R. Verbal complexity and preferences in poetry. *Journal of Verbal Learning and Verbal Behavior,* 1966, *5,* 536-540.

Kant, H. S. and Goldstein, M. J. Pornography. *Psychology Today*, 1970, *4*, 58-61.

Kimmel, E. A. Can children's books change children's values? *Educational Leadership*, 1970, *28*, 209-211, 213-214.

Kimoto, C. K. *The effects of a juvenile literature based program on majority group attitudes toward black Americans.* Ph.D. Dissertation, Washington State University, 1974.

Kingston, A. J. and White, W. F. The relationship of readers' self-concepts and personality components to semantic meanings perceived in the protagonist of a reading selection. *Reading Research Quarterly*, 1967, *2*, 107-116.

Kupperstein, L. and Wilson, W. C. Erotica and antisocial behavior: An analysis of selected social indicator statistics. *Technical reports of the Commission on Obscenity and Pornography.* Vol. 7. Washington, D.C.: U.S. Government Printing Office, 1970.

Kutschinsky, B. The effect of pornography—a pilot experiment on perception, behavior, and attitudes. In Studies on Pornography and Sex Crimes in Denmark. *New Science Social Monographs*, 1970, *E5*, 55-98.

Kvaraceus, W. C. Can reading affect delinquency? *American Library Association Bulletin*, 1965, *59* (6), 516-522.

Lancaster, J. *An investigation of the effect of books with black characters on the racial preferences of white children.* Ed.D. Dissertation, Boston University, 1971.

Lewis, I. R. *Effects of reading and discussion of stories on certain values.* Ph.D. Dissertation, University of California, 1967.

Lodge, H. C. *The influence of the study of biography on the moral ideology of the adolescent at the eighth-grade level.* Ph.D. Dissertation, University of California, 1953.

McCaul, R. L. The effect of attitudes upon reading interpretation. *Journal of Educational Research*, 1944, *37*, 451-457.

Mann, J., Sidman, J., and Starr, S. Effects of erotic films on sexual behaviors of married couples. *Technical reports of the Commission on Obscenity and Pornography.* Vol. 8. Washington, D.C.: U.S. Government Printing Office, 1970.

Mattera, G. *Bibliotherapy in a sixth grade.* Ph.D. Dissertation, Pennsylvania State University, 1961.

Meckel, H. *An exploratory study of the responses of adolescent pupils to situations in a novel.* Ph.D. Dissertation, University of Chicago, 1946.

Milgrim, S. A. *A comparison of the effects of classics and contemporary literary works on high school students' declared attitudes toward certain moral values.* Ph.D. Dissertation, New York University, 1967.

Monson, D. and Peltola, B. *A bibliography of research in children's literature.* Newark, Del.: International Reading Association, 1976.

Mosher, D. L. Psychological reactions to pornographic films. *Technical reports of the Commission on Obscenity and Pornography.* Vol. 8. Washington, D.C.: U.S. Government Printing Office, 1970.

Mosher, D. L. and Greenberg, I. Females' affective responses to reading erotic literature. *Journal of Consulting and Clinical Psychology*, 1969, *33*, 472-477.

Mosher, D. L. and Katz, H. Pornographic films, male verbal aggression against women, and guilt. Unpublished manuscript. *Commission on Obscenity and Pornography* files, 1970.

National Assessment of Educational Progress. *Literature: Responding to Literature*. Denver: Education Commission of the States, 1973.

Nelson, G. *A study of adolescent preferences for protagonists and stories as related to the qualities of independence and sex of protagonist*. M.A. Thesis, University of Minnesota, 1975.

Petrosky, A. *Individual and group responses of fourteen and fifteen year olds to short stories, novels, poems, and the thematic apperception test: Case studies based on Piagetian genetic epistimology and Freudian psychoanalytic ego psychology*. Ph.D. Dissertation, State University of New York at Buffalo, 1975.

Pollock, J. C. *A study of responses to short stories by selected groups of ninth graders, eleventh graders, and college freshmen*. Ph.D. Dissertation, University of Colorado, 1972.

Ponder, V. *An investigation of the effects of bibliotherapy and teachers' self-other acceptance on pupils' self acceptance and reading achievement scores*. Ph.D. Dissertation, University of Southern Mississippi, 1968.

Propper, M. M. Exposure to sexually oriented materials among young male prison offenders. *Technical reports of the Commission on Obscenity and Pornography*. Vol. 9. Washington, D.C.: U.S. Government Printing Office, 1970.

Purves, A. C. *Literature education in ten countries, international studies in education II*. Stockholm and New York: Almquist and Wiksell and The Halsted Press, 1973.

Purves, A. C. and Beach, R. *Literature and the reader: Research in response to literature, reading interests, and the teaching of literature*. Urbana, Ill.: National Council of Teachers of English, 1972.

Reed, J. P. and Reed, R. S. P.R.U.D.E.S. (Pornography Research Using Direct Erotic Stimuli). *Journal of Sex Research*, 1972, *8*, 237-246.

Report of the Commission on Obscenity and Pornography. New York: Bantam Books, 1970.

Rogers, J. On the metaphysichology of poetic language: Model ambiguity. *Journal of Psychoanalysis*, 1973, *54*, 61-74.

Schill, T., Evans, R., Monroe, S., and Drain, D. Effects of approval or disapproval on reading behavior of high- and low-guilt subjects. *Journal of Counseling and Clinical Psychology*, 1975, *43*, 104.

Schiller, P. The effects of mass media on the sexual behavior of adolescent females. *Technical reports of the Commission on Obscenity and Pornography*. Vol. 1. Washington, D.C.: U.S. Government Printing Office, 1970.

Shirley, F. L. The influence of reading on concepts, attitude, and behavior. *Journal of Reading*, 1969, *13*, 369-375.

Smith, J. R. An analytical study of the factors involved in learning to appreciate literature. *Indiana University School Education Bulletin*, 1933, *10*, 47-69.

Snapper, J. *A study of high school juniors' reactions to and use of literary assumptions.* Ph.D. Dissertation, University of California at Berkeley, 1958.

Somers, A. *Responses of advanced and average readers in grades seven, nine, and eleven to two dissimilar short stories.* Ph.D. Dissertation, The Florida State University, 1972.

Squire, J. R. *The responses of adolescents while reading four short stories.* Urbana, Ill.: National Council of Teachers of English, 1964.

Stout, D. A. *The responses of college freshmen to characters in four short stories.* Ph.D. Dissertation, University of California at Berkeley, 1964.

Tauran, R. H. *The influences of reading on the attitudes of third graders toward Eskimos.* Ph.D. Dissertation, University of Maryland, 1967.

Thayer, L. O. and Pronko, N. H. Some psychological factors in the reading of fiction. *Journal of Genetic Psychology,* 1958, *93,* 113-117.

Thayer, L. O. and Pronko, N. H. Factors affecting conceptual perception in reading. *Journal of Genetic Psychology,* 1959, *61,* 51-59.

Thompson, S. J. *Responses of students in grades 7-12 to selected short stories and the relationship between these responses and certain reader characteristics.* Ph.D. Dissertation, Syracuse University, 1973.

Wagener, R. E. H. *An experimental study of the effects of a program of oral reading of children's literature about Negroes on the self-concept of Negro fourth-grade children.* Ed.D. Dissertation, The University of Tennessee, 1971.

Walker, C. E. Erotic stimuli and the aggressive sexual offender. *Technical reports of the Commission on Obscenity and Pornography.* Vol. 7. Washington, D.C.: U.S. Government Printing Office, 1970.

Wallace, D. H. Obscenity and contemporary community standards: A survey. *Journal of Social Issues,* 1973, *29,* 52-84.

Weingarten, S. Developmental values in voluntary reading. *The School Review,* 1954, *62,* 222-230.

Wertham, F. *Seduction of the innocent.* New York: Holt, Rinehart, and Winston, 1953.

Wilson, W. C. and Jacobs, S. Survey of sex educators and counselors. *Technical reports of the Commission on Obscenity and Pornography.* Vol. 10. Washington, D.C.: U.S. Government Printing Office, 1970.

Young, E. C. The effect of intensive reading on attitude change. *French Review,* 1963, *36,* 629-632.

Zellinger, D. A., Fromkin, H. L., Speller, D. E., and Kohn, C. A. A commodity theory analysis of the effects of age restrictions upon pornographic materials. *Journal of Applied Psychology,* 1975, *60,* 94-99.

Zucaro, B. J. *The use of bibliotherapy among sixth graders to affect attitude change toward American Negroes.* Ed.D. Dissertation, Temple University, 1972.

Zurcher, L. A., Kirkpatrick, R. G., Cushing, R. G., and Bowen, C. K. Ad Hoc antipornography organizations and their active members: A research survey. *Journal of Social Issues,* 1973, *29,* 220-230.

III What to Do

The third section of this book is probably the most important. It concerns what teachers seem to want to know most about. It begins with Donelson's very practical article that still contains many useful suggestions for dealing with censorship, though it was written in 1974. Suhor comments on the capriciousness of censors and then describes a districtwide censorship problem that became statewide and explains how it was dealt with. He also offers some suggestions about how to change the climate by adopting the activist state of mind. Berkley describes one very good way of communicating with parents—teach them the controversial books in adult education classes at night. Shugert advises that teachers prepare written, detailed policies and rationales. She outlines how to handle a complaint and advises intelligent anticipation of possible problem areas. Her article provides suggestions for writing rationales and several examples and formats. Bartlett tells how a state department of education (Iowa) developed a model policy and rules for selection of instructional materials; he outlines the essentials of the model. In her second contribution, Shugert writes about people and organizations that may prove helpful to those trying to prevent censorship before it happens and also to those actually involved in cases. Finally, the bibliography provides a very select list of books, procedures and policies, entire issues of journals, articles, pamphlets, and portions of books for further amplification of the material in *Dealing with Censorship*.

13 Censorship in the 1970s: Some Ways to Handle It When It Comes (And It Will)

Kenneth L. Donelson
Arizona State University

During the past couple of years, I have witnessed censorship attacks on many books, films, and periodicals—everything from the "filth" of *Silas Marner* to the "controversial matter" of *I'm Really Dragged But Nothing Gets Me Down* to the "anti-Christianity" of *Slaughterhouse-Five,* from the "subversive elements" of some early Charlie Chaplin short films to the "un-Americanism" of *High Noon* to the "communist sympathies" of "Why Man Creates," from the "pornography" of the *National Geographic* to the "leftist propaganda" of *Scholastic Magazine* to the "right-wing trash" of the *National Observer.* Such attacks continue today, and to many English teachers and librarians they seem not merely to continue but to increase in number and fervor.

I believe we can expect to see even greater pressures for censorship exerted in the remainder of the 1970s. School taxes are rising, students "can't spell the way they used to," and innovative programs often irritate parents who do not understand why the programs were introduced in the first place. That magically nebulous word, "accountability," has caught the fancy of a public all too eager to find fault with an educational system whose products, the students, do not always happily accept the "traditional values" or "good old-fashioned American goals" of their parents. For years, Americans have maintained a somewhat uncomfortably ambivalent feeling about schools, an almost superstitious reverence that somehow education is good for everyone mixed with a fear of intellectualism and a dread of teachers. I suppose it comes out as a kind of "education is good *if* you don't take it and its consequences seriously" syndrome. This fear of education and the inquiring mind and the search for truth is most obviously manifested for English teachers and librarians in attacks on books that are the most likely to relate to kids' lives and their world, today and tomorrow.

The 1970s will likely see little diminution of student enthusiasm for reading real books about their very real world or parental questioning of this student enthusiasm. Indeed, an article in the November 1972 *Saturday Review of the Arts* (Patrick Merla's "'What Is Real?' Asked the Rabbit One Day," pp. 43-50) made clear that as adults head more and more toward fantasy, literature written specifically for adolescents and children heads more and more toward reality and the many unpleasant faces of our world.

Okay then. If censorship in the 1970s is likely to continue and possibly increase, what can English teachers and librarians do to prepare to meet the censor? What can they do when the censor actually comes to the school door? I would like to propose six assorted things they might try.

First, each English department should develop its own statement of rationales for teaching literature. Whatever its title, it ought to include realistic goals based on the needs and interests of specific students in a particular school. Teachers might consider Alan C. Purves's *How Porcupines Make Love: Notes on a Response-Centered Curriculum* (Lexington, Mass.: Xerox College Publishing, 1972) with its four objectives for a student response-centered literature curriculum.

> An individual will feel secure in his response to a poem and not be dependent on someone else's response. An individual will trust himself.
>
> An individual will know why he responds the way he does to a poem—what in him causes that response and what in the poem causes that response. He will get to know himself.
>
> An individual will respect the responses of others as being as valid for them as his is for him. He will recognize his differences from other people.
>
> An individual will recognize that there are common elements in people's responses. He will recognize his similarity with other people (p. 31).

English teachers intrigued with the student response-centered literature program who are concerned that the English teacher will have little work to do should take notice of the teacher's responsibilities as itemized by Purves.

> The teacher must provide each student with as many different works as possible.
>
> The teacher must encourage each student to respond as fully as he is able.
>
> The teacher must encourage the student to understand why he responds as he does.

> The teacher must encourage the student to respond to as many works as possible.
> The teacher must encourage the student to tolerate responses that differ from his.
> The teacher must encourage students to explore their areas of agreement and disagreement (p. 37).

I would hope that any statement about literature would present a number of convincing reasons in support of literary study: that literature allows young people to see themselves and their problems perhaps a little more objectively; that literature provides vicarious experiences beyond the possibilities of any one person's life; that literature frees students to meet other peoples in other places and other times, to see similarities and differences between people, and to meet a multitude of human moral and physical dilemmas; that literature exposes young people to value systems and ideas and practices different from their own, which can lead to an assessment of both the student's values and those of other people; that literature allows students to discover the world as it was and as it is, a world neither all good nor all evil, but a world all human; and above all, that literature provides deep enjoyment and satisfaction.

Second, each English department should establish a committee which will recommend books for possible use by the department. The purpose of this committee is to bring new titles and little-known or little-used older titles to the attention of their peers. I would think it helpful if a part of every departmental meeting were given over to discussions of various titles. Additionally, any discussion of books should take up the problems involved in using them with a specific class, problems of style or plot structure or censorship or student interest.

Third, each English department should work hard to win community support for academic freedom and to win that support before censorship strikes. Any community has former English teachers, librarians, and readers who may feel as strongly about censorship as the English department, but English teachers too rarely make any attempt to win friends before they need them desperately. One such group was formed shortly after a censorship episode in the Phoenix area. Named "Freedom for Readers," the group has given considerable moral support to teachers who are now aware that they do have friends outside the teaching profession who will come to their aid if censorship strikes. Perhaps similar groups can be developed in other cities.

Fourth, each English department should try to communicate to the public what is going on in English classrooms and why it is going on. Parents *do* have a right, even a duty, to know what English teachers are doing. Parents and other citizens will inevitably hear something about English teaching, but what they will hear is likely to be inexact or inaccurate. In any case, parents and citizens are likely to hear only *what* goes on, not why. And many people will be horrified to learn that their children, or any children, are reading *Soul on Ice* or *The Scarlet Letter* or *The Catcher in the Rye* or any of a number of books that have been censored by someone, someplace, sometime, for some reason. English teachers should not delude themselves into believing that they can teach any book and keep everything quiet. Surely an English department can do better than simply maintaining silence. Perhaps a discussion of "controversial" or "contemporary" literature could take place during Education Week or at some school function. Even better, an English department can set up a series of evening programs devoted to explaining why certain books are taught. In fact, going one step further, the English department might *teach* one of the "suspect" books to a group of adults, showing them how various problems could be handled in a classroom for high school students.

Fifth, each English department should establish and implement a formal policy to handle attempted censorship. Without *some* policy and form, the department is open to criticism and its members are likely to be vulnerable to censorship from any source. Obviously, a censor should be treated politely and fairly, and his objection considered carefully by a committee (presumably composed of at least the teacher in question, the English department chair, and the principal). Ultimately, a meeting should be arranged with the questioning citizen and the committee, and the results of that meeting should be forwarded to the superintendent and the school board, the legally constituted agency which must approve the decision. Because the school board must support teachers if the formal policy is to have any possibility of success, the English department should work closely with the board in devising the form and the policy in the first place. Any policy about censorship is only as good as the school board backing it. It may be true that formal policy statements about censorship have not always saved books or teachers, but any school without a policy statement is even more vulnerable. A school which has a statement and still gets clobbered is at least trying to fight censorship. That's a lot better than a school which doesn't even make a pretense of fighting.

Sixth, each English department should expect its members to prepare rationales for any book to be taught in any class. English teachers should be expected to defend their choices of books on grounds other than simple intuition or the word of some literary or pedagogical critic. In other words, English teachers should approach their choices as though they were reading them for the first time and should attempt to discover the problems involved in teaching the books or in interesting the students. While there are many things that could go into a rationale for a book, I believe that such a rationale should include answers to at least five questions: (1) Why would a teacher consider using this book with a specific class? (2) What particular objectives, literary or psychological or pedagogical, does the teacher have in mind in using this book? (3) How will the book be used to meet those objectives? (4) What problems of style, tone, or theme or possible grounds for censorship exist in the book and how will the teacher plan to meet those problems? (5) Assuming that the objectives are met, how will the students of this specific class be different because of their reading of this book?

These rationales should be written for every work to be read in common. That includes modern books and standard classics—it might be salutary for teachers to be forced to write rationales for *Macbeth* or *Great Expectations* or *Our Town* to find out just *why* teachers are using those works. These rationales should be presented both orally and in written form to the English department for approval, and they should be in the departmental files and openly available to the public. I strongly favor all demonstrations of English teacher competence in writing and speaking, thus encouraging English teachers to write and comment on rationales should be beneficial to the department and to its students.

It is not true that kids are too insensitive, stupid or unresponsive to reach out and feel and hear and see the world. But it is true that kids are often too sensitive and bright and responsive to reality to waste their time on the world explored or experienced in some English classrooms. Literature worth the students' time tells the truth as one writer sees it. Literature worth the name does not lie. As Yevtushenko wrote in his poem, "Lies," the young are not fooled by adult reticence about the hard facts of life. Our only acceptable approach to them must be to refuse to gloss over the wrong we know exists, or else

> it will repeat itself, increase,
> and afterwards our pupils
> will not forgive in us what we forgave.

If we are to have any chance as English teachers to tell the truth and to let our students explore the many visions of truth available in literature, we have to fight the censor. To fight the censor with any hope of success, we must prepare carefully before censorship strikes, not in the panic of battle. If we do not prepare in advance, or if we do not care enough to prepare, we will lose, and we will wind up losing everything, our books and our students and our freedom. And we will be forced to tell lies to the young. Perhaps they won't believe those lies, but the prospect that they might is a frightening possibility that ought to be reason enough for any English teacher to prepare to face the censor when he comes . . . and he will.

14 Basic Training and Combat Duty—Preventive and Reactive Action

Charles Suhor
National Council of Teachers of English

The most frustrating thing about censors is that you don't know for sure when they're going to attack, or why. One teacher will do a mini-course on "The Literature of Protest from Aristophanes to Jerry Rubin" without getting so much as a phone call from a curious parent, while another will be slapped down for putting *The Grapes of Wrath* on an outside reading list. A principal who rarely shows interest in English curriculum will, on hearing that something called "orgy porgy" is in *Brave New World,* suddenly start to review English teachers' booklists. A school district will move along for years with a smooth textbook and library selection process, then will unexplainedly become an open field for book-burners—as in Kanawha County, where the conflagration began with a single school board member's question about a book on dialectology.

Some censors, like the Gablers in Texas, The Heritage Foundation, the Home Circle, and Save Our Children, are organized. Sometimes they even announce their plans in advance. But most are snipers who turn up randomly and learn to shoot down books, all too effectively, as they go along.

Equally elusive is the placement of responsibility for fighting censorship in school districts that lack a well-articulated policy for dealing with complaints. A typical sequence: a teacher who is challenged, feeling isolated, goes to the department head; the department head, lacking clout, goes to the principal; the principal, not knowing literature, calls the central office; the central office, being frightened by such things, capitulates. All are intimidated, moreover, by the murky thing called "climate"—presently a stormy and mistrustful one in which the public suspects that we are telling kids that anything goes and trivializing the traditional curriculum of classical literature.

In this article I will first describe a district- and state-wide censorship problem that arose in Louisiana. The action taken there might provide one model for cooperative effort in dealing with similar problems elsewhere. Then I'll move from the concrete to the quixotic, describing ways of changing the broader climate in which specific problems arise. (It's arrogant, I realize, to claim that we can change the climate. But I've borrowed a metaphor or two to help us along. And besides, the opposite assumption—that we *can't* affect climate—absolves us from trying and is therefore absolutely self-proving.)

The Louisiana Story: A Censorship Soap Opera

There is a poem by Lisel Mueller that makes a case for soap operas as the ultimate in realism. Things really do happen, the poet says, with multiple levels of intrigue, improbable coincidences, and sudden reversals of fortune. A series of censorship-related incidents in Louisiana between 1974 and 1976 bears out the soap opera theory. The elements were all there, even to the extent that there was no clear-cut resolution to the situation, happy or unhappy, only an ambiguous merging of events into the uncertain future.

It all began in fall of 1974 with the big F, which appeared in a supplementary text in a mini-course called "News Media" at a high school in East Baton Rouge Parish. The text included an actual newspaper story that described a sign being held by a yippie at the 1968 Democratic convention. The sign said, "Fuck the cops."

A single student, thumbing through the unassigned materials, noticed the word and brought the book home to her parents. They complained to the principal, who reportedly pulled the texts from the room immediately and—in what must have been the public relations blunder of the year—called a television station to complain about dirty books in the school system. The TV coverage was splashy and inflammatory. By reporting the incident as a potential threat to the city's schoolchildren, the station turned a pesky building-level squabble into a social and moral issue in the community. Suddenly, magically, the book was news. Not only that book, but *all* of the books in the district's suspiciously "open" program of electives in English.

It was a classic instance of a media-created event. Such events are notoriously self-perpetuating. The newspapers had to run follow-up stories, reportorially, after the TV exposure aroused public interest. Naturally, letters to the editors followed and, of course, a citizens' group was formed "to get to the bottom of this thing."

The East Baton Rouge School Board, divided within itself, soon found its meetings crowded with irate citizens who had discovered that students were actually reading filth and trash written by the likes of Langston Hughes, James Baldwin, and Eldridge Cleaver. (Yes, the conflict became tinged with racial hostility.) Helen Brown, the school system's forward-looking supervisor of English, was heroically—and at first, almost single-handedly—defending the English program in this highly antagonistic climate. As the tension grew, the school system got supportive statements from the LSU and Southern University English departments, the state library association, the daily newspaper, the YWCA, and the American Library Association's Office of Intellectual Freedom.

The bottom line was the legal question, though, and a melodramatic touch arose here. Helen Brown's brother, Ossie Brown, was the district attorney, and she was faced with the possibility of being placed under injunction and prosecuted by him. As a matter of fact, she and the school superintendent did testify before the grand jury, but the jury refused to take action after conducting its investigation.

The upshot of the whole ordeal was that the English elective program held fast against the protesters. A teacher-community committee that had been set up to handle complaints even voted to retain the original media text, yippies and all, but the superintendent overruled them and pulled the book during the white heat of public debate. But the greatest damage was intangible, according to Helen Brown: the teachers were burned, and their future choice of materials would surely be affected by the fear of a reprisal from radical individuals and pressure groups in the community.

But in true soap opera style, the denouement was simply an interlude leading to the next episode. A shakeup over textbooks in a state capital is certain to have far-reaching effects on education throughout the state. State textbook adoptions in several areas were on the horizon when the furor over materials in Baton Rouge arose. A subsequent social studies adoption came under sharp criticism as being "anti-American." The outlook for English adoptions was extremely grim as rumors grew of a highly limited adoption of basal texts, with even stricter limitations on supplementary materials.

At this point a few key leaders from the State Department of Education and the Louisiana Council of Teachers of English (LCTE) got together for action that was both reactive and preventive—reactive in terms of the East Baton Rouge incident but preventive in relation to forthcoming textbook adoptions and future instances of censorship. Mari Ann Doherty, then state supervisor of English and language arts, called together a committee of twelve teachers, supervisors, administrators, and parents to develop a statement on the teaching of English. I was on the committee representing New Orleans Public Schools, where I was English supervisor.

The statement was conceived as a broad document that would cover, in nontechnical language, numerous topics—among them censorship, dialects, textbook adoption, elective programs, and testing. The statement would be submitted for approval by the LCTE and the powerful policy-making Board of Elementary and Secondary Education (BESE), as well as local school boards. The committee met as a group in April and June, corresponding on successive drafts of the statement until it was completed and ready for submission to LCTE and BESE.

Getting the LCTE approval posed no problems, but a careful strategy was set for seeking the approval of the politically sensitive BESE. Since our committee was from various parts of the state, responsibility for contacting members of BESE was parceled out. Personal visits, telephone calls, and correspondence prepared BESE members for the statement, which was published in the *Louisiana English Journal* in the summer of 1975 and sent to each board member.

The statement was placed on the BESE agenda, and our entire committee went to Baton Rouge for the meeting. Parts of the statement that were related to the censorship are reprinted below.

> *Censorship.* The student's parents have the primary right to determine what the student should or should not read in the school. However, the right to determine one's own children's reading does not extend to the right to dictate what other people's children should read. Therefore, students whose parents find a particular work in an English program objectionable should be permitted to read another work of comparable literary value, studying that work on a small-group or individual basis. Those students whose parents have no objection to the work in question should not be prohibited from reading the work on the basis of other parents' disapproval.
>
> The English teacher's responsibility in guiding the student's reading lies in selection of materials that are appropriate to the student's ability level, interests, and level of maturity. As trained educators and specialists in literature, English teachers must balance such factors as literary quality, student's interests and needs, and community mores in selection of materials. English teachers

must be prepared to interpret the rationale for reading assignments and other aspects of the English program to students, parents, and the community so that all will understand that the program is carefully designed.

The complexity of the English teacher's task in applying expertise in the various areas of English—and especially in the selection of literary materials—must be recognized by individuals, community groups, and state and local school officials. Unreasonable charges of obscenity or attempts to impose the values of a particular person or group upon an entire school district or system are inconsistent with the school's commitment to the perpetuation of democratic principles and institutions.

Attempts to impose restrictions on English programs should be met by well-established procedures to pinpoint the nature of the objection. Complaint forms like the one in the NCTE booklet "The Students' Right to Read" should be utilized to determine whether the objections raised are responsible critical judgments or ill-considered attacks on valid instructional materials. Impartial, broadly-based committees should be formed for the purpose of making recommendations for action on complaints about materials. Policies should be generated by school administrations and boards of education to assure that materials are not excluded on the whim of an individual or community pressure groups. In endorsement of the program of action as developed by the National Council of Teachers of English, we agree that a vigorous campaign should be undertaken to establish a community atmosphere in which local citizens may be enlisted to support the freedom to read.

Textbook Adoption. Recognizing that elective English programs have been generated in many parishes, we believe that an abundance and variety of English texts and supplementary materials should be adopted at the state level. Additionally, a percentage of state textbook funds should be allotted for purchase of books not included on the state textbook list but necessary for implementation of new programs. Further, textbook selection committees at the state and local levels should consist predominantly of highly qualified English teachers who are aware of current developments in the profession.

Elective English Programs. A total elective program should be well balanced. It should include such offerings as courses centered on themes, genres, skills, authors, and literary periods. Skills should be interwoven in every course, whatever the specific course titles. Parents and students should have adequate information about the nature of the courses, and students should receive counseling in order to make selections to meet their needs and interests.

BESE's fumbling inaction at the meeting was sadly anticlimactic. Most BESE members did not seem to remember having read the document at all. One had read the *Louisiana English Journal* from cover to cover, thinking that official endorsement of the entire journal was being sought. Those who had no sense of the possible impact of their approval of the document seemed to want to move on to other items on the crowded agenda. Those who had an idea of the significance of BESE's approval of open textbook adoptions and elective programs were extremely uneasy. Our known friends in BESE put in a few kind words but were not nearly as aggressive or agreeable as they had been in our face-to-face conferences. Finally BESE played it safe by referring the statement for study by a subcommittee, where it has languished ever since.

Probably, those of us who had worked in large city administrations should have realized that BESE would not deal sympathetically with the issues we had defined so sharply. There are too many resources for evasion within the political process for our naive efforts to have had the immediate impact that we envisioned. Still, BESE had heard the buzz of our gadfly committee. We became, in the time and space in which we acted, a palpable element in BESE's climate.

And the statement did have several victories. Seven or eight local school districts did adopt it as policy. In both the state textbook adoptions and the large Orleans Parish adoption, the statement was plugged directly into the work of textbook selection committees.

Wrapping up the subplot of textbook adoption: I wrote an official letter from New Orleans Public Schools to the State Superintendent of Education stating that our elective programs required a variety of materials and could not be served by traditional anthologies alone. Virginia Redd, then chair of the NCTE/SLATE Committee for Social and Political Concerns, wrote a letter at my request to the state superintendent stating that contemporary English programs require a wide selection of materials. Mari Ann Doherty continued to press for a broad textbook adoption within the State Department of Education, and she distributed the statement to the members of the English textbook selection committee.

Although the adoption was tense, few formal restrictions were put on the committee. An after-image of the censorial mood that had dominated in Baton Rouge remained, but the bad memories were counterbalanced by the action taken by the State Department of Education and LCTE. The result was an imperfect adoption (books with profanities beyond "damn" or "hell" didn't have a chance), but it was nonetheless the most expansive English adoption in the history of the state. Hundreds of titles were included, as well as a long list of audiovisual materials. Many districts were able to implement their elective program with books on the state list—which is to say, with books paid for by state-provided funds.

Changing the Climate: Some Practical Ideas and Helpful Metaphors

The Louisiana Statement was a result of action by two groups with something that might be called a power base—the LCTE, and key leaders within the State Department of Education. The positive effects of the statement on both the general teaching climate in Louisiana and the specific work of the textbook selection committee can be reasonably surmised, but not proven. In darker moments I entertain the idea that the censorship wave would have peaked by the time of the English textbook adoption, regardless of our organized efforts at turning back the censors; that our work was an empty calisthenic which, at best, gave us mutual support in a time of general uneasiness. I am haunted by the phrase applied so unkindly to G. K. Chesterton: "He mistook his own borborygmus for the rumblings of the universe."

I realize that what I'm about to describe—practical methods for individual action in combating censorship—is even more dubious than actions taken by organized groups. Although activists are a hearty group, even the most optimistic are awed by the difficulty of making a dent in the public consciousness. Feelings of futility are always lurking, despite our best efforts.

Yet individual action is absolutely necessary, because statements and pressures from organized groups like professional organizations, labor unions, and coalitions within the establishment appear contrived, self-serving, and hollow unless they are supported by innumerable statements of belief from the general public—statements circulated informally at cocktail parties and PTA meetings and formally through public opinion vehicles provided by local and national media. The tone of life in a society will be set, after all, by grassroots sentiment and the accumulated action of innumerable individuals.

The trick, then, is to psyche oneself up to the lonesome task of individual action. The most heartening view of the efficacy of individual effort that I've yet seen came from an unlikely source—a little book called *The Lives of a Cell* by Lewis Thomas, M.D., a scientist. Thomas's metaphors give us a way of seeing that every particle of action has weight in the hulking dialectic that we call the public opinion. Although Thomas was writing in *The Lives of a Cell* about the exchange of minute data among scientific scholars, the spirit of his metaphors is not violated by applying them to general interchange of ideas within a society, which I've done below.

> If you could label, by some equivalent of radioactive isotopes, all the bits of human thought that are constantly adrift, like plankton, all around us, it might be possible to discern some sort of systematic order in the process, but, as it is, it seems almost entirely random. . . . [It looks like] a collective derangement of minds in total disorder, with bits of information being scattered about, torn to shreds, disintegrated, deconstituted, engulfed, in a kind of activity that seems as random and agitated as that of bees in a disturbed part of the hive. . . .
>
> There has to be something wrong with this view. It is hard to see how we could be in possession of an organ so complex and intricate and, as it occasionally reveals itself, so powerful, and be using it on such a scale just for the production of a kind of background noise. Somewhere, obscured by the snatches of conversation, pages of old letters, bits of books and magazines, . . . and the disorder of radio and television, there ought to be more intelligible signals. . . . There may be some laws about this kind of communication, mandating a critical density and mass before it can function with efficiency. . . .
>
> [Interchange of ideas] . . . is instinctive behavior, in my view, and I do not understand how it works. It cannot be pre-arranged in any precise way; the minds cannot be lined up in tidy rows and given directions from printed sheets. You cannot get it done by instructing each mind to make this or that piece, for central committees to fit with the pieces made by the other instructed minds. It does not work this way.
>
> It sometimes looks like a lonely activity, but it is as much the opposite of lonely as human behavior can be. There is nothing so social, so communal, so interdependent. . . .

Thomas cites J. M. Ziman's comment on individual contributions to the universe of scholarly research, noting that a single insight doesn't pretend to be

> more than another little piece in a larger jigsaw—not significant in itself but as an element in a grander scheme. This technique, of soliciting many modest contributions to the store of human knowledge, has been the secret of Western science since the seventeenth century, for it achieves a corporate, collective power that is far greater than one individual can exert.

Far from being discouraged by the uncertainty of the individual's effect in such a muddled interchange, Thomas says, "What we need is more crowding, more unrestrained and obsessive communication, more open channels, even more noise, and a bit more luck."

Agitating Locally

One implication of Thomas's ideas is that it wouldn't hurt to *think local*. You simply have a better chance of being heard and of making a difference when you make some noise in your own community. As an English teacher, you are a credible source of ideas about censorship. Moreover, your background as a language specialist puts you in a favored position for writing on such topics.

The local press. In addition to the daily newspapers' letters-to-the-editor columns, a perennial resource for expressing your opinion, consider the following: *weekly papers, city magazines, op ed pages.* Many cities have weekly newspapers of different kinds—neighborhood or sectional newspapers, citywide weeklies, even weekly TV listings that include a couple of feature articles. Good writers are not that plentiful, and editors frequently welcome informed opinions on hot issues. City magazines exist in many large cities, and they too thrive on readable articles on topical subjects. The op ed page is also a spot in which many dailies will print, sporadically or regularly, well-stated opinions by the local citizenry. You have a better chance than most people at moving beyond the letters column and into short articles that take a stand on issues like censorship.

Call-in talk shows. One of the most democratic and widespread forums of public opinion is the radio call-in show. Opinions range from whacky to brilliantly argued, and that's the fun of it. Well-stated opinions on censorship are badly needed on these programs. Have you ever noticed that there is seldom a shortage of comments from conservatives, who make sweeping statements about everything from arithmetic to pornographic textbooks? Talk shows have a wide audience, yet a handful of callers presenting a censorial view often give the impression that the general public is in favor of rigid, highly controlled school programs. Here is a mass media resource that virtually anyone can use; yet we often seem satisfied to react to it with amusement or contempt, in effect leaving the opinion making to lunatic fringe.

TV editorials. Many TV stations now have editorials as part of the newscast, and they usually allow rebuttal time to appropriate respondents. In issues related to censorship, you are an appropriate respondent. If you are not cold-blooded enough to go before the cameras, contact your NCTE affiliate leaders and urge them to make replies to TV editorials inimical to English teachers' interests and to offer their services as guests on radio and TV call-in shows.

Community group programs. Every city has a variety of community groups—vital, active ones and purely social, inactive ones. Almost all have spots on the agenda that a program chair would like to fill with interesting speakers. Find out who the groups are, and become a speaker. Often, the most lethargic tea-and-finger-cookies group will turn out to include some of the most influential people in the community. Here, then, is a ready-made audience that often lacks a perspective on important social issues. Have at them.

Public officials. Do what your ninth-grade civics textbooks told you to do—write to your representatives in Congress. Minimally, politicians will tally their mail. Nowadays most Representatives and Senators answer individual letters, usually through an aide. And don't forget local public officials like the mayor, police chief, and others who frequently make comments that add fuel to the censor's fire. Or sometimes, they make helpful statements that merit your support.

Other professional organizations. Many professional organizations can be enlisted in the fight against censorship—the AFT, for example, or the NEA. Your activity within your local and state associations is another potential source of effective action.

Content—and Style

Make use of the best resources offered by NCTE and others in framing your arguments. As a popularizer, you shouldn't get too bibliographic, but you should make use of the good materials on hand. The NCTE/SLATE Starter Sheets are a good model for dealing with controversial issues in a succinct, understandable manner. Make photocopies of persuasive materials and send them to appropriate individuals, calling pertinent passages to their attention. Leave copies of relevant items from newspapers, NCTE materials, etc., in the teachers' lounge. In tipping public opinion towards a freer educational system, we need the weight of evidence as well as the force of conviction.

Then there's the matter of style. Bear in mind that no matter how cautiously you proceed, your opinion is going to be pigeon-holed by some as the rantings of a crazed radical. There is no way of controlling the reactions of those who have a compulsion to dismiss their adversaries with labels, but you can make headway with open-minded people who respond to congeniality and sweet reason. What I'm saying is that the abrasive, confrontational style of the sixties is probably ineffective today. Present times seem to call for stating your position forcefully, and pleasantly placing the opposition on the defensive.

Finally, there is the matter of *thinking national.* You will notice that most letters to influential magazines like *Time* and *Newsweek* are not written by titled individuals but by POR's—plain, ordinary readers. I know of at least half a dozen scholars with three-color stationery who wrote four-page responses to *Esquire* when John Simon attacked CCCC's *Students' Right to Their Own Language.* Yet the magazine chose to publish an extremely sprightly, brief, and brilliant letter by an untitled person I had never heard of—and a good selection it was, too.

The Saber-Toothed Gadfly

Although the activist impulse is clearly within the humanistic tradition, it actually proceeds on a series of small acts of blind faith. For example, I am writing this chapter on the faith that somebody, somewhere, will read it and make use of the ideas in it. And any move that you make in the public arena to contribute to the vast, amorphous debate on censorship is based on the faith that you can make a difference in the American educational system and in people's lives. Like Lewis Thomas, you have apparently created some metaphor which enables you to say, "My contribution has meaning and purpose," even though you are unlikely to see any concrete results from your action. You are convinced in your own mind that randomness will not win out in the end, that your contributions gather to a critical mass with those of others, and the collective force of these arguments will ultimately have an effect.

My own metaphor for the activist state of mind is the image of a saber-toothed gadfly. It's less romantic than my youthful idea that I could change the world if only people would listen to reason, and it carries no guarantees that the gadfly will be heard or felt. But it beats inaction and despondency. It also beats metaphors like the ripple effect and one little candle, being more aggressive and introducing a tinge of self-irony. Self-irony is an absolute must for activists, both as a buffer against inevitable feelings of futility and as a way of putting our tedious evangelism into perspective. If there's a final comment appropriate to this chapter, let it be an activist's revised credo: we can save the world, and maybe ourselves, by faith, good works, and a sense of humor.

Selected Bibliography

"Censorship and the Teaching of English." *Arizona English Bulletin* 17 (February 1975).

"Ideology, Censorship, and Textbook Adoptions." Speakers: George Hillocks, Charles Suhor. NCTE convention cassettes, 1976.

Perry, Jesse. "Censorship of Instructional Materials." *SLATE Starter Sheet* 1 (September 1976).

"Position Statement on the Teaching of English." *Louisiana English Journal* 15 (1975): 9–13.

Suhor, Charles. "The Case for Pop Scholarship: A Polemic for Popularizers." *English Journal* 59 (January 1970): 116–18, 121.

Thomas, Lewis. *The Lives of a Cell: Notes of a Biology Watcher*. New York: Bantam Books, 1975.

15 Teach the Parents Well: An Anti-Censorship Experiment in Adult Education

June Berkley
Fort Frye High School, Beverly, Ohio

In the final scene of Harper Lee's *To Kill a Mockingbird,* Scout Finch tells her father about the town's "bad man," Boo Radley:

> An' they chased him 'n' never could catch him 'cause they didn't know what he looked like, an' Atticus, when they finally saw him, why he hadn't done any of those things . . . Atticus, he was real nice. . . ."

So, like Mr. Arthur (Boo) Radley, in *To Kill a Mockingbird,* are most of those "awful books"—when parents finally "catch" them and get to know them, they can seem "real nice."

At Fort Frye High School, Beverly, Ohio, on the fringes of Appalachia—not more than a two-hour's drive from Charleston, West Virginia—the English department and a nucleus of parents and citizens have opened up some refreshing and unusually hopeful avenues by sharing their concerns with the "Books Our Children Read." Those "awful books" don't seem so bad after all when parents finally give them a reading in the friendly atmosphere of a community education class. There, teachers who believe in the selections approach the books, as well as the parents, with optimism and goodwill. And the students are the real beneficiaries. There is support now—where once there was mistrust—for teaching high school students books that encourage a broad, realistic view of this world and its possibilities and that affirm for the students a sense of themselves as reasoning and reasonable people.

To recognize in this community effort a response to the specter of censorship, we must know a little of the background against which the teachers of "bad books" and suspicious citizens finally emerged as good neighbors. Fort Frye School District serves a diverse community spread across a sixty-five mile span of lush river-bottom truck farms, small rolling-hill farms, rich coal fields, and strip-mined hollows. The dozens of hillsides and hamlets are peopled by those who work in or manage the many industrial plants along the Muskingum and Ohio rivers. The high school serves some eight hundred students, grades seven through twelve under one administration. The English teachers collaborate and rotate their teaching in all six grades.

Here, too, people are caught up in the changing times. Occasionally they feel that the old forms of life are simply breaking up. Some of us—but not everyone—are ready to see in this moment our opportunity to build a new and better order. As teachers, this means we must worry a lot and work hard. But our experience with good literature tells us we cannot escape the eternal questions; we know there are no longer pat answers, if ever there were. We can offer our students only reflections in a time of uncertainties; yet, so often, their parents demand that the schools prescribe directions and answers, as parents have always preferred them, straight and simple: *by the books.* Instead, we give their sons and daughters books that provoke more questions, redefine human relationships, and cast doubt on the old order.

It is tempting to recall easier, simpler times, when conflict over books read in an English class was hardly conceivable. In those days we might have been ruffled, perhaps, by the smudges on a ninth grader's composition, but were quickly mollified by learning it had been written while the student tended a 4-H calf all night at the county fair. Even today, teachers sometimes have occasion to count their blessings and forget the difficulties. Once in a while a mother brings a giant tray of home baked food to the office and says, "It's for the teachers; they've been so good to work with all my children." But mostly we are on our guard, for so often in recent years our efforts have been called into question, the censor's ignorant demands having displaced the gestures of goodwill.

I am a veteran of twenty-one years in Fort Frye High School— and the survivor of an active movement on the part of a small, vocal group of parents to dismiss me during the late '60s. I had to defend my use of the *New York Times Student Weekly*—"definitely a communist publication," some parents avowed—to teach critical reading to seniors during the anti-Vietnam War demonstrations. I have seen apparently innocuous material set off a whole community against the schools. And I have participated in the recovery, slow and painstaking, still underway today.

Our English department includes a good cross-section of native, well-educated Appalachians (one is my former student, a survivor of both the *Student Weekly* conflict and Kent State) and well-traveled intellectuals who consider teaching their highest calling. We have devoted our efforts to bringing students, materials, and ourselves together in a way that will "create a higher sense of the possible." Ours is a program that considers the creation of lifelong readers a prime objective; consequently, our offerings are diverse, as we attempt to reach every student with something of interest and value.

We teachers are fully aware that ours is a broader view of man and society than that engendered—or tolerated—in the homes of many of the students we teach. To specify our belief in fostering a positive attitude toward a democratic, pluralistic society and global brotherhood, the teachers in our school even produced a written statement. We consider our idealism defensible. We have been tested by the censorship wave of the last decade.

Our Censorship Controversy

Our students have generally supported our inclusion of a broad spectrum of topics and treatments in our curriculum. To that extent we have considered them our allies in creating understanding and community support. Imagine the dismay of one class when they learned that their textbook, Scott Foresman's *Perspectives,* was under attack in Charleston. The sensitivity of these students to the growing trend of suspicion had already been sharpened by exercises designed to measure public opinion on such issues as draft evasion and the Vietnam War itself. I encouraged them to discuss the issues with their parents. This issue-oriented approach provoked no response from the community—no notes, no calls, no parents came in—but it did engage the students in meaningful interaction with their community.

Meanwhile, signs of the censorship mentality appeared in the local community. Via the television and the newspapers, the public was apprised of censorship controversy in other communities and learned of the threat of "dirty books" in the classroom. That phrase provoked the inevitable. In our case the rumors circulated around Robert Newton Peck's *A Day No Pigs Would Die,* that bittersweet story of a Shaker boy's coming of age in rural New England, a story that moved our ex-Marine principal to tears (the weeping was unusual; the familiarity with the book was not—he read nearly everything we taught).

Friendly parents warned us: telephones were hot with the news that "there was a dirty book in junior high English." By this time, a study was undertaken and the books recalled. The superintendent examined a copy; he had been duly notified of horrors on particular pages. These he had requested the young teacher to mark for his convenience. Wisely, the teacher sent the book unmarked, with the recommendation that a book should be read in its entirety if one is to judge passages fairly and in context.

And what could a good farm family find objectionable about Peck's glowing account of a Shaker boy's attempts to raise piglets and to help his economically (but not spiritually) deprived family? To come to appreciate and finally to mourn the death of a profoundly loving father? We theorized—half in outrage, half in despair—that it must be the realism of the sow's unsuccessful attempts to mate with a neighbor's boar. Or could it be the frank description of young Robert's desperate attempts to deliver twin calves and save his neighbor's prize cow? In that effort he had sacrificed his homemade trousers to fashion a makeshift rope, then run (sans underwear) through the woods to bear glad tidings home —and acquired in the process "prickers in his privates."

We were familiar with the methods advocated by the National Council of Teachers of English for dealing with parental complaints about printed material. We sent the proper NCTE form home, but the parent did not choose to respond. Instead, we soon learned that at a civic gathering of young mothers, one parent had issued the scandalized report that we were teaching a book about "M-A-S-T-U-R-B-A-T-I-O-N." The mother actually spelled it out— whether out of modesty or inability to pronounce the term, we could not learn. One newcomer to the community left the meeting in disgust; and announcing her intention to read the book, she challenged the offended parents to do likewise, and then to face the teacher in person. But no one came. A conference was initiated by the teacher, but for one reason or another, the parent could not meet him face to face. (Perhaps by now she *had* read the book.) The fuss subsided; but the damage had been done.

Credibility is important, and in a small town, both appreciation and condemnation can flow quickly. We like the book; students who liked little else loved it; some people feared it. What can be done if challengers will not meet you face to face?

We felt, as many do, that discontent with printed material does not always come directly from the book itself; but rather, that it reflects some other dissatisfaction with the school—or the teacher or the system in general. The book becomes only the focal point, something to seize upon. Obviously, the only antidote for the situation is something to counteract this narrowing focus of unspoken disaffection. But what? Somehow the school, the teachers themselves, must re-establish confidence in their service to the community. They must make their good efforts understood.

"Books Our Children Read"

By five o'clock one winter evening, we teachers concluded our railing and lamentation with the observation that it was a pity we didn't have the parents in class instead of the students. We'd make believers of them, if only they'd read and discuss the way their children did.

"We ought to do it."

"We could invite them to come to a community education class and we could teach the books they hate—that they think they hate—and they'd see."

"We'll call it 'Books Our Children Read' and we'll invite everyone to come and discuss whatever they want—right out in the open."

"And they'll love it. They'll love the idea and they'll love the books, every one of them."

So we did. And they did.

We met with the community Education Director (Fort Frye had been chosen one of two pilot schools in the state to try community education projects), and she enthusiastically endorsed our idea. She reminded us that there were no funds available. We hadn't considered this, but we were hardly put off, since everyone was eager to share the workload. We'd begin with each department member's offering to teach one book used in the curriculum; we'd invite parents to request titles. We'd be sure to offer *A Day No Pigs Would Die* and other titles we felt might be suspect.

We announced the course in the daily and weekly newspapers, through the school newsletter, and in the community education publications, and we sent typed notes home with each student in the junior and senior high school. "Books Our Children Read," we determined, would be the best course title: they were *our* children too.

Although not all the "right" people came the first night, we presented our plan and our invitation with every member of the department present. We had a nucleus of people who were representative of a cross-section of the community. Some had students in college; some had students in our classes; one was there because she loved to read and had no one to talk to about the books.

Later, cousins and sisters-in-law joined the little group. They read a book each week, and each Tuesday night we met to discuss their reactions and to comment briefly on our reasons for selecting the book. Not once did we lecture on our philosophical platform or pass out sheets of rationale; we offered this material only as we discussed and as they asked . . . as they felt. There was often no need to explain or account for what, taken out of context, might have given rise to criticism.

We exhibited briefly lessons on writing, usage, mechanics, vocabulary—the basics—incorporated into the study of each book. We did not convince everyone that everything we did was right or sufficient; we shared our awareness that we have no final answers. Critics of the elective system saw for the first time how it is possible to integrate the language arts. Every session ended on an optimistic note.

As the weather grew cold, we added coffee and tea and the group stayed past the appointed hour. They began to browse the shelves of the classrooms and to check out other titles, to muse on the possibility of reading a series of plays, or some poetry, or Shakespeare. We showed them our videotapes, our filmstrips, our bulletin boards, samples of writings, and artwork generated by the books. They asked us to give the course again.

The second term it was even more difficult to choose the titles; they wanted to read so much. The small group increased, and we assured those who came that they were welcome to attend one, some, or all of the sessions. Most came regularly and some even changed work schedules in order to be there.

At their request on the final night, we showed them the two-volume curriculum guides which our teachers had written (all on their own time without additional pay) for the many elective courses we teach. They toured the book room—a converted classroom filled with files of student work, curriculum materials for teachers to share, and shelves of paperbacks and anthologies—an accumulation over the years that gave mute testimony to devoted effort on behalf of the community's children. No article in the newspaper, no picture, no newsletter, no brochure could have better conveyed to those parents our honest commitment than that last night of shared experience with the "Books Our Children Read."

Even while we cut the farewell cake, we began to plan another term. We'd do *Spoon River* (it had been burned in Kansas). *Hiroshima* moved our students; we'd do it too. Some people had objected to the theology in *Our Town;* we'd include it. *A Man for*

All Seasons and Paul Zindel's books, along with Chaim Potok's *Asher Lev,* would offer a variety. *Black Boy* and *Laughing Boy,* both banned in Long Island—their removal was the subject of lawsuits backed by NCTE—would interest the group. Together with the parents, we filled the blackboard with dozens of titles and then began to narrow the possibilities, partners now in the rush of life—and literature.

Today, we see every book as a bridge and we are optimistic. But we know that even this hard won confidence cannot stop irrationality. No doubt we will face it again and again. Now, however, things *are* different: if cries for censorship should come, the English department will not be obliged to stand alone; we have friends and parents who also know and love "Books Our Children Read."

16 How to Write a Rationale in Defense of a Book

Diane P. Shugert
Central Connecticut State College

"I know, I know. Everybody *says* that we ought to write a rationale for every book our students read in common. But saying is one thing, and doing is another. *Nobody* writes defenses for all those books. Too many other things to do. Thirty behavioral objectives must be sent to the principal by next week. Another conference about Harry's pyromania for this afternoon—and this one involves the psychiatrist and the probation officer as well as Harry's hysterical parent. Don't tell me what I *must* do. I must grade these required weekly themes, and all I want out of *you* is silence."

Thoughts like those must occur to most of us when presented with yet another exhortation to do something that we really "should," but if you've read this far in *Dealing with Censorship,* you've read Ken Donelson's article, "Censorship in the 1970s: Some Ways to Handle It When It Comes (and It Will)," and you know already that one of the most effective ways of dealing with censorship is to have ready, prepared in advance, *written* justifications for teaching the books you are teaching. The teachers who have rationales in hand are able to show immediately that they have thought about what they are doing. Evidence of thought alone is sometimes enough to stop a censorship incident before it gets going. In addition, preparing a written rationale really does help us to think more clearly about the books we use and to resist more strongly any attempts to remove the books from the curriculum. It may be worth a little more effort if the effort helps us to keep our jobs and our academic integrity.

So, on the assumption that it's worth a try, how is it done? For the last three years the members of the Committee on the Profession of the New England Association of Teachers of English and its chairperson (me) have been writing rationales for often challenged books and have been encouraging and assisting others to write them. Four of our rationales (two for *Go Ask Alice* and two for *The Catcher in the Rye*) are appended to this article as samples. And they required a lot, not just a little, effort.

Each rationale should include answers to the questions posed by Ken Donelson in his article:

1. For what classes is this book especially appropriate?
2. To what particular objectives, literary or psychological or pedagogical, does this book lend itself?
3. In what ways will the book be used to meet those objectives?
4. What problems of style, tone, or theme or possible grounds for censorship exist in the book?
5. How does the teacher plan to meet those problems?
6. Assuming that the objectives are met, how would students be different because of their reading of this book?

As part of the answer for each question, specific activities, methods, projects, and discussion questions should be delineated. If one prepares the rationale at the time that one plans the teaching of the book, most of the rationale is simply drawn from unit and lesson plans.

Two more questions should be answered, as well:

7. What are some other appropriate books an individual student might read in place of this book?
8. What reputable sources have recommended this book? What have critics said of it? (This answer should cite reviews, if any are available.)

The difficulties in writing rationales have to do with audience and tone. There I am, seated unwillingly at my desk, ready to write. I wouldn't be doing this if it weren't for someone "out there" whom I expect to criticize my choices, my methods, my professional competence. In addition, I may hold a most unflattering stereotype of the censor as a person of little learning and no sense, a person whose wishes and views deserve no respect. I may not have the slightest desire to justify anything to such a person. Indeed, I would probably prefer to "make him an offer he cannot refuse." It's not hard to write a short paper answering those eight questions; the problem is to do so without technical jargon, without revealing my discomfort at having to do so, and without communicating a tone of contempt for my audience.

How are those difficulties overcome? First, by acknowledging them and second, by ridding myself of the attitudes that create them. Parents and citizens are rightly concerned that their children and the society's children be properly educated. Far worse than parents who object to a book are the parents who don't care about their child. I am a professional who can claim to be expert in matters of children's reading. As a professional, I defend my choices and support my actions as a matter of course. As a servant of the Republic I have an obligation to its citizens. Keeping ideas like those uppermost helps immeasurably in catching the proper tone for the intended audience. Third, I can overcome the difficulties by writing the rationale rather hurriedly, getting the essential answers down on paper. When I am done, I ask a friend—perhaps another teacher but even better someone who is not a teacher—to read what I have written and to respond to its tone. I then revise, using my friend's response as a guide.

There are several ways to make the writing of many rationales more manageable. For sets of books that the department has approved or that several teachers use, the members of the department can share the work. Each member writes a rationale for one set. Others who will be using the books serve as editors and critics of the rationales. When an individual teacher assigns the book, he or she fills out a form which completes the rationale for that particular class as part of that particular unit. Department rationales are kept on file in multiple copies. The teacher takes a copy, adds the completed form, and keeps it handy during the time the book is being used. When the class has finished, both rationales are returned to department files as a record of what was done and as an aid to others. (Samples of completion forms for the department and for the individual teacher appear at the end of this article.)

Even easier (though less effective) is for department members to write one departmental rationale for each commonly used book. The department and the school administration make a policy that for all books recommended by the department the departmental rationale is enough. Any teacher who uses the book in any class has *a priori* approval for doing so.

Another way to share the work is to assign department members particular tasks. Several might be assigned to looking up, summarizing, and citing the pertinent book reviews. Others might cull various lists of recommended books from the National Council of Teachers of English lists, from lists in the *English Journal* and *Language Arts,* and from the American Library Association. Still others might take on the job of finding alternate books on the same theme or using the same techniques as the recommended books. Though each department member might write his or her own rationales, much of the research would already have been done.

Finally, the department might ditto the eight questions onto two pages with plenty of space after each question. Groups of teachers (either small groups or the whole department; either during department meetings or in special group meetings) then brainstorm possible answers to each question and record those on the form. Any teacher writing a rationale uses the result to provide some of the content of his or her individual rationale. A department could do one book each meeting or could divide into groups of at least three people (more would be better), thereby preparing several each meeting.

A good book rationale:

1. Is well thought out and thoroughly understood by the teacher who will be using the book
2. Answers all the questions posed earlier in this article and answers them thoroughly
3. Avoids specialized technical jargon, either literary or educational
4. Is specific
5. Maintains a tone of respect for its audience

Once the department and/or the teacher has written the necessary rationales, the defenses for particular books can be strengthened immeasurably by involving students in the process. What better way to get authoritative comments than by asking students to respond to the first six questions? The questions must be adapted, of course, by adding the negative, (e.g., For what classes is this book especially appropriate/inappropriate?); by eliminating technical terms, (e.g., for question 2, What can be learned from reading and studying this book?); or by using the conditional (e.g., for question 3, What things could be done in class to help people learn those things?). Having students respond to the questions is also one technique for meeting the book's problems (see question 5). Students' responses can be placed on file with the teacher's and the department's rationales. For once, something that students write will have a real audience and a real purpose.

There are also some shortcuts to rationales. I call them shortcuts because they're not much good. In fact, their only virtue is that they're better than nothing at all. One shortcut is to obtain some rationales that have appeared in print and to use a completion form for them. Another shortcut is simply to respond to the eight questions with brainstormed phrases, specifics, ideas, sentences. Type that up—neatly—for each book. Leave the connections, transitions, and decisions for the day *after* the censor comes. On the theory that only a few books will ever be challenged, leave the hardest work for those few.

Those two shortcuts fail on several counts to meet the test for good rationales. Especially they fail because they do not produce anything that is well thought out and thoroughly understood by the teacher who might someday need them.

Let us, as a last word, imagine the worst possible situation: Nobody has written rationales for anything. There is nothing on record to show that the teacher or department has done its professional preparation. One teacher is approached by a parent—"I want this book out of this class! Why is it here, anyway? It's disgusting, obscene, filthy, uneducated, and un-American!" When this happens, realize that the teacher's problem is the department's and the school's. Rather than leaving that teacher alone to survive or fall—and perhaps to take along the entire curriculum, everyone else's academic freedom, and the students' right to read—let the department spring to the teacher's aid. Let everyone cooperate in preparing the rationale. Even if the emergency tactic doesn't work, the loss of the book and the effort made to save it may serve to tie together the department members and to begin a process that will work *next* time.

Example Rationales

The following materials were prepared for the New England Association of Teachers of English Committee on the Profession. The Committee publishes a set of rationales for the books most often challenged—as revealed by Kenneth Donelson's survey in *Arizona English Bulletin* 17 (February 1975): 4. The set of approximately twelve rationales may be purchased at cost from Diane P. Shugert, Chair, English Department, Central Connecticut State College, New Britain, Conn. 06050.

Completion Form
Teacher's Rationale

School:
Teacher:

Title:

Grade or Course:

Approximate date(s) book will be used:

This book will be:
Studied by the whole class. _____

Recommended to individual students. _____

Part of a larger study of

Ways in which the book is especially appropriate for students in this class:

Ways in which the book is especially pertinent to the objectives of this course or unit:

Special problems that might arise in relation to the book and some planned activities which handle this problem:

Some other appropriate books an individual student might read in place of this book:

How to Write a Rationale

Completion Form
English Department Rationale

School:

Title:

Recommended grades or courses:

Ways in which the book is especially appropriate for students in this school:

Ways in which the book is especially pertinent to the objectives of this curriculum:

Special problems that might arise in relation to the book:

Ways that a teacher might handle those problems:

Some other appropriate books an individual student might read in place of this book:

Rationale for Teaching *Go Ask Alice*

When a friend, who has teenage children, recently said, "I don't see why a book like *Go Ask Alice* is included on my son's reading list for English," my immediate response was, "Why not?"

"Because the subject of drugs is so——well,——ah—sordid! I don't think kids should have to read about that when there's so many other good books to read," emphasizing "good."

Mumbling something about allowing kids to be exposed to all kinds of literature, I beat a hasty retreat to the bookstore and bought the book. After re-reading it, I'm convinced that *Go Ask Alice* is a good book that should be taught.

It is especially suitable to teach to seventh and eighth graders, even though many may have read it before. By discussing the problems that Alice has, kids this age can begin looking at themselves and understanding their own conflicting ideas and emotions.

Telling her story in diary form, Alice chronicles a little over a year in her life as a fifteen-year-old drug user and her desperate efforts to go "straight." Using her diary as the close confidant she apparently lacks, she confides her feelings of inferiority and insecurity. Her life takes a twist when her father accepts a new position in another state and the family moves. After what seems an eternity to Alice, she finally makes a friend, only to be plunged into despair when the friend goes to camp for the summer. Returning to her former town to visit her grandparents, Alice is asked to a party by a group that she had always considered THE crowd. Thrilled, she goes to the party and has her first drug trip. Continued parties, drug use and sex make her ashamed, fearful that she might be pregnant and scared of the whole scene. She returns home to another year at the new high school. When she is offered friendship, she accepts gratefully and, because they are "dopers," she begins her descent into the sordid depths of drug dependency.

Describing euphoric heights when she begins using drugs, Alice's entries quickly turn to despair and desperation, and express the guilt feelings about what she is doing to herself and her family. As her dependency increases, the changes in Alice's personality are evident in that her language becomes more and more vulgar and crude. Her life hits bottom when she is forced to become a prostitute in order to support her habit.

The descriptions of the drug scene seem accurately drawn and this is, no doubt, why kids like the book. However, it is this aspect of the book that parents most object to! I can't really believe that parents are so naive that they think that their children don't know what a prostitute is. And if they think their kids are learning new words by reading *Go Ask Alice*, ask them to monitor the lavatories and listen to their kids' conversation! Unfortunately, drugs have become a part of today's culture, and if we want our kids to withstand the pressure to use them, we must provide them with the facts, pro and con, so that they can make intelligent choices. As parents and teachers, we can't shield them from some of the unpleasant realities of life, and drugs are part of that reality.

Alice finds herself into drugs because of other pressures, and it is these pressures that I feel merit as much discussion as drugs.

Peer pressure is a common problem to young teens. To be accepted, to wear the right clothes, to "go together," and to have lots of friends are constant sources of concern. Searching for a group to belong to, Alice gratefully accepts the first offer, even though they turn out to be "dopers." Threats, taunts and lies are used against Alice by her "doper" friends when she tries to go "straight." Meanwhile, the straight kids will have nothing to do with her.

Discussing what peer pressure is, what other types of such pressure exist, how do they handle it, and how do they feel about the ways that Alice handled it are topics for class discussions. Learning to accept one another as a person is very hard to learn, but kids can certainly begin.

Thirteen- and fourteen-year-olds experience terrible feelings of loneliness. Changing high schools can be devastating. The cliques are formed and seem to wear "No Admittance" signs. The "new girl" is ignored by everyone, except those who are willing to share their misery. Once you've been tagged as a member of one group, it's nearly impossible to erase that label. This is the situation that Alice found herself in. Trying to discover why kids ignore the "new kid" and asking them why it's so hard to move from group to group will help them become less fearful of new things and situations and, hopefully, set them thinking about friendship and reaching outside of themselves. At least they will learn that their feelings of loneliness are shared by others.

Real love is shown in this book. Alice writes about her obvious enjoyment of family gatherings, and although she sometimes resents her younger brother and sister (typical), she also appreciates their support when she's struggling to stay off drugs. She remembers her grandfather's loving admonition, after she has run away from home the first time, "You have only yourself to forgive," and she takes great pride in learning how to make rolls with her grandmother. However, even with their obvious love, sympathy and support, Alice still finds herself unable to communicate her doubts and fears with them. If she had, then she may have had someone to confide in and would have been receiving some feedback to her questions, instead of having to confide her fears to an inanimate diary. Probably most of the kids in school feel this same way about confiding in their parents, and with good reason. However, learning to trust others is an important facet of maturation, and kids should be helped in learning how to do it.

One of the most poignant parts of the book concerns Alice's love for her grandparents, both of whom die during the story. She is haunted by dreams of their lying in the ground and being consumed by maggots and worms. She has many guilt feelings about her role in contributing to their deaths, yet she doesn't confide them to anyone.

Love and acceptance are also shown by her friendship with Joel, a hard working, straight, good kid. He and Alice really like each other and his friendship remains secure even after learning of her drug history. However, it doesn't seem to help her ultimately.

As she nears the end of her diary, Alice reveals her decision not to begin another one. With the help and support of Joel and her "super straight" friends, and her newly acquired inner strength, Alice faces another year in school, confident that at last she has licked the drug problem. Oh! how glad the reader is!

Three weeks later, her parents come home and find Alice dead, one of the thousands of drug deaths each year.

Perhaps the moral, if there is one, is that each person must develop his/her own inner strength. You can't depend on others to give it to you. In order to develop this inner strength, our kids must be exposed to life, its good and its bad. Literature is one of the many ways that this can be done, and *Go Ask Alice* is one of the many books that can help kids develop the needed resources to survive.

Cynthia Redman
CCTE Committee on the Profession

Rationale for Teaching *Go Ask Alice*

Go Ask Alice is either a highly edited or completely ghost written diary of a fourteen- to sixteen-year-old girl. Alice is unknowingly turned on to LSD at a party and from there experiments with all kinds of drugs, slowly becoming a pusher to support her habit. She becomes one of the dopers at school and runs away from her parents to start a boutique in San Francisco with Chris, a girl friend. She lives through the full range of sexual experiences, from homosexuality to being used for sadistic sexual purposes. Alice finally decides to go home, since she misses and loves her parents very much. She seesaws throughout the book from "reforming" to conforming. She wants to feel needed by her family (drug-free happiness) and she also wants to feel needed by her doper peers (drug high happiness). She runs away again, then returns, and again is unknowingly turned on to acid. This time she has a very bad trip and ends up scathed and battered in an insane asylum. When she finally returns home she dies of a probable overdose at sixteen years old.

Self-control is the novel's overriding theme. An important problem for Alice was that she felt she couldn't control her reactions. Alice was aware enough to know what she was doing and to write about her own deterioration, but she couldn't change what she did. Thus the book provides opportunities to discuss teenagers' needs for self-control.

Critics may object to Alice's conformity in the use of drugs and the practice of sex. But *Go Ask Alice* teaches adolescents about drugs and sex by showing them how negatively these experiences can turn out. The novel emphasizes Alice's continuous insecurity which leads her to want to conform and to want to banish all thoughts of insecurity from her mind through the use of drugs. Each drug experience, no matter how thrilling, is followed by a negative experience, such as having to sell drugs to nine year olds, or picturing the worms and maggots eating away at her dead grandfather, or being used for sadistic sexual purposes by her friend's employer. The emphasis is on how Alice is drawn into the habitual drug scene and on her lack of self-control that both causes involvement in and is fostered by drug use. Teenagers can see, then, that if Alice's first drug experience had not been positive, and if she were not so insecure, Alice would not have become drug prone.

Although sexual experiences are mentioned, they are never explicitly described in Alice's diary. She mentions a baby prostitute and comments on how lonely and burned out this girl was. When sex is mentioned, drugs have spoiled it. Though Alice enjoyed some of her sexual experiences, she bemoans the fact that all of them were under the influence of drugs. She wonders what a "real" sexual experience would be like, but she fears and avoids it.

Alice often writes about needing to talk to a responsible and friendly person who could help her analyze her feelings. Adolescent readers would find this desire all too familiar and real. The entries in the diary concerning drugs and sex provide a basis for the junior or senior high school teacher to lead discussions on the adolescent reader's own stand on drugs and his or her own values concerning sex.

Adult critics may object to Alice's negative comments about her parents: "Mother is always nagging at me." Unfortunately, this is the adolescent's reality: finding fault with his or her parents. Alice counters these negative days with overwhelmingly positive days where she writes about how lovely and wonderful her family is and about how much she loves them. Wanting to please her family and to be loved and accepted by them wins out over wanting to conform to the drug scene when Alice decides both times to return to her family and to give up drugs. Class discussion of adolescents' relationships with parents might focus on the difference between Alice's good days and bad days. Hence, although she does make some negative comments about her parents, her attitude is mostly positive.

Another set of classroom activities might probe into the themes of drugs and sex and parents as they are written about in *The Poetry of Rock* by Richard Goldstein. Poems such as "White Rabbit" by Grace Slick deal with drugs and may stimulate values discussions. Another teaching idea is splitting the class into two groups to debate whether the diary is phony or real by finding clues in the novel. A discussion of how Alice's language changes throughout the book and according to whether she is on or off drugs might profitably follow the debate.

How will adolescents be different from reading *Go Ask Alice*? Adolescent readers will identify with the moral structure of the novel in reading about Alice's need for friendship and responsible role models. That need is countered by her desire to run away from parental guidance and from threatening school situations. Those readers previously enticed or tempted into drugs or those merely considering drugs will perhaps *reconsider* having read about Alice's negative experiences and about her death at the end of the novel.

Lauren Potter
CCTE Committee on the Profession

Rationale for Teaching *The Catcher in the Rye*

Where will all the children go when Holden Caulfield can no longer catch them in the rye? Unfortunately, they will tumble heedlessly over the cliff into the adult world because they may have been denied the opportunity to meet Holden and to consider how he responded to those same questions which concern them—fear, loneliness, and disillusionment with the adult world. *The Catcher in the Rye*, although acclaimed by critics all over the world, has been criticized for vulgar and obscene language.

It is important to examine the language as a whole rather than to isolate specifically strong or offensive words. Holden's speech represents an accurate reproduction of teenage vocabulary in the 1950s. The use of expletives is typical of casual school-boy vernacular. This kind of speech appears frequently in the first third of the book, which is set in an Ivy League prep school. Any record of youthful male conversations spoken in an informal dormitory situation absolutely demands this type of language. No one can seriously contend that adolescent boys do not talk this way among themselves; indeed, the vocabulary of the 1950s seems rather tame in comparison to that prevalent in 1976. Modern adolescents will find Salinger's diction neither unfamiliar nor shocking.

Like the vernacular of all sixteen year olds, Holden's vocabulary is filled with wild exaggerations ("One of those little English jobs that do around 200 miles an hour"), vague generalizations ("All I ever meet is witty bastards,"

"It was a terrible school") and endless repetitions. The phrases, "and all," "and everything" are contained in almost every statement Holden makes. "Phony" is his only word for expressing his strong anger at the cruelty and hypocrisy he detects all around him. The few things that do meet with his approval are inevitably described with the single adjective, "nice." Both "phony" and "nice" are empty words, indicative of Holden's inability to express his deep feelings and strong opinions. In a concentrated effort to counteract "phoniness," Holden constantly affirms his own honesty by repeating, "It really was," and "I really did." The frequent use of stronger, but equally empty expressions such as "damn," "goddamn," "Christ," and "For Christ's sake," is consistent with this pattern of meaningless repetition. The vague generalizations, the empty words, and the endless repetition establishes Holden not only as a typical adolescent, but also as a character who is unable to communicate with those around him.

The selective use of certain strong expressions is absolutely essential to the novel's structure. In addition to the setting, certain situations and characters require vivid descriptions and reactions. Holden's unsuccessful encounter with a sleazy prostitute and her repulsive pimp is a notable example. Only strong words can convey Holden's fear and Maurice's brutality in this scene. In like manner, offensive language is used to describe offensive characters, from Ackley and Stradlater to Maurice and "all those phony bastards who call the Lunts angels." Since the novel is basically constructed as an interior monologue, a great number of the most vivid passages occur when Holden is simply talking to himself. There is no listener to be offended by his words. This is a key point because in this novel there is no responsible human being to whom Holden can turn. There is no one to whom he can express his doubts and insecurities, a situation all too familiar to young adults.

The Catcher in the Rye is a chronicle of a young boy's search for someone to talk to as he struggles desperately to discover honest values in a dishonest world. Holden is in the midst of a physical and emotional breakdown, and he is crying out for help. "All I ever meet is handsome bastards—when they're done combing their goddamn hair, they beat it on you." At the outset, Holden is alone on a hill, having failed to make friends at Pencey or at any previous school he has attended. His immediate roommates, Ackley and Stradlater, are too selfish and superficial to perceive their fellow student's disturbing emotional condition. Of course, like many young people, Holden feels that he cannot communicate with his parents. His is a young idealist's outrage at the corruption of the adult world. And Holden cannot talk to girls at all; witness his colossal failure with Sally in New York. He is so desperate for a listener that he turns to the prostitute for conversation instead of sex. Finally, none of the adults whom Holden meets proves helpful at all. The only people to whom he can express himself are his dead brother Allie and his nine-year-old sister Phoebe. He fails to communicate with the others partially because he cannot express his deepest feelings in words. Thus the vagueness, the empty phrases, and the meaningless repetitions also convey this character's inability to communicate with those around him.

It must be remembered that Holden's language provides valuable insights into his character—sensitive, idealistic, angry, fearful, and friendless. His is a type of character whom adolescents can readily identify with. Language is a tool which an author uses to build his characters. Salinger's purpose here is not to shock or offend the reader; his aim is rather to further the development of character, situation, and setting and thus establish important themes for his reader to consider. Where strong language isn't needed, it isn't used. Holden never uses controversial words when speaking with teachers, women, girls, or children. His unbelievably high moral standards would never permit such behavior. Because of this, he even tries to protect innocent children from the corruption of the adult world by erasing a really offensive phrase from the walls of Phoebe's school. Because he knows what's ahead, Holden has cast himself in the rather heroic role of saving children from the adult world's decay, of becoming the catcher in the rye. Unfortunately, this is an impossible goal, and it is this realization that marks Holden's passage into the adult world. He finally understands that he cannot erase all the world's words anymore than he can prevent Phoebe from reaching out for the golden ring.

When a class studies *The Catcher in the Rye*, teacher and students together could discuss the nature of Holden's language and how it fails to express what Holden so desperately tries to say. By reading and talking about Holden's inability to communicate with adults and his hatred of and isolation from his society, students may learn to better understand themselves, to talk with adults in their (and our) world, and to solve their problems as Holden could not. They might also study how all of us reveal ourselves through our language and yet how difficult it is for us to share ourselves with others or to hear what others wish to share. Holden's language might be compared with Alice's (*Go Ask Alice*), with Gene's (*A Separate Peace*), with Huck Finn's or with that of any of the narrators in *My Darling, My Hamburger*.

> Mary McLaughlin
> CCTE-NEATE Committee
> on the Profession

Rationale for Teaching *The Catcher in the Rye*

Like Melville's Ishmael, Salinger's non-heroic hero of *The Catcher in the Rye* has embarked on a journey—not a three-year whaling voyage but a sometimes tortuous, sometimes funny two-day excursion to New York which seems to last a year. (The journey of the soul will not be measured by time.) Like Ishmael, Holden Caulfield seeks truth and uncovers uncertainties. (Where do the ducks in Central Park go in the winter?) Like Ahab, the more ignominious hero of *Moby Dick,* Holden desires to strike beyond the "pasteboard mask." (For Holden, that mask is the pretentious veneer of social standard.) Like Ahab, Holden labors under the burden of his own misconceptions about reality and his inability to confront it.

The outstanding difference, however, is that Holden is as contemporary as he is classic. He follows in the best of the American tradition. His self-scrutiny is as intense as that of any Puritan. His initiation into the world of experience and his search for meaning and identity are not unlike those of Mark Twain's Huck or Stephen Crane's Henry Fleming. Yet, the young hero of *The Catcher in the Rye* unfolds his story in a subjective first person narrative which relates not only the individual traumas of Holden Caulfield but also the dilemma of modern adolescence coming to grips with itself and its world. It is not an easy dilemma for the adolescent to face, nor is it one that the academic environment ordinarily explores. Because Holden is so much like other American literary heroes, *The Catcher in the Rye* offers an excellent framework for exploring and possibly bridging the gap between the non-academic world of adolescent experience and the academic world of literary experience.

For the traditional curriculum, *Catcher* offers the study of recurring themes in American literature: the changing concept of the hero in twentieth century fiction; American culture, its influence and reflection in literature; style, tone, and characterization in the interior monologue; the advantages and limitations of the first person point of view; and other literary concerns. Its greatest contribution, however, lies in the realm most difficult to teach—that of emotion and value. Here, too, is where *Catcher*'s language and occasionally its subject matter raise questions and blood-pressures.

Attackers of *The Catcher in the Rye* focus primarily on the language, proclaiming it to be "profane," "obscene," and "unfit for human ears." These charges might be answered directly with a question: Would the reader accept a sixteen-year-old Holden Caulfield who talked like Old Spencer? Even though adults might like to think so, sixteen year olds just don't talk that way. The good adolescent reader recognizes a phony when he hears one. Holden Caulfield's language is typical of adolescents and, therefore, is necessary if Holden is to seem realistic. Furthermore, Holden's language is concerned with more than four-letter words.

Holden's manipulation of language is one area that might be explored by students. Holden may be unsuccessful at articulating his innermost feelings, but he is master of language manipulation. Conforming to the language of polite society, for example, Holden engages in inoffensive platitudes when conversing with Mrs. Morrow. He tells her what she would like to hear in the manner in which she would like to hear it. (Ironically, Holden is most phony here where his language is most polite.) Studying such situations can yield valuable insights into the conscious and unconscious manipulation of language. Role playing exercises designed to exhibit cases of language manipulation in the students' own lives would work well here.

Another possibility for language study involves Holden's inability to articulate feelings and to communicate with others. Repetition of words and phrases like "if you know what I mean" and "and all" indicate Holden's failure to formulate strong opinions and to state his thoughts clearly and specifically. Excerpts with these vague phrases may be isolated by the teacher and scrutinized by the students in groups. Questions like the following should alert students to the need for specific language in communication: What is Holden saying? Do you understand what he is saying through his effective choice of words? Do you understand what he is saying by reading between the lines or from your knowledge of the character? Can you rewrite the excerpt to illustrate accurately what you think Holden means to say? Why do you think Holden is unable to communicate? General class discussion of group conclusions might follow with some broadening to include communication gaps in students' and teacher's everyday lives.

Second to language in the dispute over teaching *The Catcher in the Rye* is adolescent sex as subject matter. Sex in *The Catcher in the Rye* is basic to the theme of growing up and the initiation into experience. To many adolescents sex is often the rite of passage into adulthood, as superficial as the physical act alone might be. Holden, however, finds sex for sex's sake repulsive. His obsession with sex and his thoughts about whether Stradlater took advantage of Jane Gallagher in the back seat of Ed Banky's car reflect Holden's consistent abhorrence for the superficial. One might even argue that Holden's view of sex in relation to Stradlater and Jane is in keeping with his self-image of protector of the innocent and is, in fact, downright moralistic. Holden is outraged, for instance, that Stradlater could have possibly had sex with Jane without knowing that she "kept all her kings in the back row." His own relationship with Jane had been platonic but intimate. ("You don't always have to get too sexy to get to know a girl.")

Holden tells the reader that he is "a pretty sexy guy." Yet, he continues to say he despises himself when he has spent the whole evening necking with some phony girl. Furthermore, he tells the reader that he always "stops" when the girl asks him to. Holden is not unlike many youths who find physical desire at war with a sense of right or propriety.

This conflict in Holden is most evident in the prostitute scene. Holden is feeling "pretty sexy" before Sunny arrives, but her banal entrance and businesslike manner turn him off completely. It is plain that Holden is not seeking physical gratification. His attempt to strike up a conversation with Sunny mirrors his need to know her as a person and to fulfill his own loneliness in more than a physical manner.

The subject of sex is therefore basic in showing vital aspects of Holden's character and in delineating the dilemma of growing up to understand oneself and one's world. Salinger never exploits the subject of sex but rather depicts what is oftentimes an excruciating trial of adolescence with both humor and pathos.

In the final analysis, *Catcher*'s strength as a teaching tool lies in its fulfillment of traditional literary objectives as well as its sensitive treatment of one adolescent's journey from innocence to experience. If the student is able to generalize Holden's plights and relate them to his own then he has not stumbled through Holden's course in vain.

Patricia C. Nero
NEATE Committee on the Profession

17 The Iowa Model Policy and Rules for Selection of Instructional Materials

Larry Bartlett
Iowa Department of Public Instruction

At about the time a group of citizens protesting the use of educational materials in Kanawha County, West Virginia, was making national headlines, Grinnell, Iowa, was involved in a similar, but less traumatic, experience. The Reverend Ben See, a fundamentalist minister, objected to the presence of three books, *The Godfather, The Summer of '42,* and *The Exorcist,* on the school library shelves and officially petitioned the local school board to have the books removed. Following established procedure, the challenged books were reviewed by a committee appointed to review the books and recommend appropriate action to the board. By majority vote, the committee recommended retention of the challenged books, and the school board accepted the majority report on a vote of four to one. The Reverend See filed an appeal with the county superintendent and hearings were held over a three-day period which resulted in a transcript of several hundred pages and which cost about $1800. The county superintendent, Dr. Richard Ploeger, affirmed the local board decision, and the Reverend See continued his appeal to the State Board of Public Instruction. After a hearing before State Superintendent Robert Benton, the State Board affirmed the decisions of the county superintendent and local board. The State Board found that the proper standard against which challenges to educational materials in Iowa are to be measured is the "appropriateness of educational materials for its designated audience" and that the ultimate determination of such appropriateness is primarily the responsibility of the local Board of Directors.

While the Reverend See and I did not agree on the specific issues of censorship which his appeal raised, we did have an opportunity to get to know each other and come to respect each other's viewpoints. He certainly was not the fire-breathing fundamentalist boob that the press had made him out to be. I found him to be a very sincere parent, concerned primarily that his children receive the best Christian upbringing possible. I also found him to be very frustrated with the entire system of review. The focal point of his frustration was the local reconsideration committee which initially reviewed his petition and made a recommendation to the Board to retain the books. He felt that, from the very beginning, the committee was stacked against him and other concerned parents in the district and that there was no chance to obtain a fair hearing.

The Reverend See's appeal and frustration, the problems in West Virginia, and my experience as classroom teacher whose principal boxed up books and locked them in his office at the first sign of complaint in the community seemed to come together all at once and direct a course of action. One of my pet projects was, and is, the development of a series of model school board policies and rules, and the censorship issue certainly was an area in which school boards needed direction.

Development of such a model involves a relatively complex procedure. I normally take responsibility for drafting an initial proposal and then present it to a committee of my peers, whose judgment I respect and who exhibit an interest in the topic. After many hours of discussion and a minimum of three complete rewrites, a draft is sent to about a dozen lawyers and educators who represent a broad spectrum of educational and legal philosophy. Their valued opinions are solicited and strongly considered by the drafting committee in compiling a final draft. The final draft is reviewed by the state superintendent and his chief advisors and then is prepared for publication and distribution. The acceptance or rejection of any or all provisions in a model is left up to each district.

My first task in developing a model school policy for dealing with censorship was to determine what the Department had done previously in regard to the issue. For over ten years, the Department had actively advocated the establishment of educational material selection policies and rules by schools to aid in achieving appropriate assignment of selection responsibility and quality selection, and to guard against unwarranted censorship of materials. As an aid in this endeavor, Department staff distributed various materials prepared and published by other professional groups. The establishment of a committee to draft a model policy and rules was completely in line with the Department's previous position. The drafting committee consisted of myself; Betty Jo Buckingham, consultant, educational media; Sharon Slezak, consultant for language arts; and Marjean Wagner, high school librarian in the Urbandale, Iowa, public schools.

The philosophy of our endeavor was established early. Our goal was to develop a model policy and rules which emphasized the ongoing nature of selection, the assignment of responsibility for selection, and continued evaluation by school staff members; and which provided for appropriate consideration and review of community concerns.

The result of our work was published as "Selection of Instructional Materials: A Model Policy and Rules" (Iowa Department of Public Instruction, 1975). The first point the model attempted to make was the important delineation between "policy" and "rules." Policy is a general statement of direction given by the governing board of a school to all concerned; and rules are the procedure developed by the school administration by which the policy is to be carried out. Rules detail the application of policy to specific circumstances. The two should not be confused nor intertwined. The model policy statement is as follows:

> Model Statement of Policy
>
> The Board of Directors of the _____
> School District hereby declares it the policy of the District to provide a wide range of instructional materials on all levels of difficulty, with diversity of appeal, and the presentation of different points of view and to allow review of allegedly inappropriate instructional materials.

After establishing the responsibility for the selection of materials in the professional staff, the rules attempt to spell out criteria for the selection of materials. By implication, those criteria would also be the standards by which challenged materials are to be judged. Here follows selected criteria:

> II. Criteria for Selection of Materials
>   A. The following criteria will be used as they apply:
>   1. Materials shall support and be consistent with the general educational goals of the district and the objectives of specific courses. . . .
>   3. Materials shall be appropriate for the subject area and for the age, emotional development, ability level, and social development of the students for whom the materials are selected. . . .
>   6. Materials shall be chosen to foster respect for minority groups, women, and ethnic groups and shall realistically represent our pluralistic society, along with the roles and life styles open to both men and women in today's world. Materials shall be designed to help students gain

an awareness and understanding of the many important contributions made to our civilization by minority groups, ethnic groups, and women.

Materials shall clarify the multiple historical and contemporary forces with their economic, political, and religious dimensions which have operated to the disadvantage or advantage of women, minority groups, and ethnic groups. These materials shall present and analyze intergroup tension and conflict objectively, placing emphasis upon resolving social and economic problems.

Materials shall be designed to motivate students and staff to examine their own attitudes and behaviors and to comprehend their own duties, responsibilities, rights, and privileges as participating citizens in a pluralistic, non-sexist society. . . .
   8. Biased or slanted materials may be provided to meet specific curriculum objectives. . . .
B. The selection of materials on controversial issues will be directed toward maintaining a balanced collection representing various views.

The word "appropriate" in paragraph three may be the single most important word in the model. On review, challenged material may be appropriate for one age level and not for another. The result under this model would be restricted use which would allow that age group for which it is appropriate to have access, but would preclude other age levels from similar access.

Paragraph six reflects the established policy of the Iowa Department of Public Instruction that schools make an affirmative effort to obtain materials which will reflect our pluralistic society. Paragraph eight recognizes the danger in too broad an exclusionary policy against discriminatory materials. There are valid reasons for using potentially offensive materials. An in-depth study of the racial problem in this country, for instance, would be incomplete without some of the pro-slavery literature and speeches of pre-Civil War America.

The selective weeding out of materials which are no longer appropriate for meeting the desired goals is an element often implicit in school rules of this nature. The panel working on the model felt that it was important to expressly authorize the process:

III. A. 4. Selection is an ongoing process which should include the removal of materials no longer appropriate and the replacement of lost and worn materials still of educational value.

In light of a recent court decision, which will be discussed later, an express authorization for regular "weeding" may be more significant than the panel originally recognized. Removal of materials judged inappropriate on a regular basis as part of an established weeding process is not as likely to draw attention or criticism as the sudden removal of materials which have achieved notoriety or which have become controversial.

The drafting committee had its most difficult time in approaching the problem of procedures involved in handling challenges to instructional materials, and that is where the majority of non-traditional features are found. All of the models the committee previously reviewed differed from each other in only a few minor respects. The committee was at first split between those who wanted to follow the earlier models and those who were concerned that the earlier models did not appear to be working smoothly. The committee struggled for several months and made little progress. Then in July, 1975, another panel member and I attended a workshop on censorship presented by Robert Foley, director of staff and curriculum for the Cedar Rapids, Iowa, Community School District. We were exposed to a philosophy and approach to censorship completely foreign to those we had been reviewing.

In the early 1970s, the Cedar Rapids schools had put a policy into practice that was a distinct departure from the others we had seen, and it had appeared to work well. Fully recognizing the uniqueness of Foley's views, we were at first skeptical, but by the end of the workshop, he had sold us, and nearly everyone else in attendance, on the non-traditional approach. Most of the persons present were ready to go back to their schools and try to develop a policy built around the Cedar Rapids approach; however, most were reluctant to tread unfamiliar waters. When they learned that some of us at the Department were working on a model policy and rules which would be widely distributed throughout the state, they encouraged us to utilize the Cedar Rapids approach.

The two of us came back to the committee resolved to do just that, but we were not sure that we would be able to persuade the other two committee members. As it turned out, the others readily accepted the concept and we set about to adapt the Cedar Rapids philosophy and bits and pieces of other models to some of our own ideas and blend them into a model that would utilize the best of each.

Here follows the section of the model, including committee comments, which deals with challenges to materials:

IV. Objection
   A. Any resident of the school district may raise objection to instructional materials used in the district's educational program despite the fact that the individuals selecting such material were duly qualified to make the selection and followed the proper procedure and observed the criteria for selecting such material.
      1. The school official or staff member receiving a complaint regarding instructional materials shall try to resolve the issue informally. The materials shall remain in use unless removed through the procedure in Section *IV. B. 6. e.* of this rule.
         a. The school official or staff member initially receiving a complaint shall explain to the complainant the school's selection procedure, criteria, and qualifications of those persons selecting the material.
         b. The school official or staff member initially receiving a complaint shall explain to the best of his or her ability the particular place the objected to material occupies in the educational program, its intended educational usefulness, and additional information regarding its use, or refer the complaining party to someone who can identify and explain the use of the material.

(Comment: The vast majority of complaints can be amicably disposed of in the first stages when the school officials and staff are frequently reminded of the school's procedures. A quick personal conference can often-times solve the problem where a shift into a more formal procedure might inflate the problem. While the legal right to object to materials is not expressly stated, it is implied in such provisions as the right to petition the government for redress of grievances.)

      2. In the event that the person making an objection to material is not satisfied with the initial explanation, the person raising the question should be referred to someone designated by the principal or person in charge of the attendance center to handle such complaints or to the media specialist for that attendance center. If, after private counseling, the complainant desires to file a formal complaint, the person to whom the complainant has been referred will assist in filling out a Reconsideration Request Form in full.
      3. The individual receiving the initial complaint shall advise the principal or person in charge of the attendance center where the challenged material is being used, of the initial contact no later than the end of the following school day, whether or not the complainant has apparently

been satisfied by the initial contact. A written record of the contact shall be maintained by the principal or other person in charge of the attendance center.
4. The principal or other person in charge of each attendance center shall review the selection and objection rules with the staff at least annually. The staff shall be reminded that the right to object to materials is one granted by policies enacted by the Board of Directors and firmly entrenched in law. They shall also be reminded of ethical and practical considerations in attempting to handle resident complaints with courtesy and integrity.

B. Request for Reconsideration
1. Any resident or employee of the school district may formally challenge instructional materials used in the district's educational program on the basis of appropriateness. This procedure is for the purpose of considering the opinions of those persons in the schools and the community who are not directly involved in the selection process.
2. Each attendance center and the school district's central office will keep on hand and make available Reconsideration Request Forms. All formal objections to instructional materials must be made on this form.
3. The Reconsideration Request Form shall be signed by the complainant and filed with the Superintendent or someone so designated by the Superintendent.
4. Within five business days of the filing of the form, the Superintendent or person so designated by the Superintendent shall file the material in question with the Reconsideration Committee for reevaluation. The Committee shall recommend disposition to the office of the Superintendent.
5. Generally, access to challenged material shall not be restricted during the reconsideration process. However, in unusual circumstances, the material may be removed temporarily by following the provisions of Section *IV. B. 6. e.* of this rule.
6. The Reconsideration Committee
   a. The Reconsideration Committee shall be made up of eleven members.
      (1) One teacher designated annually by the Superintendent.
      (2) One school media specialist designated annually by the Superintendent.
      (3) One member of the central administrative staff designated annually by the Superintendent. (This position will normally be filled by the supervisor or person responsible for the district's media services.)

(4) Five members from the community appointed annually by the Executive Committee of the Parent-Teacher-Student Association.
(5) Three high school students, selected annually from and by the Student Advisory Committee.

(Comment: Subsections (4) and (5) represent a departure from the traditional approaches of handling challenged school materials and may well be the key to the success or failure of this model. A committee with a majority of lay members should be viewed by the community as being objective and not automatically supportive of prior professional decisions on selection. Much of the philosophy regarding the Committee structure was borrowed from the policy of the Cedar Rapids Community School District, Cedar Rapids, Iowa.

Use of the Parent-Teacher-Student Association in this model is merely illustrative. Whether the non-educators are selected from the P.T.S.A. or other groups interested in the community's schools is not important. The important thing is the establishment and maintenance of the Committee's credibility with the community through a majority of nonprofessionals. An appointed committee will generally be more objective than a voluntary committee.

The method of selecting students for the Committee will depend greatly upon the size and organization of the district. A district with several high schools may want to have one student from each on the Committee while a district with one high school may want one student representative from each grade. Student selection of the representatives to this Committee is very important. Any responsible student group or groups may be used when a Student Advisory Committee does not exist in the district.)

b. The chairperson of the Committee shall not be an employee or officer of the District. The secretary shall be an employee or officer of the District.

(Comment: It is vital to the operation of this model that a community member chair the Reconsideration Committee. Credibility is the watchword.)

c. The Committee shall first meet each year during the third week in September at a time and place designated by the Superintendent and made known to the members of the Committee at least three school days in advance.
d. A calendar of subsequent regular meetings for the year shall be established and a chairperson and a secretary selected at the first meeting.

(Comment: While many districts may not feel the need to hold regular, perhaps monthly meetings, it is important to establish a sense of continuity and regularity about the Committee. The notoriety and excitement caused by emergency meetings when challenges arise in a community may be the unnecessary fuel to cause an ordinary healthy situation to become distorted beyond proportion. It is wiser to cancel unnecessary meetings than to call unexpected ones. Lack of frequent challenges to school materials probably means that one or more of the following is present: (1) satisfaction with the selection process, (2) lack of community interest, (3) belief in the futility of communication with school district officials, or (4) undue influence on the selection and weeding processes.)

e. Special meetings may be called by the Superintendent to consider temporary removal of materials in unusual circumstances. Temporary removal shall require a three-fourths vote of the Committee.

f. The calendar of regular meetings and notice of special meetings shall be made public through appropriate student publications and other communications methods.

g. The Committee shall receive all Reconsideration Request Forms from the Superintendent or person designated by the Superintendent.

h. The procedure for the first meeting following receipt of a Reconsideration Request Form is as follows:
  (1) Distribute copies of written request form.
  (2) Give complainant or a group spokesperson an opportunity to talk about and expand on the request form.
  (3) Distribute reputable, professionally prepared reviews of the material when available.
  (4) Distribute copies of challenged material as available.

i. At a subsequent meeting, interested persons, including the complainant, may have the opportunity to share their views. The Committee may request that individuals with special knowledge be present to give information to the committee.

j. The complainant shall be kept informed by the Secretary concerning the status of his or her complaint throughout the Committee reconsideration process. The complainant and known interested parties shall be given appropriate notice of such meetings.

k. At the second or a subsequent meeting, as desired, the Committee shall make its decision in either open or closed session. The Committee's final decision will be, (1) to take no removal action, (2) to remove all or part of the challenged material from the total school environment, or (3) to limit the educational use of the challenged material. The sole criteria for the final decision is the appropriateness of the material for its intended educational use. The vote on the decision shall be by secret ballot. The written decision and its justification shall be forwarded to the Superintendent for appropriate action, the complainant and the appropriate attendance centers.

(Comment: The state open meeting law should be reviewed for its application to this provision.)

l. A decision to sustain a challenge shall not be interpreted as a judgment of irresponsibility on the part of the professionals involved in the original selection or use of the material.
m. Requests to reconsider materials which have previously been before the Committee must receive approval of a majority of the Committee members before the materials will again be reconsidered. Every Reconsideration Request Form shall be acted upon by the Committee.
n. In the event of a severe overload of challenges, the Committee may appoint a subcommittee of members or nonmembers to consolidate challenges and to make recommendations to the full Committee. The composition of this subcommittee shall approximate the representation on the full Committee.
o. Committee members directly associated with the selection, use, or challenge of the challenged material shall be excused from the Committee during the deliberation on such materials. The Superintendent may appoint a temporary replacement for the excused Committee member, but such replacement shall be of the same general qualifications of that person excused.

(Comment: The Committee should never be placed in the position of appearing to defend itself, its members, or the school staff. The Committee must maintain a nonadversarial position.)

p. If the complainant is not satisfied with the decision, he or she may request that the matter be placed on the agenda of the next regularly scheduled meeting of the Board.

(Comment: These requests should comply with existing board policy and rules regarding the board agenda.)

While the comments provide the flavor of the philosophy of the model, a few additional points need to be made. Notice that paragraph A allows any resident of the district to raise an objection. By implication, this precludes nonresidents who have no ties to the community from utilizing the objection process. That paragraph also exonerates good faith selection of materials by professional staff which may later be considered inappropriate. Hopefully, adversary roles will be lessened under this policy. A situation of professionals opposing parents should not be allowed to develop.

Paragraph A.1. provides that most challenged materials will remain in use until the challenge has been completely processed. This is designed to aid in the elimination of harassment. If materials are removed as soon as an objection is filed, a person merely needs to file an objection to achieve his or her goal of censorship. In one Iowa school district, the absurdity of the absence of such a provision was shown, when in retaliation for the immediate removal of a challenged book, residents opposed to censorship filed challenges to the schools' dictionaries and encyclopedias.

The provisions of Section A.4. are very important in that every staff member should have at least a general knowledge of the rules provisions. Time after time, I have seen schools with infrequent challenges to materials start the objector down the wrong path. Most often, the objector is told to come to a board meeting, the opposite end of the procedure from which to start, to make his or her objection.

As the comments within the provisions of paragraphs B.6.a. and b. point out, the key to the success or failure of this model is the maintenance of a committee with a majority of lay members and a lay person as chairperson. Many persons, including the Reverend See, have told me that appearances before review committees dominated by educational professionals gives a complainant a feeling of futility. It is very important to establish credibility in the committee through a majority membership of noneducators.

It was intriguing to me that Bob Foley took the position, at his workshop on censorship, that the Cedar Rapids schools welcomed inquiries into the appropriateness of educational materials. He felt that lack of inquiries and objections in some school districts were more likely the result of a lack of community interest or a belief in the futility of communication with school officials than satisfaction with the selection process.

Paragraph B.6.e. provides the mechanism by which materials may be removed from use in a rapid manner. The committee intentionally made this procedure difficult to implement so that librarians and administrators could not arbitrarily remove materials from use after an objection had been made. In order to obtain the three-fourths vote of the committee necessary for immediate removal, the material in question will have to appear inappropriate on its face to a good cross-section in the reconsideration committee.

Paragraph B.6.k. is the only one in the model with which I do not personally feel comfortable. Its language was a result of a compromise in which I did most of the compromising. The paragraph allows the decision to be made in either open or closed session and upon a secret ballot. A closed session for deliberation appears to run counter to the general philosophy of openness and credibility threaded through the rest of the model. While the secret ballot also runs this contrary course, my objections are lessened by a recognition of community pressures which can be applied to reconsideration committee members. The provisions of paragraph B.6.m. are designed to eliminate repetitious reviews which may be the result of harassment.

As the final paragraph implies, the ultimate authority for a final decision on appropriateness of educational materials in most states rests with the local school district board of directors. This was the basis of the ruling of the Iowa State Board of Public Instruction in the Reverend See appeal, 1 D.P.I. App. Dec. 82, and federal courts in *President's Council v. Community School Board*, 457 F.2d 289 (2nd Cir. 1972), and *Williams v. Board of Education*, 388 F.Supp. 93 (S.D., W. V. 1975). A third federal court ruled the same way in a case arising in Ohio, but was overturned on appeal in *Minarcini v. Strongsville City School District*, 541 F.2d 577 (6th Cir. 1976). The *Minarcini* decision has important implications for the entire country, but especially for Ohio and the other states in the Sixth Circuit. The court in *Minarcini* found no constitutional problem with the local board of education controlling the curriculum and textbooks under Ohio law; however, removal of certain books from the library was a different matter. The court held that the Strongsville School Board violated the First Amendment to the United States Constitution when it removed books from the library which it found to be objectionable. Some of the language of the opinion found at pages 581 and 582 is instructive:

> A library is a storehouse of knowledge. When created for a public school it is an important privilege created by the state for the benefit of the students in the school. That privilege is not subject to being withdrawn by succeeding school boards whose members might desire to "winnow" the library for books the content of which occasioned their displeasure or disapproval. Of course, a copy of a book may wear out. Some books may become obsolete. Shelf space alone may at some point require some selection of books to be retained and books to be disposed of. No such rationale is involved in this case, however. . . .
>
> Neither the State of Ohio nor the Strongsville School Board was under any federal constitutional compulsion to provide a library for the Strongsville High School or to choose any particular books. Once having created such a privilege for the benefit of its students, however, neither body could place conditions on the use of the library which were related solely to the social or political tastes of school board members.

The result of the *Minarcini* decision has been interpreted by some people to strengthen the need for a determination of appropriateness by the local board. This is not the correct interpretation, since the result seems to be almost foreign to most educators. The concept that books, once placed upon a school library shelf, cannot later be removed when found inappropriate flies full face into the concepts of professional judgment and local determination of appropriateness. For this reason, the committee that drafted the model discussed in this article has not seen fit to alter its provisions. Until the Iowa Board of Public Instruction or a court with jurisdiction in Iowa rules to the contrary, we feel that the proper criteria for such final decisions is, and must remain, the appropriateness of the material for its intended educational use, and the most appropriate body to make that determination, with input from the community and educators, is the local board of directors.

18 A Body of Well-instructed Men and Women: Organizations Active for Intellectual Freedom

Diane P. Shugert
Central Connecticut State College

For the last five years I have hacked my way through the jungle of censorship and labored in the garden of intellectual freedom. Much of what I have done has been pure drudgery—plowing the stony soil of English teachers' indifference to their own responsibilities and their students' rights to academic freedom, for example. Much has been disheartening and frightening. I have had a recurring nightmare in which I slash with my hoe at the face of the English department head who once told me, "We have no censorship problems in *my* school. I simply remove any books I disapprove of from the book room." I have been pricked by the thorn of insult and strangled with the vine of ignorance. But one part of the garden blooms luxuriantly, "a wonder of summer with apples, pears and red currants" where "sweet singers suddenly come in the morning." For me, no part of my work with censorship has been more satisfying than finding out about and working with people who cultivate and nurture our freedom to teach, to write, to speak, and to learn.

Nothing gives one greater courage and strength to go on than having contact with others who care about the same things we do, and perhaps the best service we can offer to other English and language arts teachers is that of helping them to see that they are not alone. One way of doing that is to make use of the information and people available through organizations that are concerned with First Amendment and academic freedoms.

At the end of this article is a list of such organizations, their national offices, and phone numbers. Rather than listing each one with an annotation I have decided to describe some ways to use the whole list, then to inventory some of the needs that various organizations can meet and name the specific organizations which best satisfy them, and finally to comment more thoroughly on a few of the organizations whose names are not self-explanatory or whose services are unusual or unique.

Using the List

To begin with, you might want to write to them all and ask them to send you their catalogs of publications and position papers concerning censorship and anything else that they will send you for free. Some of these groups publish little about censorship but have taken stands opposing it. Others publish so much that even their membership materials will give useful censorship information. By looking at authors listed in their catalogs and reading titles and annotations one can get a good idea of who is active in censorship matters and what each organization's special interests are.

Another way to use the list is to refine it. All the addresses are national offices, and unless you happen to live in the organization's home state, chances are that few people you contact there will be able to visit your school or talk to your legislator. It's a long way from the executive secretary of a national organization to a citizen in your school district who can help you support *The Catcher in the Rye* before your school board. You might want, then, to use this list as a starting point, to ask those organizations which have state affiliates to send you the address of your state's affiliate. Through the state affiliate you can get the names of people who are especially interested in censorship matters. (Another way of locating some state affiliates is to ask your state office of public instruction.)

You will want, too, to refine the list by supplementing it. One address you'll want to add is that of your state office of public instruction or state board of education. Another whole set of addresses that is missing from the list is that of religious groups. Many religious organizations support intellectual freedom, and many ministers, priests, and rabbis are willing to assist in censorship controversies. In fact, so many are supportive that listing the organizations here is impossible. Some citizens and professional groups are also missing (League of Women Voters, American Orthopsychiatric Association, etc.). A letter to the National Ad Hoc Committee Against Censorship asking for the names and addresses of organizations which comprise its membership will serve as a beginning for all of those.

In all cases, if you want to reach someone who is local—who is from your state or your town—you will eventually have to reach local organizations.

Inventory of Needs

All the listed organizations provide many services. Under each service I list only a few of the most useful organizations for that purpose and sometimes the subject(s) that each one handles especially well. For local resources and consultants be sure to check with state affiliates also.

Publications. American Civil Liberties Union (teachers' and students' rights). American Library Association (all aspects of freedom to read). Freedom to Read Foundation (significant court cases). National Council of Teachers of English (everything particularly pertinent to the English classroom).

Speakers. Here, the problem is to get people who know something and who speak especially well. LAWYERS: American Bar Association. First Amendment Lawyer's Association. JUDGES: First Amendment Lawyer's Association. Your area may also have an organization of state judges or of federal judges. State supreme court judges' offices are listed, usually, in the phone book under the state government. DOCTORS: National Ad Hoc Committee Against Censorship for the names of the psychiatric associations that belong to the Committee. WRITERS: P.E.N. Writer's Guild of America, Inc. The publisher of a particular writer whose books are often challenged. PUBLISHERS: Association of American Publishers. National Ad Hoc Committee Against Censorship. The publisher of a textbook series which has been attacked. LEGISLATORS: Local offices of the American Civil Liberties Union, National Education Association, American Federation of Teachers. Those groups keep track of state legislation and legislators' opinions. The chair(s) of the judiciary committee(s) (where most obscenity legislation is studied) of your state legislature. REPRESENTATIVES OF RELIGIONS: National Ad Hoc Committee Against Censorship. American Civil Liberties Union. TEACHERS OTHER THAN ENGLISH TEACHERS: National Council for the Social Studies. National Science Teachers Association. Speech Communication Association. American Association of School Librarians. Freedom to Read Foundation. American Library Association Office of Intellectual Freedom. BUSINESS PERSONS CONNECTED WITH PUBLISHING: (booksellers, theater owners, magazine publishers) Media Coalition, Inc. ENGLISH TEACHERS: National Council of Teachers of English. NCTE also maintains a list of speakers from other professions who have been especially helpful to English teachers.

Legal advice. First Amendment Lawyer's Association. American Civil Liberties Union. Local chapters of the American Federation of Teachers and the National Education Association.

Crisis help. Freedom to Read Foundation. National Council of Teachers of English. Your state affiliate of NCTE. Local chapters of the American Federation of Teachers and the National Education Association.

Preparing guidelines for selection of materials and for handling complaints. National Council of Teachers of English and your state NCTE affiliate for how-to-do-it information, for samples, and for consultants. American Library Association. For other points of view on the matter: American Association of School Administrators, National Association of Secondary School Principals, National Association of Elementary School Principals, and the National School Boards Association.

Lobbying. National Ad Hoc Committee Against Censorship. Media Coalition, Inc. American Civil Liberties Union. National Education Association. American Federation of Teachers. Through the Freedom to Read Foundation you can learn how to establish or join regional ad hoc lobbying groups. One publication must be mentioned here: Kenneth P. Norwick, *Lobbying for Freedom* (New York: St. Martin's Press, 1975). Excerpts available free as a pamphlet from National Ad Hoc Committee Against Censorship.

Money. If you become involved in a court case, these organizations *might* provide financial and/or legal support, and/or they *might* file *amici curiae* briefs which support your interests. Freedom to Read Foundation. American Civil Liberties Union. Association of American Publishers. American Federation of Teachers. National Education Association. The publisher of the work which has been attacked might also file on your behalf.

More About Some of the Organizations

The National Council of Teachers of English, the American Library Association's Office of Intellectual Freedom, and the Freedom to Read Foundation are groups which are very much concerned with censorship in the schools. They keep active committees going all over the country, participate in most coalitions against censorship, maintain offices and staff, follow legislation and court cases, publish information, try to keep current lists of consultants, and try to help individual teachers who are embroiled in censorship controversies. A call to the executive secretary of the Freedom to Read Foundation almost always gives the caller some information and help. A call to the National Council of Teachers of English or to the chair of the Censorship Committee or president of your NCTE affiliate will also elicit good advice, publications, and a referral to someone who can consult on almost any problem. Nearly all the listed organizations have taken formal positions opposing censorship and favoring intellectual freedom.

The Media Coalition, Inc. and the National Ad Hoc Committee Against Censorship are loose affiliations of other organizations which have banded together to act more effectively against censorship.

P.E.N. is an international organization whose primary function is to bring pressure to bear on foreign governments to free imprisoned writers and artists and/or to permit them to emigrate.

The American Civil Liberties Union and the First Amendment Lawyer's Association are interested in all forms of censorship and only incidentally in school censorship. The First Amendment Lawyer's Association is a very informal, loose affiliation of (as of this writing) 102 attorneys from everywhere in the United States who specialize in First Amendment cases.

Lou Willett Stanek describes the activities of the American Library Association, the National Council of Teachers of English, the American Civil Liberties Union, the Media Coalition, Inc., and the National Ad Hoc Committee Against Censorship in considerable detail in *Censorship: A Guide for Teachers, Librarians, and Others Concerned with Intellectual Freedom* (free from Dell Publishing Co., Inc., 1 Dag Hammarskjold Plaza, New York, N.Y. 10017).

Unfortunately, we, unlike Darwin's body of well-instructed men, have to labor for our daily bread. When I first began to work against censorship, I was almost overwhelmed by all the things that needed doing and all the people that I was told I "should" and "must" get to know. The effort is worth it, though, for there is great intrinsic satisfaction in the results. It all bears fruit, as in that talk I had with Jerzy Kosinsky about countries where books aren't banned—because no one is allowed to print anything objectionable. And it bore fruit in the anti-obscenity-law testimony given jointly with a dedicated First Amendment lawyer, with the owner of my favorite movie theater, and with the person who runs the bookstore I most admire. I hope you, too, will join us.

National Organizations Concerned with Intellectual Freedom

American Association of
  School Administrators
1801 North Moore St.
Rosslyn, Va. 22209
703-528-0700

American Association of
  School Librarians
50 East Huron St.
Chicago, Ill. 60611
312-944-6780

American Bar Association
1155 E. 60th St.
Chicago, Ill. 60637
312-947-4000

American Civil Liberties
  Union
22 East 40th St.
New York, N.Y. 10016
212-925-1222

American Federation of
  Teachers
11 Dupont Circle N.W.
Washington, D.C. 20036
202-797-4400

American Library Association
Office for Intellectual
  Freedom
50 East Huron St.
Chicago, Ill. 60611
312-944-6780

Association of American
  Publishers
1 Park Ave.
New York, N.Y. 10016
212-689-8920

*First Amendment Lawyer's
  Association
Suite 1200
1737 Chestnut St.
Philadelphia, Penn. 19103
215-665-1600

*Freedom to Read
  Foundation
50 East Huron St.
Chicago, Ill. 60611
312-944-6780

International Reading
  Association
800 Barksdale Rd.
Newark, Del. 19711
302-731-1600

**Media Coalition, Inc.
342 Madison Ave.
New York, N.Y. 10017
212-687-2288

*National Ad Hoc Committee
  Against Censorship
22 East 40th St.
New York, N.Y. 10016
212-686-7098

*Has no state affiliates.
**An umbrella group which consists of many organizations.

Organizations Active for Intellectual Freedom

National Association of Elementary School Principals
1801 North Moore St.
Rosslyn, Va. 22209
703-528-6000

National Council for the Social Studies
Suite 406
2030 M St. N.W.
Washington, D.C. 20036
202-296-0760

National Council of Teachers of English
1111 Kenyon Rd.
Urbana, Ill. 61801
217-328-3870

National Education Association
1201 16th St. N.W.
Washington, D.C. 20036
202-833-4000

National Association of Secondary School Principals
1904 Association Drive
Reston, Va. 22091
703-860-0200

National Science Teachers Association
1742 Connecticut Ave. N.W.
Washington, D.C. 20009
202-265-4150

*P.E.N. American Center
156 Fifth Ave.
New York, N.Y. 10010
212-255-1977

Speech Communication Association
5205 Leesburg Pike
Falls Church, Va. 22041
703-379-1888

*Writer's Guild of America East, Inc.
22 W. 48th St.
New York, N.Y. 10036
212-575-5060

*Writer's Guild of America West, Inc.
8955 Beverly Blvd.
Los Angeles, Calif. 90048
213-550-1000

National School Boards Association
1055 Thomas Jefferson St. N.W.
Washington, D.C. 20007
202-337-7666

Your State Department of Public Instruction, State Department of Education

Through the Media Coalition, Inc., the National Ad Hoc Committee Against Censorship, and the Freedom to Read Foundation (all listed above), *many* other organizations can be reached, such as the American Association of University Professors, the National Council of Churches of Christ, the American Booksellers Association, the U.S. National Student Association, The Newspaper Guild, and the Child Study Association.

A Selected Bibliography

James E. Davis
Ohio University

Books

Anderson, A. J. *Problems in Intellectual Freedom and Censorship.* New York: R. R. Bowker Co., 1974.

Armitage, Gilbert. *Banned in England: An Examination of the Law Relating to Obscene Publications.* London: Wishart, 1932.

Barker, Lucius J., and Twiley W. Barker, Jr. *Civil Liberties and the Constitution.* Englewood Cliffs, N.J.: Prentice-Hall, 1975.

Bennett, D. M. *Anthony Comstock: His Career of Cruelty and Crime.* New York: Liberal and Scientific Publishing House, 1878.

Boyer, Paul S. *Purity in Print: The Vice-Society Movement and Book Censorship in America.* New York: Charles Scribner's Sons, 1968.

Busha, Charles H. *Freedom versus Suppression and Censorship; With a Study of the Attitudes of Midwestern Public Librarians and a Bibliography of Censorship.* Littleton, Colo.: Libraries Unlimited, 1972.

Clor, Harry M. *Obscenity and Public Morality: Censorship in a Liberal Society.* Chicago: University of Chicago Press, 1969.

Combatting Undemocratic Pressures on Schools and Libraries: A Guide for Local Communities. New York: American Civil Liberties Union, 1964.

Craig, Alex. *Suppressed Books: A History of the Conception of Literary Obscenity.* Cleveland: World, 1963.

Ernst, Morris, and Alan U. Schwartz. *Censorship: The Search for the Obscene.* New York: Macmillan, 1964.

Fellman, David. *The Censorship of Books.* Madison: University of Wisconsin Press, 1957.

Frank, John P., and Robert F. Hogan. *Obscenity, the Law, and the English Teacher.* Urbana, Ill.: National Council of Teachers of English, 1966.

Haight, Anne Lyon. *Banned Books: Informal Notes on Some Books Banned for Various Reasons at Various Times and in Various Places.* 3rd ed. New York: R. R. Bowker Co., 1970.

Hove, John. *Meeting Censorship in the School: A Series of Case Studies.* Urbana, Ill.: National Council of Teachers of English, 1967.

Levine, Alan, et al. *The Rights of Students: The Basic ACLU Guide to a Student's Rights.* New York: Avon Books, 1973.

Lewis, Felice Flannery. *Literature, Obscenity, and Law.* Carbondale: Southern Illinois University Press, 1976.
McCoy, Ralph E. *Freedom of the Press: An Annotated Bibliography.* Carbondale: Southern Illinois University Press, 1968.
Moon, Eric, ed. *Book Selection and Censorship in the Sixties.* New York: R. R. Bowker Co., 1969.
Nelson, Jack, ed. *Captive Voices: High School Journalism in America.* New York: Charles Scribner's Sons, 1974.
Nelson, Jack, and Gene Roberts, Jr. *The Censors and the Schools.* Boston: Little, Brown, 1963.
Responsible Academic Freedom: Challenge to Ridgefield (Report by Professional Inquiry Panel of the Professional Rights and Responsibilities Commission of the Connecticut Education Association). Hartford, Conn., November 15, 1973.
Rubin, David. *The Rights of Teachers: The Basic ACLU Guide to a Teacher's Constitutional Rights.* New York: Avon Books, 1972.

Procedures and Policies for Materials Selection

American Association of School Librarians. *Policies and Procedures for Selection of Instructional Materials.* Chicago: The Association, 1970.
American Association of School Librarians. *School Library Bill of Rights for School Library Media Programs.* Chicago: The Association, 1969.
American Library Association. *Library Bill of Rights.* Chicago: The Association, 1967.
———. *Intellectual Freedom Manual.* Chicago: The Association, 1974.
Boyer, Calvin J., and Nancy L. Eaton. *Book Selection Policies in American Libraries: An Anthology of Policies from College, Public and School Libraries.* Austin, Tex.: Armadillo Press, 1971.
Iowa Department of Public Instruction. *Selection of Instructional Materials: A Model Policy and Rules.* Des Moines: State of Iowa Department of Public Instruction, 1975.
Rosenberg, Max. "Criteria for Evaluating the Treatment of Minority Groups in Textbooks and Other Curriculum Materials." *Audiovisual Instruction* 15 (May 1970): 21-22.
———. "Evaluate Your Textbooks for Racism, Sexism." *Educational Leadership* 31 (November 1973): 107-09.
"Try Out This Model School District Policy on Censorship." *American School Board Journal* 60 (May 1973): 44.

Entire Issues of Journals

Arizona English Bulletin 11 (February 1969).
———. 17 (February 1975).
Focus: Teaching English Language Arts 3 (Fall 1976).
Journal of Research and Development in Education 9 (Spring 1976).
Iowa English Bulletin Yearbook 25 (Fall 1975).
New England Association of Teachers of English. *The Leaflet* 8 (May 1969).

Articles, Pamphlets, and Portions of Books

"Academic Freedom in the Public Schools: The Right to Teach." *NYU Law Review* 48 (December 1973): 1176-99.

Berger, Alan S., John H. Gagnor, and William Simon. "Pornography: High School and College Years." In *Technical Report of the Commission on Obscenity and Pornography, Vol. 9: The Consumer and the Community,* pp. 165-208. Washington, D.C.: U.S. Government Printing Office, 1972.

Berninghausen, David K., and Richard W. Faunce. "An Exploratory Study of Juvenile Delinquency and the Reading of Sensational Books." *Journal of Experimental Education* 33 (Winter 1964): 161-68.

Boaz, Martha. "The Student Does Have the Right to Read." *California School Libraries* 41 (January 1970): 63-67.

Booth, Wayne. "Censorship and the Values of Fiction." *English Journal* 53 (March 1964): 155-64.

Boyer, Paul S. "Boston Book Censorship in the Twenties." *American Quarterly* 15 (Spring 1963): 3-24.

Broderick, Dorothy. "Censorship—Reevaluated." *School Library Journal* 18 (November 1971): 30-32.

Burress, Lee. "How Censorship Affects the School." *Wisconsin Council of Teachers of English, Special Bulletin* 8 (October 1963): 1-23.

"Children's Rights: One to Agonize Over." *American School Board Journal* 60 (March 1973): 41-42.

Collier, James. "The Language of Censorship." In *Language in America,* edited by Neil Postman, Charles Weingartner, and Terence Moran, pp. 57-70. Indianapolis: Pegasus, 1969.

"The Debate: Whether and How to Censor 'Objectionable' School Books." *American School Board Journal* 60 (May 1973): 38-39.

Donart, Arthur C. "The Books They're Banning and Why." *American School Board Journal* 60 (May 1973): 42-43.

Donelson, Kenneth. "The Censorship of Non-Print Media Comes to the English Classroom." *English Journal* 62 (December 1973): 1226-27.

———. "Some Tentative Answers to Some Questions about Censorship." *English Journal* 68 (April 1974): 20-21.

Donelson, Kenneth, ed. *The Student's Right to Read.* Rev. ed. Urbana, Ill.: National Council of Teachers of English, 1972.

Donlan, Dan. "Parent versus Teacher: The Dirty Word." In *Diversity in Mature Reading: Theory and Research,* 22nd Yearbook, Vol. 1 edited by Phil L. Nacke, pp. 224-31. Boone, N.C.: National Reading Conference, 1973.

Escott, Richard H. "Intellectual Freedom and the School Administrator." *School Media Quarterly* 2 (Winter 1973): 118-21.

Faigley, Lester. "What Happened in Kanawha County." *English Journal* 64 (May 1975): 7-9.

Fessler, Aaron L. "Selective Bibliography of Literary Censorship in the United States." *Bulletin of Bibliography and Dramatic Index* 20 (May-August 1952): 188-91.

Gaines, Ervin J. "Censorship and What to Do about It." *Minnesota English Journal* 5 (Winter 1969): 5-9.

Hardy, Clifford A. "Censorship and the Curriculum." *Educational Leadership* 31 (October 1973): 10-11, 13.

Hare, William. "Controversial Issues and the Teacher." *High School Journal* 57 (November 1973): 51-60.

Jones, Harry, and Ray Lawson. "Intellectual Freedom and the Handling of Complaints." *School Media Quarterly* 2 (Winter 1973): 116-18.

———. "Intellectual Freedom and Materials Selection." *School Media Quarterly* 2 (Winter 1973): 113-16.

Kosinski, Jerzy. "Against Book Censorship." *Media and Methods* 12 (January 1976): 20-26.

Mallios, Harry C. "The Emerging Law of Due Process for Public School Students." *High School Journal* 57 (November 1973): 83-90.

Mangione, Anthony R. "Implications of Censorship: Past, Present, and Future Threats." *Ohio English Bulletin* 15 (September 1974): 24-31.

McLaughlin, Frank. "Selecting and Defending Controversial Books." *School Paperback Journal* 1 (September 1965): 8-11.

Obler, Eli M. "'Just Like the Child in the Family': Paternalistic Morality and Censorship." *Library Journal* 98 (September 1973): 2395-98.

Poe, William S. "How to Deal with Controversy in Your Community." *American School Board Journal* 159 (August 1972): 30-32.

Ritchie, Richard M. "Due Process and the Principal." *Phi Delta Kappan* 49 (June 1973): 697-98.

Schimmel, David, and Louis Fischer. "On the Cutting Edge of the Law: The Expansion of Teachers' Rights." *School Review* 82 (February 1974): 261-79.

Scott, Gloria S. "Paperbook Censorship: An Idea Whose Time Has Gone." *Media and Methods* 11 (May/June 1975): 14-15.

Tedford, Thomas. "What Every English Teacher Should Know about the Supreme Court Obscenity Decisions." *English Journal* 63 (October 1974): 20-21.

Veix, Donald B. "Teaching a Censored Novel: *Slaughterhouse-Five*." *English Journal* 64 (October 1975): 25-34.

Whaley, Elizabeth G. "What Happens When You Put the *Manchild in the Promised Land*?: An Experience with Censorship." *English Journal* 63 (May 1974): 61-65.

White, Mary L. "Censorship—Threat Over Children's Books." *Elementary School Journal* 74 (October 1974): 2-10.

Wilson, W. C., and Sylvia Jacobs. "Pornography and Youth: A Survey of Sex Education and Counselors." In *Technical Report of the Commission on Obscenity and Pornography, Vol. 5: Societal Control Mechanisms*, pp. 369-73. Washington, D.C.: U.S. Government Printing Office, 1971.

Contributors

Larry D. Bartlett, Administrative Consultant with the Iowa Department of Public Instruction, is a frequent speaker on school law issues. He was a social studies teacher and department head in the Omaha, Nebraska, public schools. He received his J.D. degree from the University of Nebraska and is a member of the Iowa and Nebraska bar associations. He is currently a Ph.D. candidate in educational administration at Iowa State University.

Richard Beach is a professor of English Education at the University of Minnesota. He received a B.A. degree from Wesleyan University, an M.A. degree from Trinity College, and a Ph.D. from the University of Illinois. He is co-author with Alan C. Purves of *Literature and the Reader: Research in Response to Literature, Reading Interests, and Teaching of Literature.* He has published articles and book chapters on various aspects of teaching English.

Gertrude Berger is a professor of education at Brooklyn College of the City University of New York. In addition to her activities in the field of censorship, she is active in the field of women's studies. Among her publications is "Changing Roles of Women," which appeared in the *Journal of Research and Development in Education.*

June Langford Berkley is Chair of the English Department at Fort Frye High School, Beverly, Ohio, and part-time instructor in the Education Department at Marietta College. She is the author of a number of curriculum guides selected by NCTE for the national curriculum exchange and is a regular contributor to regional and state education journals. A past president of the Southeastern Ohio Council of Teachers of English, a founder and member of the executive committee of the Conference on Ohio English Departments, she has served two terms on the NCTE Board of Directors and appeared on NCTE national convention programs.

Lee Burress is Professor of English at the University of Wisconsin—Stevens Point. He has written a number of articles on American literature, folklore, and censorship. He is currently president of the Wisconsin Council of Teachers of English.

James E. Davis, Professor of English and Chairman of the English Department at Ohio University (Athens), is the author of over thirty articles and sections of books on the teaching of English. He is a frequent speaker at NCTE conventions and has been a member of that organization's board of directors since 1972. He has also served as president of the Southeastern Ohio Council of Teachers of English and the Ohio Council of Teachers of English Language Arts and as editor of the official publications of both organizations.

Kenneth L. Donelson is a professor of English at Arizona State University. He received B.A. and M.A. degrees in English and a Ph.D. in English education from the University of Iowa. He is co-author of *Teaching English Today* and editor of *The Students' Right to Read* and the 1976 edition of *Books for You*. He has published nearly 200 articles on censorship, adolescent literature, film, and the English curriculum. He has been chair of the Conference on English Education, a member of the Executive Committee of the National Council of Teachers of English, and editor of the *Arizona English Bulletin*.

Allan Glatthorn teaches at the Graduate School of Education of the University of Pennsylvania and has been director of the NCTE Commission on Curriculum. He holds A.B., M.Ed., and Ed.D. degrees from Temple University, has been an Alfred North Whitehead Fellow at Harvard University and a John Hay Fellow at the University of Chicago. He taught high school English and psychology, and before joining the faculty of the University of Pennsylvania was principal of the Abington High School. He is coauthor of *Five American Adventures*, *The Next Five Years*, and *Composition: Models and Exercises*.

Robert F. Hogan is Executive Director of the National Council of Teachers of English. Before coming to work for NCTE in 1962, Hogan was assistant director of the Commission on English for the College Entrance Examination Board. During his tenure with NCTE, Hogan has represented the organization and its membership on numerous national committees and commissions, including the Ad Hoc Committee on Copyright Law, the New York State Joint Legislative Committee on Censorship, and the President's Commission on Obscenity and Pornography. He has published widely in professional journals.

Edward B. Jenkinson, Professor of English Education and Director of the English Curriculum Study Center at Indiana University, is the author or editor of more than twenty books on the teaching of English, speech, and journalism. A former vice president of NCTE, he recently completed a six-year term as vice president, president, and immediate past president of the Indiana Council of Teachers of English. He is also completing a three-year term as chair of the NCTE Committee Against Censorship.

J. Charles Park, Professor of Educational Foundations and Counselor of Education at the University of Wisconsin—Whitewater, has been a student of right-wing pressure groups and public education for fifteen years. He has spoken to a number of educational organizations about pressure groups in education and is in the process of preparing a series of educational articles on the growth of the New Right.

Robert T. Rhode, Associate Instructor in English at Indiana University, became involved in research on First Amendment rights when he served as a graduate assistant in the Indiana University English Curriculum Study Center. He combines his talents as a musician and artist in teaching literature.

Diane P. Shugert, Associate Professor of English at Central Connecticut State College, is president of the Connecticut Council of Teachers of English and is CCTE censorship chair. She is also Censorship Committee chair and SLATE representative for the New England Association of Teachers of English. She edits and distributes the "NEATE Rationales for Controversial Books" and has conducted sessions for meetings of NCTE, CEE, NEATE, and CCTE.

Robert C. Small, Jr., is Associate Dean, Graduate Studies and Research, Virginia Polytechnic Institute and State University. He is co-author of *Literature for Adolescents* and author of *The New Fiction* and *View Point and Point of View.* He is director of ALAN (1977–present) and currently program chair and participant in NCTE, CEE, and VATE. He is also editor of the *Virginia Association of Teachers of English Bulletin* and is chair of the NCTE Committee to Revise *Books for You.*

Charles Suhor, Deputy Executive Director, Internal Affairs, for the National Council of Teachers of English, is a former English teacher and English supervisor for New Orleans Public Schools. In the past he has served in numerous NCTE groups, including SLATE, Committee to Review Curriculum Bulletins, Commission on the English Curriculum, and the New Orleans and Louisiana Affiliates of the Council. His articles and poetry have appeared in many publications.